COMMUNITIES WITHOUT BORDERS

COMMUNITIES WITHOUT BORDERS

IMAGES AND VOICES FROM THE WORLD OF MIGRATION

DAVID BACON

FOREWORDS BY CARLOS MUÑOZ JR. AND DOUGLAS HARPER

ILR Press
an imprint of Cornell University Press
Ithaca and London

Cornell University Press gratefully acknowledges the support of the Rockefeller Foundation toward the publication of this book. Sole responsibility for the supervision, direction, and control of the conduct of the project lies with Cornell University Press.

First published 2006 by Cornell University Press
First printing, Cornell Paperbacks, 2006

Design by Scott Levine

Printed in Canada

Library of Congress Cataloging-in-Publication data

Bacon, David, 1948–
    Communities without borders : images and voices from the world of migration. / David Bacon; forewords by Carlos Muñoz Jr. and Douglas Harper.
        p. cm.
    Includes bibliographical references and index.
    ISBN-13: 978-0-8014-4499-9 (cloth : alk. paper)
    ISBN-10: 0-8014-4499-3 (cloth : alk. paper)
    ISBN-13: 978-0-8014-7307-4 (pbk. : alk. paper)
    ISBN-10: 0-8014-7307-1 (pbk. : alk. paper)
    1. Alien labor, Mexican—California.   2. Alien labor, Guatemalan—Nebraska.   3. Immigrants—California—Social conditions.   4. Illegal aliens—California—Social conditions.   5. Immigrants—Nebraska—Social conditions.   6. Illegal aliens—Nebraska—Social conditions.   7. Transnationalism.   8. Oaxaca (Mexico : State)—Emigration and immigration.   9. Guatemala—Emigration and immigration.   10. California—Emigration and immigration.   11. Nebraska—Emigration and immigration.   I. Title.
    HD8081.M6B333 2006
    331.6'2720794--dc22
                            2006017141

Cornell University Press strives to use environmentally responsible suppliers and materials to the fullest extent possible in the publishing of its books. Such materials include vegetable-based, low-VOC inks and acid-free papers that are recycled, totally chlorine-free, or partly composed of nonwood fibers. For further information, visit our website at www.cornellpress.cornell.edu.

Cloth printing   10 9 8 7 6 5 4 3 2 1
Paperback printing   10 9 8 7 6 5 4 3 2 1

CONTENTS

FOREWORD ON THE TEXT

On March 24, 2006, I witnessed the largest protest march for immigrant and civil rights in the history of the United States. It took place in the streets of Los Angeles, California. It was estimated that a million people marched on that day. Approximately five million people—overwhelmingly Latino immigrants—marched in the streets of numerous cities throughout the nation during the months of March and April. The massive protests ended with a national economic boycott on May Day (May 1) aimed at making the nation aware of the importance of undocumented immigrants to the economy of the United States.

It took courage for Latino undocumented immigrants to come out of the shadows by the millions to protest the social injustice of proposed anti-immigrant congressional legislation. In particular, the mass demonstrations were a response to the Sensenbrenner Bill (HR 4437) that was passed by the U.S. House of Representatives in early March. The Bill proposed making illegal entry into the United States a felony crime. Those protesting made clear to the U.S. Congress, and the nation as a whole, that they were hard-working men and women and not criminals or terrorists bent on endangering the security of the United States. They simply wanted to be treated with respect and as equals to other workers whose hard labor contributes to the U.S. economy.

Their struggle has generated a passion for social justice throughout the nation that has not happened since the 1960s when the southern civil rights movement led by Dr. Martin Luther King Jr., the California farm worker movement led by Cesar Chavez and Dolores Huerta, and the southwestern Chicano civil rights movement made a similar impact.

The undocumented Latino workers, who appear in this photographic investigation of migration by David Bacon, are some of the people who organized and were part of the millions who marched across our nation to protest the Congressional effort to criminalize them. In particular, the immigrant workers in the city of Omaha, Nebraska, who appear in the book, organized the shutdown of every meatpacking plant in that city and other surrounding towns during the economic boycott held on May Day.

The oral histories, flushed out by David Bacon's insightful interviews, dramatically tell us the poignant stories of why Guatemalan and Mexican workers endure the arduous journey across the border to the United States in the quest for work and a better life. Bacon's extraordinary photography captures their humanity as it is etched in their faces. They are the faces of a people who have experienced a life of hard struggle for survival in their homelands and in the United States.

David Bacon, however, does not present them as victims of oppression but as a strong people who have courageously struggled against all odds armed with the heroic legacies of struggle of their indigenous ancestors. The fact that Latino undocumented workers include indigenous people is not a well-known fact, either in the U.S. Congress or the nation as a whole. They are the direct descendants of the original Americans, the indigenous peoples of all the Americas. The U.S.–Mexico Border did not exist when their ancestors traveled throughout the continent to establish and maintain contact with each other or in search of a better life. The border was created by an expanding U.S. empire after it waged war against the sovereign nation of Mexico in 1848 in order to take over half of that nation's territory.

The people Bacon has photographed and interviewed have not had the freedom of movement that their ancestors enjoyed before the border was imposed on them. But they have created transnational communities enabling them to maintain their ties to their homelands and to survive as unwelcome "foreigners" in their ancestor's lands, now known as the United States. David Bacon has given voice to a people whose vulnerable condition has forced them to live in silence until now.

Carlos Muñoz Jr.

FOREWORD ON THE PHOTOGRAPHY

In *Communities without Borders*, David Bacon weaves visual and narrative threads into a gorgeous fabric that will force citizens and politicians to confront his simple assertion that those who contribute to our society economically should also be allowed to participate in it politically.

Bacon presents us with transnational communities in Mexico, Guatemala, and the United States. His photographs show us how and why borders are crossed; they document political repression and movements among exploited workers; and they show us the cultural invigoration that immigrants bring their new communities. We see the vitality of social and political movements and are thrust into the shameful memory of Bracero camps in California. Further, his photos place us directly into the work that drives migration: We share, vicariously, the tedium and pain of labor; the efforts to create shelter; and the pleasures of community arising from collective work and political organizing.

The success of this ambitious project is largely attributable to Bacon's skill as a photographer—namely, his ability to bring his political and social vision into the individual photographic frames.

His portraits of immigrants from Oaxaca who live in a field in the Sonoma County wine country where they work are apt examples. In one photograph, a man sits on a makeshift mattress in the middle foreground; behind him other workers sit on discarded mattresses that lack sheets or blankets. The men are bundled against the cold, and we can see flimsy canvas covers that constitute some sort of roof in this improvised shelter. The workers face ahead attentively, listening to an unseen speaker. Bacon's vertical framing makes this an extraordinary photograph: it draws attention to two sets of footwear—a man's worn work boots and a woman's sandals—

placed carefully side by side, in front of the makeshift bed. We recognize, startled, a reflection of our own carefully lined shoes in the comfortable bedrooms we retreat to, after we have enjoyed the wine made from the grapes these workers have harvested.

Bacon's photographs of children of Mexican immigrant meatpackers in school in Madison, Nebraska, explore the language barrier and more. In one photograph Bacon fills the frame with two young Hispanic students, a boy and a girl. The room has that wonderful clutter of an energetic elementary schoolroom. On the wall in the upper corner of the photo is a map of the world, cropped to feature Central and South America. The essential message of the image is the immigrant child who cannot understand his English-speaking teacher. His hand is on his head in exasperation; he's turned beyond the camera so we see the full force of his frustration. In the next frame he is sitting across from a blonde-haired girl, and he is rocking back in his seat confidently. His hand is in the air; he is volunteering an answer to the stern teacher in the background. Here is the promise of the future, and we learn through the accompanying text that the immigrants are not only contributing to the economies of this small Nebraskan town but also revitalizing its social institutions. Immigrant children now represent a majority of pupils in this rural district. The school now has enough students to justify its existence.

To remind us of the history of the exploitation of Mexican and Central American workers in the United States, Bacon photographed the deserted buildings and empty spaces left over from the Braceros program, which between 1942 and 1964 oversaw the official exploitation by the United States of south-of-the-border workers. The first of these images shows an abandoned camp from that era, in use even until the 1980s. It is a carefully composed image of deserted buildings, juxtaposed with a discarded bicycle rim in the foreground that reminds us: movement, movement. The second of these photos shows us the toilets and urinals available to the workers, lined up side by side, allowing less privacy than found in a common jail. This grim image is expanded to one of promise by a beam of sunlight that extends from a high window into the forlorn room.

In one powerful image in the book, Bacon shows us a makeshift memorial for those who have died trying to cross the border. There are six narrow crosses fastened to the wall; these carry dates on the horizontal axis and a tally on the post of the number of people who died in each of the years. They read 1995: 61; 2000: 117. In the center of the display is an abstracted crucifix made from work clothes fastened to a flat surface that reaches higher than the iron fence that separates the two countries. Bacon's photograph is formally satisfying: objects piled against the wall that might have been flowers in a different memorial (could these be discarded canisters of the ashes of unknown victims?), a glowering sky, and strong light and shadow.

There are numerous other photos that simultaneously excite one's sociological imagination and satisfy one's artistic instincts. One image shows a Mayo woman who gleans beans from the harvested field as she rises out of the ground like a plant herself (the black-and-white film melds her likely colorful clothes with the greens and browns of the land and crops). Another photo shows fecund grapes dominating the frame; a worker is in the background, bundled against the cold. In yet another image, a traditional Oaxacan woman cooks over charcoal and wood, lit by slanting rays shining through the spaces between the wide boards of her house. Utensils, food, posture, expression combine to communicate the visceral reality of peasant life. These and other images are breathtakingly beautiful, and they are analytically dense.

Communities without Borders is inviting, compelling, and relevant. David Bacon's successful marriage of sociology and documentary, and thus science and art, will no doubt teach Northerners some global realities they need to know better and with any luck inspire those of the South to continue their struggle for dignity and justice.

DOUGLAS HARPER

INTRODUCTION

The Roots of Migration

In 1982 Guatemalan army troops filled the roads through the highlands above the small city of Huehuetenango. They were the brutal emissaries of the country's propertied elite, terrorizing small towns to turn them against armed rebels and their effort to upend Guatemala's unjust social order. Soldiers carried Armalite rifles, gifts of U.S. president Ronald Reagan, for whom rural villages were just another theater of the cold war. For the indigenous people of these highland towns, such as the Mams and Qanjobales, however, the war was not cold at all. That year the soldiers also swept into the small village of San Miguel Acatan. Accusing the townspeople of using church youth groups to recruit guerrillas, they began killing political activists. Finally, after the army shot down teenagers in front of the church, many families fled.

"Helicopters chased and bombed them, as they ran through the mountains, all the way to the [Mexican] border," recalls Francisco Martin Quixic, who now heads the San Miguel parish council. Refugees wound up living in tent camps a hundred miles north in Chiapas, Mexico. "For those who stayed behind, there was no work—just devastation. You couldn't even buy salt or vegetables here anymore."

It was also in 1982 that indigenous Mixtec, Zapotec, and Triqui farm workers from the Mexican state of Oaxaca, living in migrant labor camps in the northwestern state of Sinaloa, began to rise up against filthy living conditions and backbreaking labor. Radical young Mixtec organizers launched strikes and, together with left-wing students from the local university in Culiacan, faced down growers, armed guards, and police.

Oaxaca's Mixtec, Zapotec, and Triqui laborers were recent arrivals in Sinaloa but had already been migrating within Mexico for two decades. Starting in the late 1950s, when Mexican policies of rural development and credit began to fail, the inhabitants of small Oaxacan villages traveled first to the nearby state of Veracruz. There they found work unavailable in Oaxaca, cutting sugarcane and picking coffee for the rich planters of the coast.

Then Sinaloa's new factory farms a thousand miles north, growing tomatoes and strawberries for U.S. supermarkets, needed workers too. Soon growers began recruiting southern Mexico's indigenous migrants, and before long, trains were packed with Oaxacan families every spring.

Over the next twenty years, Guatemala's Qanjobal and Mam refugees and Oaxaca's indigenous farm workers moved north through Mexico. Eventually they began crossing the border into the United States. Today, both of these migrant streams have developed well-established communities thousands of miles from their hometowns. In Nebraska, Los Angeles, and Florida, Huehuetenango highlanders affectionately call their neighborhoods Little San Miguel. Triquis, living just below the U.S. border in Baja California, name their settlements Nuevo San Juan Copala in honor of their Oaxacan hometown. In Fresno and Madera, California, the Mixtec community is so large that signs in grocery stores list sale items not just in Spanish but in a tongue that predates the Spaniards' arrival by centuries.

U.S. Immigration Policy, Guest Workers, and Misperceptions about Migrant Communities

Indigenous migrant streams have created communities all along the northern road from Guatemala through Mexico into the United States. Their experience defies common preconceptions about immigrants. In Washington, D.C., discussions of immigration are filled with wrong assumptions. U.S. policy treats migrants as individuals, ignoring the social pressures forcing whole communities to move as well as the networks of families and hometowns that sustain them on their journeys. Government policy often requires the deportation of parents caught without papers, who have to leave behind their children born in the United States. Sometimes this arbitrary Alice-in-Wonderland world does just the opposite, deporting undocumented young people who have no memory of the place they were born but to which they find themselves forcibly relocated.

Policymakers see migration simply as a trip from point A to point B. They assume that people make decisions about when to leave home, where to go, and how to live based almost entirely on economics—the need for a job. What U.S. immigration policy does not take into account is the equally strong drive for community. Proposals for guest workers, which have acquired new political momentum in recent years, are the latest form of this denial of one of the most basic aspects of human life. By definition, guest workers are admitted to the United States on a temporary basis, contracted to employers. They have no right to settle in communities, send their children to school, practice their culture and religion, or speak their language. They can't vote or exercise fundamental political or labor rights. They can only come if an employer, or a gang boss recruiter, offers them a job. Without constant employment, they have to leave. The assumption is that they are here to work, and only to work.

The bracero program was the largest and longest such guest-worker scheme in U.S. history. It began in 1942, lasted twenty-two years, and involved more than four million migrant contract workers who were housed in barracks, shipped from job to job, and deported if they went on strike. Mostly Mexican citizens, they were isolated from, and pitted against, the communities around them, as employers sought to create a labor surplus to drive down wages. Modern guest-worker programs serve the same economic purpose. But the results of denying migrants the ability to build communities and participate in the broader society are disastrous.

There is no denying the importance of the universal human need for work. But the dislocation of communities worldwide, which forces people to migrate in search of employment, has never been a voluntary process. In Washington, dislocation is a dirty, unmentionable secret of the global economy. Sergio Sosa, Guatemalan organizer of Omaha Together One Community in Nebraska, emphasizes that "Mams and Qanjobales face poverty and

isolation, even the possible disappearance of their identity. But they didn't choose this. People from Europe and the U.S. crossed our borders to come to Guatemala and took over our land and economy. Migration is a form of fighting back. Now it's our turn to cross borders."

When migrants do cross those borders, though, they confront a second dirty secret of globalization—inequality. Inequality is the most important product of U.S. immigration policy, and a conscious one. This policy's basic thrust, not limited just to guest-worker programs, assumes that immigrants should not be treated as equals of the people around them or have the same rights. The philosophy underpinning it would reverse a four-hundred-year history of struggle in the United States to expand the rights of all people. U.S. policy denies the reality that the migration of people is as much a product of the global economy as the migration of capital.

The Making of Migrant Communities: Abuse, Activism, and Organization

Migration is a complex economic and social process in which whole communities participate. Migration creates communities that today pose challenging questions about the nature of citizenship in a globalized world.

While he was still living in a settlement of bamboo-and-plastic tents in the reeds beside California's Russian River, Fausto Lopez, a Triqui migrant farm worker from Oaxaca, became president of California's Sonoma County chapter of the Indigenous Front of Binational Organizations (FIOB). Also known as the Frente, it is a truly binational organization, with chapters all along the migrant trail dedicated to fighting for the rights of indigenous Oaxacan migrant workers. He brought fellow Triquis from their impromptu encampment to marches and demonstrations in California's state capital, demanding driver's licenses and amnesty for undocumented immigrants. Lopez and his companions were living in conditions most Americans equate with extreme poverty, yet they saw themselves not as victims but as social actors, with a right to acceptance both in Mexico and the United States.

"Indigenous Oaxaqueños understand the need for community and organization," says Rufino Dominguez, who left Oaxaca in 1984 as a young man and who now coordinates the FIOB. "When people migrate from a community in Oaxaca and settle in a new place, they form a committee comprised of people from their hometown. They are united and live near one another. This is a tradition they don't lose, wherever they go."

Just as migrants carry community with them, they also carry those traditions of social rights and organization. The desire for community is as important and necessary to survival as the need to find work or to escape hunger and state violence. David Fitzgerald, a *Los Angeles Times* photographer turned academic, says that "community lies at the heart" of the questions posed by migration.

Indigenous migrants from Mexico and Central America overwhelmingly belong to transnational communities like those of Oaxaca's Mixtecs and Triquis or Guatemala's Mams and Qanjobales. The Mixtec scholar Gaspar Rivera-Salgado and Jonathan Fox, an authority on Oaxacan migration at the University of California in Santa Cruz, refer to "Oaxacalifornia" as a "space in which migrants bring together their lives in California with their communities of origin more than 2,500 miles away." They might have equally referred to Pueblayork, the nickname bestowed on New York by a similar flow of indigenous migration from the Mexican state of Puebla. Migrants from Guatemala's Santa Eulalia don't yet call their Midwest community Nebraskamala, but there are enough migrants living in Omaha and surrounding meatpacking towns to make such a nickname inevitable.

People retain ties to their communities of origin and establish new communities as they migrate in search of work. They move back and forth through these networks, at least to the extent the difficult passage across borders allows. Their ties to each other are so strong, and the movement of people so great, that in many ways they belong to a single community that exists in different locations, on both sides of the borders that formally divide their countries.

For Oaxacans, the formation of communities outside their home state began long before they migrated to the United States, when they became the workforce for industrial agriculture in the northern Mexican states of Sinaloa and Baja California. Dominguez, like many other migrants from Oaxaca, went first to Sinaloa before continuing north across the border. Responding to abusive conditions for migrants that were the scandal of Mexico, he formed the Organization of Exploited and Oppressed People. The strikes Dominguez helped organize in Sinaloa put industrial agricultural companies' abuse into the public eye. That abuse was recalled by Jorge and Margarita Giron, who also migrated from Oaxaca to the fields of Sinaloa.

"When they were irrigating, we took off our shoes and went into the fields barefoot, even if it was freezing. Going in like that made us sick, but there were no rubber boots," remembers Jorge, from the Mixtec town of Santa Maria Tindu, who now lives with his family in Fresno, California. His wife, Margarita, recalls that "when you had to relieve yourself, you went in public because there were no bathrooms. You would go behind a tree or into the tall grass and squat. People would bathe upstream while downstream others would wash their clothes and even drink the water. That's why many came down with diarrhea and vomiting. Others drowned in the river because it was very deep. The walls in the camp were made of cardboard, and you could see other families through the holes. In the camps you couldn't be picky." The strikes, they say, forced improvements.

While bad conditions kept the cost of tomatoes low in Los Angeles, they were also a factor motivating people to keep moving north. Dominguez followed the migrant trail to San Quintin on the Baja California peninsula, where he and his friends organized more strikes. Finally he crossed the border into the United States, winding up in California's San Joaquin Valley. There he again found Mixtec farm workers from his home state. "I felt like I was in my hometown," he recalls. And just as they had in northern Mexico, Oaxacan migrants in California organized themselves, forming the Frente by using the network of relationships created by common language, culture, and origin.

Labor organizing was part of the mix here too. In 1993 FIOB began a collaboration with the United Farm Workers (UFW). "We recognized that the UFW is a strong union representing agricultural workers," Dominguez explains. "They in turn recognized us as an organization that tries to gain rights for indigenous migrants." But it was an uneasy relationship. Mixtec activists felt that UFW members often exhibited the same discriminatory attitudes toward indigenous people common among Mexicans back home.

Fighting racism in Mexico, however, had given indigenous migrant communities an important advantage when they faced it in the United States. According to Rivera-Salgado, "the experience of racism enforces a search for cultural identity to resist [and] creates the possibility of new forms of organization and action." The FIOB is one of those new forms. "We wanted to tell a different story—that our people were stripped of our culture," Dominguez asserts. "They imposed a different God on us, and told us that nature wasn't worth anything. In reality nature gives us life. Our purpose was to dismantle the old stereotypes, to march, to protest."

Even among other organizations of Mexican immigrants in the United States, the FIOB is unique. Members adopt one overall political program every two years, while chapters address the distinct problems of indigenous communities in each location.

In Oaxaca in the mid-1990s the Frente began to help women organize weaving cooperatives and development projects, to sustain families left behind in small, depopulated towns after the men migrated. Taking advantage of its chapters in the United States, the Frente began selling their clothes, textiles, and other artisan work in the United States to support the communities in Mexico. This activity was an embarrassment to the Oaxacan state government, however, which is still run by Mexico's old ruling party, the Party of the Institutionalized Revolution (PRI). Government hostility grew even sharper because FIOB leaders, such as high school teacher Romualdo Juan Gutierrez, not only voiced outspoken criticism but allied themselves with Mexico's left-wing Party of the Democratic Revolution (PRD). In 2003 Gutierrez was arrested and held in jail until a binational campaign of telegrams and demonstrations won his release.

"You can't tell a child to study to be a doctor if there is no work for doctors in Mexico," Gutierrez says. "It is a very daunting task for a Mexican teacher to convince students to get an education and stay in the country. If a student sees his older brother migrate to the United States, build a house, and buy a car, he will follow that American dream." Like many others on the left in Mexico, Gutierrez accuses authorities of relying on remittances from workers outside of Mexico to finance domestic social services and public works, which are really the government's responsibility. "The money brought in by immigrants is Mexico's number-one source of income, but the state government only recognizes the immigrant community when it is convenient."

In Baja California, FIOB activists fight for housing for indigenous migrants. They seek to enforce the old Constitutional right of people to settle on vacant land, a right largely eliminated by the neoliberal economic reforms of the former president Carlos Salinas de Gortari. Militants like the indigenous Triqui activist Julio Sandoval led land invasions in the state's agricultural valleys. Large growers, who supply produce for the U.S. market, have been so threatened by this that Sandoval was locked up for three years in an Ensenada prison. Interviewed at FIOB's 2005 binational congress in Oaxaca, Sandoval declared that "as Mexicans, we have a right to housing, and we will force the government to respect us." Binational pressure was indispensable to winning his release.

The FIOB in Depth

The FIOB started in California as an organization of two indigenous groups from Oaxaca—Mixtecs and Zapotecs—and then broadened to include all Oaxacan indigenous groups. At the 2005 assembly in Oaxaca, members voted to expand its reach again, to include indigenous organizations beyond Oaxaca, from Puebla, Guerrero, and Michoacan. It views itself as representing the interests of all indigenous people of Mexico, in communities both there and in the United States. The FIOB has become much more political than previous cross-border organizations, like the hometown clubs of immigrants from the same village or state.

Mexican indigenous communities in the United States live at the social margin, and the FIOB's activity confronts that fact. It is an organization of cultural activists, mounting an annual celebration of Oaxacan dance, the Guelaguetza, every year. Its organizers work for California Rural Legal Assistance, speaking to farm workers in their indigenous languages about their rights. In fact, the FIOB has won the right to Mixtec translation in California courts, a right still not recognized in most of Mexico. It knits different communities together through basketball tournaments (unlike most Mexicans, Oaxacans prefer this sport to soccer) and leadership training groups for women.

The FIOB's organizing strategy is based on indigenous culture, particularly an institution called the *tequio*, "the concept of collective work to support our community," Dominguez explains. "We know one another and can act together. . . . Wherever we go, we go united. It's a way of saying that I do not speak alone—we all speak together." Preserving the culture depends on keeping the Mixtec language alive, too. "We still speak it, even though five hundred years have passed since the Spanish conquest. We are preserving our way of dancing, and rescuing our lost beliefs."

Part of this culture is a participatory democracy with roots in indigenous village life. The organization's binational assemblies discuss bylaws and political positions in detail. In one of the Frente's defining moments, the 2001 Tijuana assembly removed a longtime leader who was no longer accountable to the FIOB's members. A woman, Centolia Maldonado, played the central role in this difficult process—a recognition of new sex roles that are, in part, a product of the migration experience.

The political platform adopted at the FIOB's 2005 assembly maintains a focus on the problems faced by transnational communities. It condemns U.S. guest-worker proposals, arguing that such proposals treat migrants only as temporary workers rather than as people belonging to and creating communities. The organization also calls for extending the rights of citizenship by implementing the Mexican government's 1996 decision to allow its citizens in the United States to vote in Mexican elections.

Discrimination in Mexico is not the only obstacle to preserving indigenous culture. It's not easy for Mixtec and Triqui parents in Fresno to convince their children, born in the United States, to hold fast to languages and traditions that are light-years removed from California schools and movie theaters. California's ban on bilingual education and discrimination from local school authorities make cultural preservation even harder. But the experience of forty years of migration proves that economic and social survival depends on maintaining the identity, language, and those progressive traditions that hold a community together.

Transnational Communities from a Global and Historical Perspective

Ruben Puentes, director of the transnational communities program at the Rockefeller Foundation, which has supported cultural development among Mexican indigenous migrants, asks, "Is there today a growing culture of migration itself, a kind of cultural capital which helps communities survive?" He argues that this developing transnational culture does not get adequate consideration in the debate around immigration policy.

Transnational communities play a growing role in the political life of their home countries, changing the very definition of citizenship and residence. In 2004, for instance, Jesus Martinez, a professor at California State University in Fresno, was elected by Michoacan residents to their state legislature. His mandate is to represent the interests of the state's citizens living in the United States. Transnational migrants insist that they have important political and social rights, both in their communities of origin and in their communities abroad.

U.S. electoral politics can't remain forever immune from these expectations of representation, and they shouldn't. U.S. democracy is based on the idea that those who make economic contributions should have political rights. That requires recognition of the legitimate social status of everyone living here. Legalization isn't important just to migrants. It is a basic step in the preservation and extension of democratic rights for all people.

Transnational communities are a global phenomenon. They exist at different stages of development in the flow of migrants from Algeria to France, Turkey to Germany, Pakistan to the United Kingdom, South Korea to Japan, and from developing to developed countries worldwide. According to Migrant Rights International, over 170 million people live outside the countries in which they were born—a permanent factor of life on the planet.

Migration across the U.S.-Mexico border, of course, is not new. In its earliest moments, it wasn't migration from one country to another at all. Before 1848, the states that today receive the most migrants were part of Mexico—California, Arizona, New Mexico, Nevada, Texas, Colorado, Utah, and parts of others. Mexicans coming north now "return" as immigrants to a land from which their countrymen were dispossessed two centuries ago. Facing down the media-hyped border patrols of nativist Minutemen (a self-styled anti-immigration militia whose members mount demonstrations at the border), today's immigrant rights demonstrators often wear T-shirts declaring, "We didn't cross the border—the border crossed us!"

Current transnational organizations are part of a long historical process. From the beginning, immigration to the United States led to the formation of associations based on towns and countries of origin. Irish immigrants were and are a support base for anticolonial movements back home. The Flores Magon brothers, immigrants from Oaxaca, organized the Liberal Party and the first battles of the Mexican Revolution while living in barrios along the railroad lines from Los Angeles to St. Louis in the first decade of the 1900s. Sun Yat-sen's statue on the edge of San Francisco's Chinatown honors his efforts to organize the Chinese Nationalist Party among Toishan migrants originally brought to build U.S. railroads.

While almost all immigrants have organized for similar purposes, the U.S. color line enforces vast differences in their treatment. Assimilation into mainstream culture was accessible to Europeans. Immigrant communities from Latin America and Asia faced a hypocritical exclusion, which demanded that they give up their culture, language, and identity and yet maintained a color line denying them equal social status.

The roots of this inequality lie in slavery. Any attempt by Africans to recreate their culture in the United States was viciously suppressed for slavery's 250 years. Even the current concept of the "illegal" person has its roots in the Black Codes, used to define who could be enslaved and who couldn't. Chinatowns and Manilatowns owe their existence not simply to the desire for community and group identity but to a century of social segregation.

Immigrants subjected to racism and xenophobic exclusion organized hometown associations, at least in part, to resist. In the 1920s, when a generation of Filipino men were recruited to provide contract labor to growers in western states, U.S. policy forbade the entry of Filipina women, while local laws prohibited marriage between Filipinos and white women. Hometown associations, such as the Sons of Garcia Hernandez, helped migrants locate jobs, filled their need for community and family, and even organized defense against anti-Asian riots. Progressive trends in the U.S. labor movement learned early to use these traditions. The network of Filipino hometown associations, for instance, was an important base for Filipino radicals such as Chris Mensalves and Ernesto Mangaoang, who organized workers in the Alaskan fish canneries in the late 1940s.

Transnational Communities Today

Today's migrants often come with experience in the radical social movements of their homelands. Sergio Sosa, a church lay worker during Guatemala's civil war, organized young people in highland towns. They wrote songs and formed troupes creating their own theater, he explains. "But that was the time of repression and scorched earth policies. Many of the youth involved were seen as guerrillas, and all our activities were prohibited." The massacre in San Miguel Acatan was one consequence.

When Qanjobales and Mams came to Nebraska, their experience dovetailed with efforts to organize meatpacking workers already underway in the church parishes of South Omaha. Using social networks to organize people is part of Latin American culture, Sosa says. "The art is to know how to transform these social networks and connect them with African Americans and Anglo-Saxons. I think Latinos can do many things, and this is our moment. But we can't do them alone."

Transnational communities, while often originally formed around a single indigenous ethnic identity, don't exist in isolation. In South Omaha's organizing ferment, the organizing styles of Guatemalans and Mexicans blend together as people reinterpret various traditions of collective action. The alliance between South Omaha's immigrants, the United Food and Commercial Workers, and Omaha Together One Community (an organizing project started by the Industrial Areas Foundation) successfully organized a union in one of the city's main meatpacking plants.

Sosa and another activist from Guatemala's Santa Eulalia, Francisco Lorenzo, then started Grupo Ixim with other local Guatemalans. The word *ixim* means "corn" in Guatemala's twenty-three indigenous languages. "It also means the common good—the way that, inside an ear of corn, all the grains are together," Sosa says.

Like many immigrant groups, Grupo Ixim first gelled around practical goals. "For example, if a fellow countryman were to pass away, we would quickly mobilize to gather money and send the body to Guatemala," explains Jesus Martinez, a meatpacking worker (no relation to Jesus Martinez the Fresno professor). Ixim also had cultural purposes—from ensuring that young people learned indigenous languages to preserving the heritage of the marimba, a musical symbol of Qanjobal and Mam culture. Santa Eulalia is famous for making the instruments, but the town's young people now leave Guatemala as migrants instead of following their fathers into the marimba workshops. Ironically, groups like Ixim in migrant communities in Nebraska are now a major market that keeps those workshops alive. "Our purpose is to pass on our culture to our children," Martinez says. "It is important for them to know where we came from."

Groups like Ixim have also been organized in Chicago, Los Angeles, and other U.S. cities. In the Nebraska group, tension surfaced in 2003 between those who saw its function mainly as cultural preservation and others who wanted more politics. When Rodolfo Bobadilla, bishop of Huehuetenango

and a former disciple of the assassinated Salvadoran archbishop Oscar Arnulfo Romero, visited his parishioners living in Omaha, a heated debate broke out in a back room during the welcoming fiesta. Martinez, Sosa, and their allies proposed to give the bishop a letter to take home, expressing the sentiment of Guatemalans in the United States about the country's national election. Former general Efrain Ríos Montt, the president who ordered the bloodiest massacres of the 1980s, was once again a candidate. Ixim's activists wanted to remind their countrymen about this terrible past, the principal reason why many Guatemalans now live in exile.

"I don't think it is a political move. It is just a call to consciousness," Martinez said at the time. But the letter provided convincing evidence that even those who left Guatemala long ago (in his case, twenty-two years) still feel they belong to a community partly located in Nebraska and partly in Santa Eulalia and San Miguel. "We must not forget the people in Guatemala," he cautioned. "As citizens of our country, it is our obligation to take an active role in who becomes president." In the end, the group at the fiesta voted to send the letter.

Bobadilla's visit was also evidence of the close relationship between church parishes in Omaha and the diocese of Huehuetenango. Sosa and Lorenzo even took the daring step of inviting non-Guatemalans to join Ixim, and brought North Americans to Santa Eulalia with groups of migrants returning home. This effort sought to provide the resources of affluent U.S. parishes to the poor ones of Huehuetenango. "We can't just organize Guatemalans," Sosa explains. "We have to open our own internal borders and let strangers into our lives."

He and other transnational community activists see migration itself as an act of resistance to globalization. Sosa believes indigenous communities have to preserve their own identities but also find allies in the countries to which they've migrated. Bobadilla agrees: "If they are going to stay here, while they should keep their own culture, they should begin to integrate themselves in U.S. culture as well. Otherwise they will always live separately. It will take a lot of years for immigrants to integrate themselves into this country. People must reside here and plant their roots."

The Costs of the Global Flow of Workers

Emigration has complicated social costs and benefits in communities of origin. It threatens cultural practices and indigenous languages. It exacerbates social and economic divisions in small rural towns as families with access to remittances sent home by relatives bid up land prices beyond the reach of families without that access. San Miguel now boasts a number of large modern houses built by refugees of 1982 who live in the United States. For the town's young people, migration doesn't seem a choice forced by war and massacre. Instead, it promises a standard of living higher than what they can achieve in Guatemala, even with a university degree.

With no economic development at home, migration has become a necessity. The ability to emigrate increasingly determines social and economic status in communities of origin. At the same time, poverty in industrial countries is increasingly defined by migration status.

U.S. immigration policy threatens to institutionalize this global flow of migration, as well as the roles of countries that employ it (such as the United States) and those that produce the migrants (such as Mexico and Guatemala). The main mechanisms for organizing the flow are guest-worker programs. Corporate interests have successfully made them the centerpiece of almost all reform proposals, whether made by Republicans or Democrats. As guest workers, migrants are considered only as workers to be directed to the industries where they can be used most profitably. At the same time, their communities of origin are assigned the function of providing a labor pool for the production of future workers.

Rich countries offer no support for their externalized labor reserves. Instead, home communities depend on remittances from migrants. Mexican president Vicente Fox boasted in 2005 that some of the world's most impoverished workers now send home more than $18 billion annually—a contribution to the economy approaching oil and tourism. At the same time, his government's policies for encouraging foreign investment are guaranteed to produce more migrants. Economic reforms cut subsidies on food, transport, and other necessities for poor families; meanwhile, wages are kept low by making it difficult to organize militant independent unions. Lack of rural credit and a flood of cheap U.S. agricultural imports make it almost impossible to earn a living as a small farmer. As economic pressure ratchets up and people leave, guest-worker programs step in to recruit labor for U.S. businesses.

This is not simply a U.S. or Mexican policy but an aspect of globalization. In 2005, Mode 4 of the General Agreement on Trade and Services proposed a worldwide system in which migrant labor would be contracted globally and funneled into industries in developed countries. Dependence on immigrant labor is growing in all industrial countries, and guest-worker programs are becoming popular as a result. Transnational migrants are increasingly viewed simply as workers in the global economy. Yet as that global economy reinforces economic inequality and desperation, migrant labor has also become one of its most important products.

The FIOB's Los Angeles coordinator, Odilia Romero, predicts that "expanded guest-worker programs will lead to the wholesale violation of migrants' rights." In previous periods, when U.S. immigration policy valued immigrants only for their labor power, it produced extremely abusive systems. The memory of the bracero program, which ran from 1942 to 1964, is so bitter that even today defenders of guest-worker schemes avoid association with the name "bracero." But before the braceros came, Filipinos were treated the same way—as a mobile, vulnerable workforce, circulated from labor camp to labor camp for over half a century. And before them the Japanese and Chinese, all the way back to slavery.

Today, guest workers are brought from tiny Guatemalan, Honduran, and Mexican towns to the pine forests of the eastern and southern United States. Their experience is remarkably similar.

U.S. immigration policy doesn't deter the flow of migrants across the border. Its basic function is defining the status of people once they're here. A policy based on supplying guest workers to industry, at a price industry wants to pay, has inequality built into it from the beginning. An immigration policy that denies community inevitably produces rootless people vulnerable to exploitation. It undermines workplace and community rights and affects nonimmigrants as well. It inhibits the development of families and culture, denying everyone what newcomers can offer.

The alternative is a policy that recognizes and values transnational communities. A pro-people, anticorporate immigration policy sees the creation and support of communities as a desirable goal. It reinforces indigenous culture and language, protects the rights of everyone, and seeks to integrate immigrants into the broader U.S. society.

The UN's International Convention on the Protection of the Rights of All Migrant Workers and Members of Their Families proposes this kind of framework, establishing equality of treatment with citizens of the host country. Both sending and receiving countries are responsible for protecting migrants, and both retain the right to determine who to admit into their territories and who has the right to work. Predictably, the countries that have ratified it are the sending countries. Those countries most interested in guest worker schemes, like the United States, have not.

"Another amnesty is part of the alternative also," Sosa says, "but ten years from now we're going to face the same situation again if we don't change the way we treat other countries. Treaties like the Central American Free Trade Agreement ensure that this will happen." Today working people of all countries are asked to accept continuing globalization, in which capital is free to go wherever it can earn the highest profits. Sosa argues that migrants must have the same freedom, with rights and status equal to those of anyone else. "I come from a faith tradition," he concludes. "Faith crosses borders. It says, this world is our world, for all of us."

A Word about This Book

Communities without Borders is a photographic look at transnational communities. The images were taken over a three-year period from 2000 through 2003. They tell the story of the Guatemalan exodus to Nebraska and of the Oaxacan communities created along the road from Oaxaca's Santiago Juxtlahuaca, through Maneadero in Baja California, to California's Madera and Sonoma counties. Through oral histories, *Communities without Borders* also presents the words and memories of Sergio Sosa, Rufino Dominguez, and other community members and leaders. They offer not only the raw material of their experience but also the conclusions they've drawn about its meaning and their answers to the broader political and social problems facing their communities.

When I began this project, I realized that a complete picture required a historical perspective on the border itself and on the key role of the bracero experience in postwar migration. Migration across what is now the U.S.-Mexico border predates the border's existence. When we compare the story of Mexican gold miner Joaquin Murrieta (1829–53) with the current history of the miners on both sides of the border in recent times, it's easier to see not just the development of the second-class status of Mexicans and Latinos living in the southwest United States but the ways their communities fought against inequality for the last 150 years.

On one side of the border, Alfredo Figueroa describes how hard it was to grow up as a Chicano in Blythe, California, before World War II. On the other, Antonio Murrieta, descendent of Joaquin Murrieta, explains why the history of his famous family is important to an understanding of how Mexicans see the status of undocumented immigrants in the United States today. Figueroa recalls that his grandfathers were jailed for singing about Joaquin Murrieta, while Antonio Murrieta remembers that his family name prevented an uncle from even crossing the border into the United States. The Oaxacans and Guatemalans who are now establishing communities in the United States are inheriting this history.

Communities without Borders describes the roots of transborder mining communities in the indigenous Mayo culture of southern Sonora, Mexico, and the efforts by present-day Mayos to preserve it. In this book I also examine the more recent history of these mining communities, which, like those of the Oaxacan Mixtecs or Guatemalan Qanjobales, are in some ways larger communities divided by the U.S.-Mexico border. This examination focuses on solidarity among miners, who historically have supported one another during strikes and efforts to improve mine conditions. That solidarity reached a high point during the 1998 strike in Cananea, a gold and silver mining city twenty-five miles south of the U.S. border, when miners lost a desperate effort to prevent layoffs generated by privatization. As a consequence, many joined their Oaxacan and Guatemalan brothers and sisters as undocumented migrants in the United States.

I would be remiss if I didn't present some perspective on the future of transnational migration. Since powerful political interests in Washington imagine that future as one of new guest-worker programs, this book looks at the largest such program—the braceros—during its heyday. The photographs in this section include images of one of the few camps still standing, in Blythe, California. Former braceros describe the abuse and hard life they endured. Rigoberto Garcia also remembers a more complex reality. He recalls strikes among braceros, and he explains that some of those contract laborers, like his brother, drew upon that experience when they helped to start the United Farm Workers. Many Mexican workers and their families eventually did gain U.S. legal residence after years in the bracero program. Garcia got his green card because a Japanese farmer saw the connection between his workers kept behind barbed wire in camps and his own experience in internment camps during World War II.

Today's guest workers describe experiences very similar to those of the braceros. Edilberto Morales recounts the terrible accident in which fourteen of his friends and coworkers drowned in Maine as they rushed to work in the pine forests, thinning trees at the end of the work season. His is a cautionary tale of debt—the effect of its pressure on families back in Guatemala and on the workers struggling to send home the money to help them survive. The stories of these guest workers present a disturbing vision of a possible future, should U.S. immigration policy ignore the reality of transnational communities and instead respond only to the desire by large U.S. businesses to set up another bracero system as a ready source for labor.

The United States (and other developed countries) face a fundamental

A former labor camp for braceros in Blythe, California

choice—a system imposing second-class status on migrants valued only for their work or vibrant communities of resourceful people, developing their own culture and deepening that of the communities around them. Braceros or equality.

Acknowledgments

Support from the Rockefeller Foundation made *Communities without Borders* possible. Robert Bach, Ruben Puentes, and Tomás Ybarra-Frausto understood the importance of documenting transnational communities well before this project began, as part of their overall commitment to supporting those communities. My wife, Lillian, a lifetime civil and immigrant rights activist, helped me see that the immense sacrifice made by families is the key to understanding the human reality of migration. She kept our own family going during the many months I spent on the road and helped sort through the photos and narratives each time I got back.

I've been an immigrant rights activist myself for a quarter century. Being part of this political and social movement helped me understand the world presented in this book. *Communities without Borders* is a product of that partisanship and commitment. I'm responsible for any omissions or errors made here, but I owe a lot to wonderful comrades and coworkers in People United for Human Rights, the Northern California Coalition for Immigrant Rights, the Labor Immigrant Organizers Network, and the many unions and community organizations in which I've worked over the years. Thanks to you all.

I interviewed several undocumented people while working on this project. Some of their names have been changed.

COMMUNITIES WITHOUT BORDERS

PART ONE

GLOBALIZING FARM LABOR

OAXACANS CREATE A NEW KIND OF CROSS-BORDER COMMUNITY

Juan Guzman, a Chatino from Oaxaca, lives under a bridge outside of Graton, California, in the middle of the wine-grape country of Sonoma County. He was getting day-labor jobs on the street in Graton but hadn't worked for a week.

A tent encampment of Triqui farm workers from Oaxaca in the middle of the grape fields near Geyserville, California. Their homes are bamboo structures, built using the same technique used to build animal enclosures in their hometown in Mexico.

Fausto Lopez helps Fernando, a Triqui boy who came to California to work, build his first house in their tent encampment.

Two Triqui farm workers from Oaxaca sit in the kitchen of their tent encampment near Geyserville.

This group of Triqui farm workers is part of a transnational community extending from Geyserville all the way to Oaxaca.

When Estela Guzman and her daughter, Jaquiline, first arrived in Geyserville, California, from Oaxaca, they lived in the tent camp. Later Estela moved to an apartment with her husband, Sebastian, where they had to pay rent but where raising a baby was safer and easier.

Fernando, a thirteen-year-old boy, washes pans in the settlement set up by migrant Triqui farm workers in the reeds near the Russian River.

A Mixtec farm worker gets a haircut from a friend in a camp on a hillside outside Delmar, near San Diego.

Domingo, a Oaxacan migrant, sits inside his tent on a Delmar hillside.

Chatino indigenous immigrants from Oaxaca live outdoors in a field in Sonoma County's wine country.

Children of migrant Mixtec families play in a trailer park in the fields near Madera, California.

Raul Dominguez, a Mixtec immigrant from San Miguel Cuevas, Oaxaca, picks grapes.

A teenager works picking wine grapes in a Napa Valley field.

A farm worker prunes grapevines outside Madera, California.

An older worker ties grapevines to wires after the pruning.

Rufino Dominguez, coordinator of the Binational Front of Indigenous Organizations, and Eduardo Stanley, a local journalist, host a Spanish-language radio program for Oaxacan and other Mexican migrant farm workers on KFCF-FM in Fresno, California. The program covers community issues and informs people about their labor and immigration rights.

Mixtec basketball players participate in the tournament organized every year by the Binational Front of Indigenous Organizations. While soccer is the national sport for most Mexicans, Mixtecs in Oaxaca and California love basketball.

Oaxacan basketball players get ready to play.

Members of the Binational Front of Indigenous Organizations vote in Tijuana to expel a former leader, Arturo Pimentel, for failing to be accountable to the membership of their organization. The profoundly democratic process of the Frente is based on the communal decision-making tradition of indigenous communities in Oaxaca.

The residents of Cañon Buenavista, a community of indigenous farm workers created by land invasions in Maneadero, Baja California Norte, take the husks off tomatillos.

A family takes the husks off tomatillos in Cañon Buenavista.

A young boy gets ready to pick tomatoes on the ranch of the Santa Cruz Packing Company, owned by the Castañeda family, in San Quintin, Baja California Norte.

Migrant Mixtec farm workers in Maneadero, Baja California Norte, harvesting cilantro for export to the United States.
Wages are so low that the whole family, including children, has to work to earn enough to live.

One of several storefront telephones in Juxtlahuaca, Oaxaca, where most families don't have private phones of their own. On the side of the store are listed the main towns in northern Mexico where the town's residents go in search of work. The latest destination is written on the cloth banner—the United States.

A woman in the FIOB office in Santiago de Juxtlahuaca wears a cap sent her by her daughter, who works for a strawberry grower in Santa Maria, California.

In her home in Agua Fria, Oaxaca, Centolia Maldonado's mother cooks in the traditional way over charcoal and wood.

The Flor Mixteca (Mixtec Flower) brings vegetables to the weekly market in Juxtlahuaca, Oaxaca, from the small towns in the surrounding hills.

A barber gives a boy a haircut in Santiago de Juxtlahuaca.

On the wall of a building in Santiago de Juxtlahuaca, the government promises young people that it will support them if they finish their schooling.

A Triqui woman walks through the street on market day in Santiago de Juxtlahuaca, Oaxaca.

A Triqui woman weaving cloth in Yosoyusi, Oaxaca. Yosoyusi is the hometown of Julio Sandoval, who was imprisoned in Baja California for leading housing struggles among Triqui migrant farm workers.

With the help of the Binational Front of Indigenous Organizations, women weavers in Juxtlahuaca, Oaxaca, have formed a street sellers' and artisans' organization to send their textiles to California, where family members living there can sell them at a better price.

A Triqui woman during a meeting of a street sellers' and artisans' organization in Santiago de Juxtlahuaca wears a traditional *huipil*.

Women weavers listen during a meeting of street sellers and artisans in the office of the Binational Front of Indigenous Organizations in Santiago de Juxtlahuaca.

1

Indigenous people from Oaxaca have been migrating within Mexico and to the United States for decades. Many were braceros during that program's twenty-two-year run from 1942 to 1964. In Mexican agricultural valleys from Sinaloa to Baja California, Oaxacan migrants are the backbone of the labor force that made corporate agriculture possible.

As a result, communities of Oaxacans have settled in a broad swath that extends from their state of origin through Veracruz, where they went first as the labor force in the sugar harvest, through northwest Mexico's fields of tomatoes and strawberries, into the valleys of California's San Joaquin and Oregon's Willamette rivers, and to Washington state, Florida, and beyond.

In Madera, California, restaurants bear Mixtec names. During meetings of Florida's Coalition of Immokalee Workers, people can be heard talking softly in the same language at the back of the room. Los Angeles furniture shops employ Zapotec-speaking workers, and Triqui-speakers are an important constituency in Oregon's PCUN union for farm workers.

Settlements of Mixtecs, Zapotecs, Triquis, and other Oaxacan indigenous groups along the three-thousand-mile-long migrant stream from Oaxaca to the Pacific Northwest are bound together by shared cultures, languages, and social organizations that people carry with them from place to place. While dispersed inside Mexico and the United States, the movement of people has created larger communities, located in different places simultaneously.

Some of the organizations among Oaxacan migrants are based on common towns of origin—a general phenomenon among immigrants to the United States. But Oaxacans have also developed the Frente Indigena de Organizaciones Binacionales, the Indigenous Front of Binational Organizations, which unites different language groups in order to promote community and workplace struggles for social justice.

Near Santa Rosa, California, Triqui migrants created a community of makeshift homes along the banks of the Russian River, near the vineyards that produce the wine and wealth of Sonoma County. At first glance the migrants seem to be living in unimaginably difficult conditions—sleeping on mattresses dragged into the bushes, cooking on rough fireplaces in the reeds, and taking shelter out of doors.

But this community has strong cultural bonds holding people together, creating a support network that provides food and companionship for migrants just arriving from the south with no work and no money. In the cattails of a riverbank, this group built homes of bamboo, lined with plastic from the local Home Depot. Their grandparents used similar traditional techniques to erect structures in Oaxaca. Workers living here belong to the Frente—in fact, Fausto Lopez, the tiny community's leader, was the president of the Sonoma County chapter when it was first organized.

Led by Lopez and Lorenzo Oropeza, who left the fields to become a community worker for California Rural Legal Assistance, the people living under the trees have walked in marches calling for driver's licenses for undocumented workers. They've spoken out for a new immigration amnesty that would allow people to play a more open role in the political and social life of the county where they live.

Living under a tree did not rob them of their voice or their organizational skills.

Lopez and Oropeza also look for answers to the problem of cultural preservation. How can Triqui-speaking farm workers migrate to the United States for work, while still ensuring that their children speak their language and preserve the cultural bonds that allow them to survive? Lopez sent his wife and child back to Oaxaca for that reason before leaving Baja California for the United States. Oropeza is equally concerned that indigenous migrants learn to protect themselves from exploitation in the jobs they now depend on.

FAUSTO LOPEZ
THE MAN IN THE REEDS
Geyserville, California, May 2003

While living in plastic-covered tents near the Russian River, Fausto Lopez and other members of this Triqui settlement tried to find solutions to the complex problem of ensuring that their children maintain their language and ethnic identity, while advocating for the rights of migrants in the United States. Fausto here says there were no problems with the local residents around them, but a youth gang burned out the settlement a year after I interviewed him.

My father was a corn farmer in Oaxaca. When I was a child, my entire family spoke Triqui. When I started going to school, the teachers there spoke Triqui and began teaching in our language. Then they started speaking Spanish. I learned how to do math and other subjects in Spanish, but I didn't really understand what I was saying.

I left my town, Yosoyusi, for Baja California in 1987. When I left, there were about five hundred inhabitants. I went back to visit in 1998, and there were new homes and more development. About half the town's population has migrated to other places to work—Mexico City, Sinaloa, Sonora, and Baja California. Some people work and return home, while others never go back.

In 1990 I went to Ensenada [seaport in Baja California] and worked there for ten years. I started to speak with other workers—Mixtecos, Zapotecos, and others that spoke Spanish. I met other people from Durango and Zacatecas and other states who also only spoke Spanish. That is how I learned Spanish. It seemed simple to me because I practiced daily.

After my family joined me, we lived on a ranch and harvested squash, cabbage, lettuce, watermelon, and corn. Because the harvest rose dramatically, I became the supervisor of the packing department, and later I worked in the office.

Fausto Lopez in his shelter of bamboo and plastic

In Baja California our community got organized as more and more Triquis arrived. Many needed housing and we organized ourselves to find land for it. We named our new settlement Nuevo San Juan Copala, which comes from the name of the Triqui area in Oaxaca. Now there are more Triquis near Ensenada than any other indigenous group. More and more Triquis are arriving in the area, and there's still not enough housing. The majority stay and never return to their hometowns.

Because the pay wasn't enough for clothing and medical expenses as our family expanded, I left for the U.S. in 1999 with my father. My cousins in the U.S. called me and asked me to join them. The first time I crossed the border we walked for two days through Nogales, Arizona, in January. It was very cold. Since then, I've always crossed with coyotes, but ones I've known for a long time. In 1999 it cost me $600, and today it costs $800, but there isn't a lot of walking involved—just a day.

When I first immigrated to the U.S., I left my wife and children in Ensenada. When the school year ended, I sent them back to Oaxaca, so that my children would learn Triqui. Here in California that wouldn't be possible. In Ensenada they were taught some Triqui through books in school, but that isn't the same as an environment like Oaxaca, where people speak it. I want my children to learn Spanish but also keep our traditions, which I feel that they are losing. I have spoken with Zapotec and Mixtec parents who feel the same.

My wife and I are trying to preserve our culture. We teach our children Triqui as well as Spanish. Things are changing so much that young Triqui children are learning Spanish a lot sooner. The television, radio, and music that surrounds them is all in Spanish, as well as the books and newspapers.

The people I know here [in the U.S.] are all immigrants with no money or home. We are all Triquis from Copala, but from different communities. In 1999 there were only two families living here. One family had been here five or six years. Now there are ten of us.

When we first arrive, we build small huts out of anything. Our great grandfathers made similar homes in Mexico, using large leaves to make a roof. We use plastic sheets from Home Depot. We all save money by living like this. In 1992 there was a fire close to our community. When the sheriff and firefighters arrived, they put out the fire. Later they returned and removed thirty people living here. But we came back, and since then we haven't had a problem with the local people.

The majority here work in the grape harvest. We work by the hour in the planting season, and during the harvest by piece rate. We earn nine dollars [per hour] if the field is far away, and eight dollars if it's close.

We relax and play sports together and talk about the maintenance of our community. Everyone cooks for themselves. I enrolled in two English classes at the adult school here, but I couldn't continue. Our work hours are so long that I don't have time to go to class.

When you see Fernando, a thirteen- or fourteen-year-old boy who lives with you, how does that make you feel?

He's like a part of our family, and I feel sad because he's so young. He should not be here. He should be in school. But he's here for the same reason as the rest of us. He's been here for three weeks and just started working.

In the last few years I met Lorenzo [an organizer for the Indigenous Front of Binational Organizations (FIOB) and California Rural Legal Assistance], and he guides us. Lorenzo began talking to us about how to organize ourselves and how to speak with our supervisors. FIOB helped us a lot on work-related problems and life skills. I think it's a wonderful organization.

I joined FIOB because Lorenzo speaks my native language. He works with all Oaxaqueños, not just Triquis. He is Mixteco and we are Triqui, but since we're from the same state we're all the same. Then our local group elected me to represent them. I traveled to various parts of the state with Lorenzo and met with other leaders. I'm learning a lot.

A lot of us farm workers don't know our rights, and FIOB teaches us. We also work for amnesty for immigrants, because so many of us cross the border illegally, and so many die in the process. An amnesty would create more opportunity for all of us.

I don't want to be apart from my family. The fact of the matter is that it is necessary. I am here so that they have a better life. I want my children to go to school and hope to give them a home when they are older. I never had the opportunity to have a home as a child. I am doing all of this for my family.

LORENZO OROPEZA

A COMMUNITY ORGANIZER

Santa Rosa, California, March 2003

Lorenzo Oropeza was a migrant farm worker most of his life. He now uses his experiences as a community organizer to teach indigenous workers how to defend themselves.

I come from a Mixtec family. Although my parents spoke Mixteco to each other, they spoke to us in Spanish. My grandparents, may they rest in peace, spoke to me in Mixteco and that is how I learned. When we were old enough to go to school, the teachers spoke to us in Spanish. The majority of people my age don't like speaking Mixteco, but I do. We must maintain our language even though we don't speak it perfectly.

When I was thirteen or fourteen years old, my father took me to work with him. I plowed the land with two oxen to prepare for farming rice. And by the time I was fifteen years old I was also going to Sinaloa with him as a migrant. There I met a friend who told me to come to California. I told my father I was going with my friend, and he began to weep.

We crossed the border at noon and in half an hour we were already in San Ysidro. There was only a chain link fence with holes everywhere. Now it is more difficult. I couldn't find work for a month. My fellow countrymen helped me by giving me food. I wouldn't eat all day, and in the evenings we would gather and all eat together. When I think about the living conditions migrants endure today, those conditions haven't changed since 1973 at least, when I got here.

The first time I went to San Diego I was eighteen years old, and there was still money to be made. So I soon began migrating to California every year. I would finish the harvest season and then leave. In November I would return home to harvest the rice. In the U.S. we would live all together and never venture into the cities for fear of the border patrol. We would send money to our families and build homes or establish businesses in Mexico.

Lorenzo Oropeza in an outdoor training on labor rights

After I married, I lived and worked with my father another ten years. It was hard when my wife and I separated from him. From 1973 to 1993 I only came seasonally. Then in 1992 my wife came to the U.S. for the first time, here to Sonoma County. I lived on a ranch owned by my boss, in a trailer home. When my wife arrived she asked me if we were going to live there. I told her yes, and she said she was sad to leave a nice home in Oaxaca to live in these conditions. She was here for four months and then went back.

Unfortunately, now in my hometown there are only about 250 people. In 1973 the population was 1,000 or more. The first men who came to the United States came as braceros in 1945. They would meet in Guaymas and then be transported here. The majority began migrating later, but that is how we got the idea. When I first came, migrating was already common. I began to think that I should come, since everyone else was doing it. Our state is so poor it is a necessity to emigrate simply to feed your family. In

Yucuyachi, my hometown, only the elderly are left. The young are living in various parts of the United States.

People from my hometown live in Santa Rosa, Santa Maria, San Jose, and San Diego, California. All of these communities are tied together. In each city we have a committee that meets monthly to discuss the needs of our people here. We also have a larger committee from the different cities. With donations from our people and the Yucuyachi government, we were able to improve the center of our town. We paved the streets, rebuilt the church, and changed the plumbing for the public drinking water.

We give money and do the work ourselves. Returning to help wasn't difficult in the seventies or eighties. Now it's extremely difficult and expensive, so the town government finds people who need the money to do it. It's easy to go back home but not easy to return. Still, the majority of our people living here go back to visit every year.

When we first arrived, I would tell my family we were going to return to Mexico because we built our house there. But we are still living here, while my parents live in our house in Mexico. My children were born and raised here. They're not used to the temperature and way of life there. They understand Mixteco and can ask for basic things like food. I always told them they had to learn the language. Now I have two granddaughters who can count to twenty in Mixteco.

I learned about the Binational Front of Indigenous Organizations when I began working for California Rural Legal Assistance in 2000. In Sonoma County we now have fifteen to twenty workers who belong.

The people who live out by the river in Geyserville are very active, and we're trying to organize the community near Graton. We give people in both communities food baskets, clothing, and transportation. They come to all our marches and meetings.

I am interested in educating people. Many of my fellow immigrants are farm laborers. They may not be in this country legally, but they still have rights. I want to help them feel more secure. Sometimes people organize themselves, but most are reluctant for fear of losing their job. We come

from a very poor country and simply want to earn money to send back home. The majority live on the grower's property.

When I was working with California Rural Legal Assistance, a group of Oaxaqueños asked me to help them because they weren't being paid fairly. I told them that they had to organize themselves and as a group demand what they were owed. When they did, the owner fired them all. As they were leaving the premises, the owner stopped them and told them he would pay them the right amount. If people stick together, they can win their rights.

2

The dispersal of indigenous people from Oaxaca is so large, and their concentration in California so great, that they often jokingly call the state Oaxacalifornia. But despite this dispersal they have found a way to unite, not just around language and their towns of origin but through their identity as indigenous Oaxacan migrants. Because their communities exist on both sides of the border, one center of activity lies in Fresno and another in Oaxaca itself. A third is located close to the border, in Tijuana and Ensenada.

The Frente Indigena de Organizaciones Binacionales began in 1987 at meetings in California's Central Valley and in Los Angeles and San Diego. At its founding on October 5, 1991, it was called the Frente Mixteco Zapoteco Binacional because the founders wanted to unite immigrants belonging to three Mixtec organizations and two Zapotec ones. Soon the organization had to change its name. Triquis and other indigenous Oaxacan people wanted to participate but felt the Frente's name excluded them. It became the Frente Indigena Oaxaqueña Binacional, the Indigenous Oaxacan Binational Front. In 2005 it broadened its scope again, including migrant communities with origins outside of Oaxaca, like Mixtecs from Puebla and Guerrero, or Purepechas from Michoacan.

Soon after its formation, the organization began looking for a strategy that would reflect the reality of Mexican indigenous communities. It used the celebrations of the five-hundredth anniversary of the arrival of Christopher Columbus in the Americas as a platform to dramatize its call for indigenous rights. When the Zapatista army rose in Chiapas on January 1, 1994, the day the North American Free Trade Agreement went into effect, the Frente immediately mounted actions to pressure the Mexican government to refrain from using massive military force to crush it. From Fresno to Baja California to Oaxaca, Frente activists went on hunger strikes and demonstrated in front of consulates and government offices. That experience solidified the organization's binational character, sparked the development of cross-border tactics, and contributed to its activist identity.

Activism was hardly a strange idea, however. Rufino Dominguez, FIOB's coordinator, has a long history as a strike leader in the fields of northern Mexico, where indigenous Oaxacans first began fighting for their rights as migrant workers. Jorge and Margarita Giron remember not only how abysmal the conditions were that provoked those strikes but also the improvements that resulted.

These experiences undoubtedly played a role in the decision by Frente leaders in the mid-1990s to forge an alliance with the United Farm Workers in California. The same year that Cesar Chavez, the UFW's founder, died in Arizona, the Frente began a collaboration with his successor, its new president Arturo Rodriguez. The union organized a month-long peregrination from Delano to Sacramento, recapitulating its seminal march in 1967, to dramatize to California farm workers its renewed commitment to field organizing. The pact with the Frente had a similar aim for the union—to win support among a key group in the fields, the growing community of Mixtec-speaking migrants from Oaxaca. Frente leaders, however, continue to have very mixed feelings about the alliance, in part because they encountered among the Mexican members of the union the same discriminatory attitudes toward indigenous people common in Mexico.

Nevertheless, organizing Oaxacan migrants around their rights as workers continues to be a bedrock activity for the FIOB in California. Irma Luna describes her early life in rural Oaxaca, speaking Mixtec and not knowing Spanish, and then her remarkable journey to the United States and her transformation into a workers' rights advocate. Oralia Maceda had her baptism of political fire in Oaxaca, but also came north to Fresno, where she uses her activist skills to reach out to constituencies in the Oaxacan community who have traditionally not had a strong voice. Women in FIOB have begun to change the traditional domination of community political life by men, and both Luna and Maceda have worked to develop participation by women and young people. Because of the strong pressure on children and teenagers in the United States to assimilate into a dominant lifestyle of mass consumption, maintaining a connection to faraway home communities is difficult. Winning the interest of youth in indigenous languages and cultural practices is even harder.

Dominguez and other activists use Mixtec-language programs on the radio to inform and organize their communities. Many Oaxacans are fanatical basketball players, and migrants from the same hometown form teams, with playoffs and a championship in Madera, California, every year. The Guelaguetza cultural festival, begun in Oaxaca, now also unfolds in Fresno and Los Angeles.

The Frente's organizing strategy is based on the culture of Oaxacan communities, particularly the tequio, the concept of collective work and collective responsibility. The FIOB newsletter is even called "Tequio." The tequio is a crucial institution in Oaxacan hometowns, which depend on it to repair roads and carry out public works, and to fill political positions at town assemblies. Jorge Giron describes his election by his home community while he was in California and his decision to accept the responsibility and go home to serve.

Many Oaxacans living in the United States express deep concern about the difficulties of transmitting their traditions and language to their children. The pressures of assimilation are intense, and although institutions like the tequio are well adapted to life in a Oaxacan village, migrants have yet to incorporate them into the responsibilities they owe to their communities in the United States.

RUFINO DOMINGUEZ
ORGANIZING ACROSS THE BORDER

Fresno, California, November 2001

Rufino Dominguez is FIOB's binational coordinator, and much more. He articulates its politics and the vision that has taken FIOB a giant step beyond hometown associations. In his history as organizer and strike leader, one can see the roots of FIOB in the social struggles of Oaxacan migrants as they began their migration through northern Mexico. Dominguez eventually confronted the high personal cost of sacrificing family to the demands of the movement, a familiar dilemma for organizers everywhere.

My father was a carpenter and an artist. He was also a *curandero* [healer] and treated people's illnesses. He and my mother grew corn and beans to survive. I don't know when the migration of our people first began, but it was already going on when my father was young. At first many indigenous people went to Veracruz to work harvesting sugarcane. They say the people went walking. My father went to Veracruz, and he could count the days it took to get there.

Then people went to Mexico City to work on the construction of the metro. After that they went to Sinaloa to work in the fields, and then to Sonora and Baja California.

The first people from Oaxaca who came to the U.S. were single men in the bracero program. They didn't come in large numbers, but there were some. They were recruited in Mexico City, where many indigenous people were already living. Then it began to grow, and by the 1980s whole families were migrating. This had never been seen before. That was the time of the economic crisis, when living conditions were the worst.

Back then people traveled in stages, that is, first to Sinaloa, then to Baja California, and finally to the U.S. But now very few do that. Most people come here directly and go back to Oaxaca. Many of us have our families

Rufino Dominguez in a workshop of FIOB members in Tijuana

here, or people from the same town. We have a place to go to, and someone who pays for the travel. That did not exist before.

But even those who live in the U.S. migrate. Many from Fresno go to Oregon in May to pick strawberries. From there they go to Washington to pick apples or cherries. When the grape season is over others go to Corning in the northern Sacramento Valley to harvest olives. People from the same town in Oaxaca for the most part migrate to the same areas. The majority of people from my town, San Miguel Cuevas, live in Kerman or Fresno. Our families live together—it is rare for people to be alone.

As a boy, I studied with a religious group, the Marist Brothers. That's where my social consciousness began. When I graduated from high school, I was one step away from being one of them, but at the last moment I didn't go. They had a beautiful life, but they didn't get married and they couldn't organize, something I was passionate about. Even though they spoke about the need to stand up for justice, they would only talk and not actually do it.

So when I was fifteen I returned home. I started to organize, and my life took off. A hacienda owner, Gregorio Platon, was abusing his authority by charging migrants for traveling to Sinaloa to work. He put those who didn't pay in jail. He burned the homes of five families and killed three people. After two years of fighting, we got him out, but a friend was killed and I was tortured. The town rescued us—otherwise we wouldn't be alive today.

In 1984 I migrated to Sinaloa. I saw a lot of discrimination toward indigenous people. The bosses would say, "You donkey, put some strength into it!" So I started the Organization of Exploited and Oppressed People, with the help of the Independent Confederation of Farm Workers and Small Farmers. Benito Garcia, a Mixteco from San Juan Mixtepec, helped us, and we organized marches and strikes. From there I went to Baja California, where we organized thousands of people, too.

Finally, I crossed the border into the U.S. to Selma, California. When I arrived I felt like I was in my hometown. People asked me to continue my work here. I didn't even know how to drive, or where the sun rises and where it sets. But we began.

The Frente Mixteco Zapoteco Binacional was founded on October 5, 1991, in Los Angeles to unite three Mixteco and two Zapoteco organizations. It took off in 1992, when the governing bodies of the world were celebrating the famous five hundred years since the discovery of the Americas. They said that Christopher Columbus was welcomed as a grand hero who brought good things. But they wouldn't talk about the massacres or the genocide in our villages. All the indigenous organizations on the American continent protested against this celebration.

We wanted to tell a different story—that our people were stripped of our culture. They imposed a different God on us and told us that nature wasn't worth anything. In reality nature gives us life. Our purpose was to dismantle the old stereotypes, to march, to protest. After that we thought, Why not keep organizing for human rights, labor rights, housing, and education? There are many problems in our communities.

In 1993 with California Rural Legal Assistance we organized a project to educate indigenous immigrants about labor rights in our own languages. Many bosses don't pay their workers for months, and sometimes for years or never at all, because many people don't have their documents. When they are deported, the patron keeps the workers' wages. They often pay below minimum wage, forcing us to live in subhuman conditions in places where we shouldn't have to live at all. But if someone doesn't know the language, they can't demand their rights. Workers must learn their rights so that they can demand them.

That same year we also began a collaboration with the United Farm Workers under its new president, Arturo Rodriguez. We recognized that the UFW is a strong union representing agricultural workers. They in turn recognized us as an organization that tries to gain rights for indigenous migrants.

Even within the UFW, though, some people still thought we were ignorant or retarded. They'd call us Oaxaquitas or Oaxacos [meaning little people from Oaxaca] to make fun of us. Some people in the union said that indigenous people were *rompehuelgistas* [strikebreakers] or *equiroles* [scabs]. In '84 there was a strike in Merced, and we were called these names. But the people from the union spoke to us only in Spanish. They didn't understand that our people spoke only Mixteco or Zapoteco, so many times, because of the language barrier, we couldn't understand each other.

Finally, I criticized them during public events. This treatment doesn't live up to the political ideals of the union, I told them. They should welcome indigenous people and be more open-minded. We are not Oaxaquitos or Oaxacos. We are Oaxaqeños. Not everyone who comes from Mexico, or from Latin America, speaks Spanish. Indigenous languages need to be respected and recognized. In reality, although we felt the union didn't take us seriously, that campaign was historic because the union finally recognized us in a formal way.

Indigenous Oaxaqueños understand the need for community and organization. When people migrate from a community in Oaxaca, in the new places where they settle they form a committee comprised of people from their hometown. They are united and live near one another. This is a tradition they don't lose, wherever they go.

We use the tequio, the concept of collective work to support our community. We know one another and can act together. For instance, when a community gathers to build a school, the government doesn't send workers to gather rocks or sand for construction. People from the community do it. They each take turns, carrying five rocks or a bag of sand. The whole town is obligated to help, and if people don't, there are consequences, like going to jail or getting fined.

Wherever we go, we go united. It's a way of saying that I do not speak alone—we all speak together. Our people in Oaxaca don't care if we have been here for ten years. They send us notices telling us, "Rufino, you have to return to serve the community as a secretary, to be a council person, or a president." Mexican law doesn't recognize that we, living here, have political rights. But in our indigenous communities, we do.

If that existed in the United States, it would be very interesting, very different from the way we live here. For those that live in the U.S., the obligation of the tequio is to send money to our communities of origin, to return when asked to assume responsibilities, and to contribute work to a community project. If we have a position here, we are obligated to send money to contribute to the development of the community there. But if we get a notice to serve, we have to go for a year or two, depending on the position. We give our time for free. We're not earning anything—we're cooperating.

Here that tradition of mutual assistance exists, too. For example, when someone dies here, it is rare that they are also buried here. Most return. Over four hundred people from my hometown, San Miguel Cuevas, live in the United States. Fifteen years ago we decided that every person must contribute thirty dollars to send the body of anyone who dies back to our town. This is an example of the tequio. We think about what would happen if we were to die, and we all expect we would help each other.

Beyond organizing and teaching our rights, we try to save our language. Even though five hundred years have passed since the Spanish conquest, we

still speak it. We are preserving our way of dancing, and we are rescuing our lost beliefs—that nature is something sacred for us, just as it was for our ancestors.

Years ago, in many communities in Oaxaca people discriminated against us for speaking a different language, for dressing differently—because our skin is darker and we have straight hair. Many of us felt, Why should I speak this language if all they do is laugh at me? Why should I dress this way if the world says I am a native and ignorant? I felt that way, going to high school in a large town, away from where I'd grown up. The girls would laugh at me, and I felt embarrassed. I said, I'm going to stop speaking Mixteco because they laugh at me every day. I'm going to stop walking next to my mother because she dresses in a traditional manner. It was the racism from the mestizo—people who do not consider themselves indigenous. Many stopped speaking the language and denied being indigenous. It wasn't their fault. It was the lack of education and the racism that surrounded them.

When I was young, I didn't know how to appreciate who I was, what I spoke, or what I had. I didn't know what it was to be indigenous. Now I know my identity, and I'm proud of it. I know that I am Mixteco or a "Nusami," as we say in our language.

But losing your culture is much easier in the U.S. Many indigenous children now speak only English, not Spanish or any indigenous language.

I got married in 1984 and came here with my wife. But since 1979 I've spent my life struggling and demanding our rights. So in 1999 I got divorced because I was away from home too much. I spent more time on the community than on my family, and my wife couldn't take it. She told me that I had to choose between them or the struggle. It was very painful, but I said I had to continue. I don't know. If I'd stayed with my family, I would have become closed and gone crazy. I have four children, all boys. One is in his last year in high school and the rest are small. I see them every eight days. That's the sad part of my life.

People in my community said, "We always thought nobody would ever want to live with you because you're always going from one place to another." Very pessimistic, huh? My wife and family thought that because I preferred this work it was obvious that I didn't love them, that it was irresponsible for me not to give them the time that they deserved or needed. But it was hard for me to see so many problems and not do anything about them. I wanted to make a difference. So it was very difficult for me to say no. I have something in my blood that I can't remove so easily. We are very complicated and difficult individuals. We have the ability to communicate, but we don't use it at that critical moment.

In this country, the rights of women are well respected, but those same laws increase divorce. It's still not too common in our community, but more people get divorced now. With time it will be something normal, I think.

Raul Dominguez and his family in their Madera trailer park

RAUL DOMINGUEZ
A GRAPE WORKER
Madera, California, October 2002

Raul Dominguez is a grape worker in California's Central Valley. Although he speaks Mixteco and tries to hold on to his indigenous culture, his children live in a world of English—in school, on television, and among friends. He wonders whether they will all ever live in Mexico again.

I reached the fifth grade. I came here after that and started working. Work, earn money, and send money to help my parents—that's what I thought of doing. Before I left I saw men return to our town from the United States and they were always well dressed with new shoes, while we who lived in Mexico didn't even own shoes. We just wore huaraches. The people who returned from the United States always had money, and in Mexico you work hard and still don't have enough money. That's why I decided to come to the U.S.

As a child I wanted to be in a musical group and play an instrument. In Mexico there isn't money for that. If we asked, our parents got mad and asked why we needed it. When I came to the United States, I bought myself a guitar. That was my dream. I came in 1988 with my brother Damian and returned after the grape harvest was finished. That was the first time, and I liked it. Since then, I've gone back and forth quite often.

We crossed the border by ourselves, through the hills near San Ysidro. We walked for three hours and got a taxi that took us to Bakersfield. When I arrived we lived in migrant housing, where many other people from San Miguel Cuevas were living. The second time we came to the United States we were robbed in Mexico City. A taxi driver told us he would take us to the bus station. It was dark and he told us we were being followed by police officers. He drove into an alley, and then he and his friends pulled us out of the cab and beat us up. They searched our belongings and took what we had. I was scared, because they had a gun.

Margarita and I got married and came to the U.S. together in 1989. We do seasonal work in the fields. It's hard when the children get sick or when you lose a job. We still send a little money to Mexico, since my mother is still there. I send her about three hundred dollars a month when I'm working, and the rest goes for my wife, children, and the rent.

It is more difficult living in the U.S. now, since what happened in New York [on September 11]. It's more difficult to cross the border now. A lot of people going through the desert die from the heat. Everyone is saying that the Border Patrol and police are going to get us, and we feel very insecure. Still, as long as we're working everything should be fine.

Right now I'm working the grape harvest. I work from six in the morning until six in the afternoon, and I earn about a hundred dollars a day. You get off of work very tired, and the harvest only lasts about twenty days. We used to work the olive harvest in Fresno, but we don't move around much now, because the children would miss a lot of school. Daisy is in fourth grade. We want her to get an education because there are many opportunities for her here.

When she first began school, she was taught in both English and Spanish, but now her classes are only in English. At first her homework assignments were in Spanish and we understood them, but now we don't. In Mexico, when your school day is over, you still have to go home to work in the fields. Here, kids get home and study or read. It is not as hard. There, if you don't pass your exam, you stay in that same grade until you learn the material. Here, if you learn you learn, and if not you still get passed to the next grade. In Mexico there are some children that are thirteen or fourteen years old and are still in third or fourth grade.

As a child in San Miguel, we spoke Mixteco and not Spanish. I learned to speak Spanish in the third grade. My wife and I speak Mixteco to each other, but we speak Spanish to my daughters. They know a little Mixteco, but they know more Spanish. When they speak with each other they use English. Television is all in English. They understand Mixteco but they don't speak it, and learning it is difficult for them. We have taken them to Mexico, but they ask us when we are going to return to the U.S. They are not accus-tomed to the food or school there. Most of the children born in the United States don't like to go back to Mexico.

I think we'll eventually return to Oaxaca, but you never know because the years go by and we're still here. I think our daughters will live here in the United States.

IRMA LUNA
KEEPING MIXTECO ALIVE
Fresno, California, July 2002

Irma Luna never went to school in Mexico. It was only after being smuggled across the border by her brother that she began to learn Spanish and English, but she fought to retain her Mixteco heritage. Today she is a workers' rights advocate in the fields of the San Joaquin Valley, where she helps other indigenous women overcome domestic violence.

I was born in Sinaloa in April 1972 in an agricultural camp where my parents worked. We slept on the floor on cardboard and plastic and cooked on the floor. We washed our clothes in the canals and brought our water back from there. In those days very few people migrated to the United States. People would migrate to other states in Mexico to work.

I was four or five when my mother passed away. I don't remember her—I just have some pictures. My father and I returned to San Miguel Cuevas, and I have very good memories of my hometown. I never went to school. My father registered me in first grade, but I would not go, so he took me out. Instead I began working with him. He cultivated the land and I went to the hills and took care of the sheep, cattle, and horses. I didn't play much with other girls—they talked about things like homework and I talked about the animals, so we couldn't relate.

Irma Luna tells the foreman of a labor crew to respect the rights of indigenous Mixtec workers.

I would leave the house early in the morning and not return until almost sunset. There wasn't a lot of time to play—we were very poor and I didn't have any dolls. Life for a ten-year-old little girl with no schooling, living with a stepmother, was difficult. It was a life of a girl with no shoes and little clothing, taking care of cattle in the hills. My oldest brother, who migrated to the United States in 1978, knew that I wasn't in school or learning how to cook at home. I was eleven when he returned to San Miguel Cuevas. When I saw him packing to go back to the United States, I brought my two changes of clothes, put them under my arm, and said, "Let's go, I'm ready." He asked me, "Where are you going?" and I said, "I'm ready to go to the North."

My brother had a green card, but I didn't have any papers, so he told me he couldn't take me. I had no idea what kind of papers they were talking about, and I started crying. His wife tried to talk to me in Spanish, because she doesn't speak Mixteco. When my brother told her I wanted to go with them, she said she would take me. They didn't have children of their own.

As we were driving they started to talk about how we were going to get me across. My sister-in-law's sister had three children born in the United States, so my brother put me with them as if I was a fourth child. Those children were very light skinned with blonde hair and I was dark skinned with black hair. They were laughing, saying that I was going to look like a fly in a glass of milk, but they couldn't think of another option.

My brother told me to pretend I was asleep. The next thing I know an official is looking under the seat and talking to me. I couldn't understand him, but after ten minutes we got into the car again and continued on our way. An hour later we stopped. They got out, and began cheering and laughing because we had made it. I thought about all I'd heard over the years about how difficult it was to cross the border. I suppose they all prayed a lot, and my father too, because I crossed so easily.

My father told my brother that he could take me for a year, and then I had to return because there was work to be done at home. But a year and half after I left he passed away. My brother told me that we no longer had a mother or father or anyone to take care of me back home. To everyone's surprise, twenty years have passed and I'm still here in the United States.

I owe everything to my brother. I see a lot of parents who bring children ten and twelve years old, like I was, intending that they'll work to help the family. Thank God, my brother had a stable job in a butcher shop so I didn't have to work. He wanted me to go to school.

When I first came I didn't speak Spanish or English. My brother told me I had to leave the Mixteco language behind. Nobody around us spoke it. My sister-in-law registered me in school, but I was very scared because I didn't know how I was going to communicate. There were only a handful of Latinos. The Caucasians wondered why I didn't speak Spanish if I was from Mexico. They looked at me as if I were a Martian. I learned English at school and Spanish at home. I even began to wonder why I should speak my native language if nobody was going to understand me, but in my heart I knew that I couldn't forget. Sometimes when I was alone or in the shower, I would talk to myself in Mixteco, to reassure myself that I wasn't forgetting. My brother would refuse to speak it, saying I had to learn to speak Spanish.

Four years later, my other brothers arrived, and I started speaking Mixteco regularly again. To this day, though, with my older brother I only speak Spanish. Sometimes my husband asks me why I speak Mixteco with all of my brothers except him. The words just don't come out in Mixteco when we're talking.

You can say you forgot your language and not speak it, but you cannot really forget it. Many people come to this country for one or two years and then return to Mexico saying that they forgot how to speak Mixteco. A lot of times it is because of peer pressure. They get ridiculed. They want to be like the rest. I'm happy I didn't forget. Perhaps I wanted to when I first arrived because of the pressure from other kids. But now I'm even a Mixteco court interpreter.

In 1997 my husband and I came to Fresno and never left. I soon joined an organization supporting indigenous rights [the FIOB] as a volunteer, working as an instructor about domestic violence.

The subject of domestic violence is taboo in the Oaxaqueño community, but it happens often. Many women are used to taking abuse. Divorce and separation are not options, and they feel they have to stay in that environment. After I began to work on the domestic violence team, I noticed that when I spoke about it, people would slowly leave the room. Others would ask why I was telling women to call the police on their husbands. When I would go to the radio station to talk about my project, listeners called to ask why I was giving this information to women.

I wasn't telling them simply to call the police. Everything has a consequence, which will not only be felt by the man. Of course, he's the one going to jail, paying the fine, and attending domestic violence workshops. But they also risk loss of their driver's license and green card. Children suffer the most. The money a husband pays in fines is money that could be spent on his children, and we know that farm work is not well paid.

It is a problem that goes back to Mexico, but there is a lot of pressure in the United States, too. I am not saying that people earn a lot of money here, but you do earn more than in Mexico. It is a lot easier to go to the store after

work, buy a six-pack of beer, and go home intoxicated, but then the problems start. Many times families have to share a home, maybe with three families in one apartment, because no one earns enough money to rent their own. The pressure can start there. Immigration only adds to the domestic violence problem. But now there is more support in towns in Oaxaca for women to report their husbands, and many women send their husbands to jail after receiving a brutal beating.

Now I am a community worker and help people working in farm labor. When they don't have portable bathrooms, or if their employer refuses to pay them their wages, I go to the work site and investigate. I inform the employer that it is easier to solve the problem right there instead of risking a fine by the state later. It is important to solve the problem immediately—if the employer simply pays a fine two months later, the workers still don't have water.

I knew I wasn't going to be a woman who would just stay at home and have about ten children and wait to see what life imposed on me.

ORALIA MACEDA
CHANGING THE WAY MIXTECOS SEE WOMEN AND YOUNG PEOPLE
Fresno, California, February 2002

It is not easy to be a young activist in an organization whose leaders are much older, in a community where tradition and age are valued highly. To be a woman activist is even more difficult. Oralia Maceda confronted both problems. She gained her political consciousness and organizing skills in Oaxaca and then learned to use them to promote change in the Mixtec community within the United States.

In my community, San Francisco Pastaguacla in Oaxaca, there is a river. The land is irrigated, and my father grows corn, beans, and tomatoes. After

Oralia Maceda referees a
FIOB basketball tournament

Pastaguacla and does not have land, he then farms my uncle's land. So we help each other, and everyone has a small piece to cultivate.

One person provides land, fertilizer, a tractor, and seeds. Another provides the labor. When it is time to harvest the corn, the whole town is involved, and both parties provide a big meal. If they need twelve chickens to feed everyone harvesting the corn, each family kills six. Three dishes of chili for one family, three for the other. The two families take the food to the field where everyone's harvesting the corn.

Afterwards, a load of harvest corn—two sacks of corn carried on a donkey—is given to one family, usually first to the owner of the land. The first three donkey loads go to one family and then the next three to the other. There are other arrangements between people, too. If I have enough corn to eat, then I just rent my land, and whatever profit the farmer receives from the harvest is theirs.

It is a very old system. My father goes in halves with somebody else, because if he sows corn alone, he'll have too much at the end of the harvest. It doesn't have a high selling price. In our town, everyone helps each other. If my father is harvesting somewhere else, other people will take tortillas to my mom to feed the crew of workers. And if I bring tortillas to a crew, I'll receive a basket of corn in return.

When we were very young, we all needed to work. When I was six I had to bang cans together to scare birds away so they would not eat the tomatoes. At seven I started picking tomatoes. Fortunately, I'm a middle child. My three older siblings had to harvest more. When I came home from school, I would put my backpack down and run out to harvest squash. Sometimes my dad would ask me to plant three grains of corn and one bean seed, and then cover it with dirt. They were simple tasks that I could do easily.

My older brother started getting involved in political parties when he was in high school, asking people to vote. He was too young to vote himself, but he didn't care. He would ask my grandma whom she was voting for, and she would say for the Mexican flag. He would reply that the Mexican flag meant voting for the PRI [Mexico's old ruling party], and they were not doing anything for us. That was a big conflict in my family. My dad was a

the tomatoes are picked, he sows squash. They were really good times when the prices were high, but sometimes the whole harvest was thrown on the riverbank for the animals to eat. He had no transportation, so if a box of tomatoes cost 120 pesos in the market in Tepiaca, my dad would get only 60.

He has his own land, like most people in town, but everything is for the community. Whoever wants to work in the field can do so. If my uncle has land and he is in the United States, and my father is here in San Francisco representative of the PRI, and my brother was for the PRD [Mexico's main left-wing party] in '94, when Cuauhtémoc Cardenas ran for president.

He would come home late and talk about his meetings. My sisters and I would turn the lights off as soon as we heard him coming and pretend to be asleep. Then one day the Frente [the Indigenous Front of Binational Organizations] had a workshop about human rights. My brother asked me to go for him. I refused, but my mom told me to go see what he did all day long and why he came home so late. When I got there, they had a speaker and a video about human rights. They talked about the Agreement of San Andres, the autonomy of indigenous people, and why we needed to support the Zapatistas.

I wondered why in school no one had told me about this. So I started to think. I am still upset that no one told me before that I was an indigenous person or taught me the language. As a child, when I would say a word in Mixteco, my grandpa would get mad and say that word is only used by Indians. My mom was not allowed to speak in Mixteco. When I got involved with FIOB, I realized that I was indigenous, too. Now when I speak to my dad on the phone, I try to talk to him in Mixteco. He is surprised that in the United States I am learning it.

I understood why my grandpa did not let us speak our language and be who we are. When he was younger he went to Veracruz and was treated very badly because he only spoke Mixteco, and he had to learn Spanish. He did not want his kids to go through the same experience, to suffer like he did.

When I was younger I thought I would never go to the U.S. But I had two sisters and a brother here. My sisters have kids, and I wanted to meet them. Then I had the chance to come without going through the desert. So I planned to stay for a month. I arrived in 1998, when I was twenty-two, and I've been here since.

When I got here, it was really hard. My sisters are much older, so when I was little I did not spend a lot of time with them. I felt like I was nobody, since I didn't understand so many things. I had an opportunity to go to school back home, but here I was only a housekeeper, just cleaning where the cat or dog sleeps.

Finally Gaspar Rivera [a Mixtec scholar] told me about a FIOB meeting in Arvin Lamont, and they asked me to share my experiences in Oaxaca. Rufino asked me if I was interested in working with women, and I agreed. When I told my sisters about the job, they didn't want me to go, but I said cleaning houses was not my ideal job, and they finally agreed.

I had no idea how to start and was very discouraged, but I asked people for help. At first there were no women involved in FIOB. Rufino asked me to share my experiences in Oaxaca, and we started going to different cities—Fresno, Selma, Santa Maria, and Santa Rosa. Once we had a women's conference, but there were more men than women. We encouraged them to bring their wives, since it is important for all people to know their rights. In Oaxaca you are not allowed to go to the agency [local government office] and sit with the presidents, just because you are a women. Another issue was my age. I would advise older women how to care for their children and they would get upset. They felt, How can she tell us what to do if she has no kids?

Today, women sometimes participate more than men. The biggest obstacle for women is the lack of time. They have to work in the fields and take care of their families. They don't have child care. When they come to meetings they worry about their kids and get distracted. Transportation is much more difficult here. In Oaxaca I can take a bus anywhere. Here there is no transportation in rural areas.

I believe men have to be more conscious of women's needs so they can participate. But it is women's responsibility to find out how and get involved. Right now there is room for women and their ideas to develop.

The way we work here is different. In Oaxaca there was more control over how I did things. When a job was assigned to me, I had to get my ideas approved by the coordinator. Here I have more freedom and support. Sometimes when things go wrong I ask Rufino why he did not warn me. He tells me that if I have an idea and it goes wrong, I will learn from it. Here we try to educate our people. In Oaxaca, FIOB is very political because of the PRD/FIOB alliance—we go to the streets and march with five or six hundred people. Over here we don't have the same political rights.

Politics affects us, and I do some indirect political activity. We ask people to register and vote, and I believe in the near future we will participate politically here, too.

I told my mom not to ask me again to quit, because it would be the same as if I asked her to stop going to church. I told them, this is my life and I like it here. My family got the message.

JORGE GIRON CORTEZ AND MARGARITA DE GIRON
SACRIFICING FOR YOUR FAMILY
Madera, California, April 2002

Before coming to the United States, Jorge and Margarita Giron worked as migrants in northern Mexico, where they endured terrible conditions in the camps. But their ties to their hometown are so strong that not only do they fulfill their tequio responsibilities while living in Madera, but they plan to go back once their children are on their own. For them, the dream of returning has never weakened.

JORGE: We are from the town of Santa Maria Tindu, Oaxaca. We don't have land there, and that's why we left to find work. I left when I was twelve. I went with relatives, first to Veracruz and then to Sinaloa. There I worked stringing tomatoes, harvesting them, and fertilizing the land so the tomatoes grow.

They paid me half the normal salary, which in those times was twenty-two pesos, so I would get twelve. But I worked very fast, and the boss recognized that and soon paid me the full salary. Later we worked in other areas, in Sonora and Baja California.

MARGARITA: When I married my husband, my parents knew that his

Jorge and Margarita Giron

family was poor. We left town after we were married. We weren't stable. When there was no more work we'd go to another place.

Five years after I was married I returned to my town, because my husband and I had an agreement that I would stay there two or three years with his mother while he worked in Sinaloa. So he left and I stayed. Ten years passed and he came for me again. I haven't been back. I do go to visit, but not to stay. We've been married for thirty years.

JORGE: We lived in the labor camps, made of steel sheets. During the hot season it was unbearable. In the morning we would huddle around the foreman, and he would give us buckets for the tomato harvest. When they were irrigating, we took off our shoes and went into the fields barefoot, even if it was freezing. Going in like that made us sick, but there were no rubber boots. We worked from sunup to sundown. Candlelight was our only form of light.

The towns and cities were far away. We would go there only on Sundays, so the camps provided everything. There was a store that gave us food on credit. On Saturday we would get paid and pay our debt.

The roof was flimsy, and when it rained everything got wet. We would put everything up on a table to avoid having things swept away by the water, which would even take bowls and pans with it. Everything was bad in those times.

MARGARITA: When you had to relieve yourself, you went in public because there were no bathrooms. You would go behind a tree or into the tall grass and squat. People would bathe upstream while downstream others would wash their clothes, and even drink the water. That's why many came down with diarrhea and vomiting. Others drowned in the river because it was very deep. The walls in the camp were made of cardboard, and you could see other families through the holes. In the camps you couldn't be picky.

JORGE: Finally, students came from the universities and began to protest on behalf of the workers. Then the movement spread to Baja California. CIOAC [the Independent Confederation of Farm Workers and Small Farmers] organized most of the strikes. They wanted workers' rights, better salaries and jobs, better housing, running water, and transportation to and from work.

When the students came we would leave the fields and in solidarity stop working. Then the police would come and take away the students. The bosses began to cut the workday to eight hours, and when they needed a couple of extra hours they paid double. Before, if we worked ten or eleven hours, we were paid the minimum. Now houses are made of better materials, with electricity and running water. After that movement, things got better.

In 1979 we came to the other side as *mojados* [undocumented immigrants]. In those days the border patrol was very vigilant. We couldn't go to the store. When we went to work, our ride would pick us up early, because the border patrol would set-up at their checkpoints at 5 a.m. We would go at 2 a.m. and sleep in the field. It was very cold. We would wait until the sun came up to go to work. Thank God, the whole time I was here I was never caught by immigration.

Some ranchers would protect their workers. They had devices that alerted them when the border patrol was coming. They would tell us to hide and we would run. When the border patrol left they would tell us it was safe to come out.

With time and luck I helped my family fix their papers. Now we're all here legally. We're still seasonal workers. After pruning season we go to Oregon to work in the strawberry fields or whatever work is available. Once that's over we come back here to the grape harvest.

Last year I was appointed mayor of Santa Maria Tindu for a year. Each town forms an assembly, and the townspeople elect the mayor—an obligation we have to fulfill, to be responsible for the town for a year. You don't receive a salary. In bigger towns those in a similar position get paid, but we don't. I went in January and stayed through February. Then I returned to the U.S. but went back again in August, September, and October. I turned over my position after the year was up and came back here. My family stayed here. My daughter and son were in school, so I couldn't take them with me.

Anybody who was born in Santa Maria Tindu can be called upon for this duty when they turn eighteen. It's their obligation to fulfill this commitment if they're called upon. If the clinic needs repairs, then you are called upon to fulfill your tequio. Schools or roadways may also need repairs, and all of those things are our responsibility. A tequio means you will be working with your community. When there is a job to be done, we call upon the people to step up and help, and we let them know what days they will be needed.

It is a very important custom because we're giving back to the community. If you are in town, you must fulfill this commitment. But if you are out of the area, you can't be forced into it. They know that poverty drives us to leave. Those who are financially secure, who own small business, don't have to leave. We do, though.

About three years ago the census reported 1,700 people in Tindu, but not all live there. The majority are in the U.S. When it was easy to obtain visas, a lot of people fixed theirs and helped their families obtain them. Now they're buying homes. That's why there are so few in Tindu now, and so many in Madera, California.

We have an executive committee in Madera of people from Santa Maria Tindu. They collect sixty dollars a year, and when there is a job to be done, like paving a road, we use that money. The town puts up 20 percent of the money needed. The state government of Oaxaca provides another 50 percent, and we provide the rest. If someone becomes ill, I think they also should be able to expect some type of support.

MARGARITA: Every person's responsibility is to give back to the town. Women do it, too, if they are single. Widows also have to participate, or they must look for someone who is willing to work for them. If they ask for a donation, everyone must cooperate. Our children, who are twenty-one and twenty-two years old, also have the obligation to give back to the community.

JORGE: I don't know if they will, though. They don't understand these things because they didn't grow up over there. If they are approached to donate they will, but they are not likely to fulfill their tequio. The parents are usually the ones to fulfill it.

My children don't speak Mixteco because they were raised in Baja California and didn't learn. We don't use it here in our family. There are areas in Oaxaca where mostly older men speak only Mixteco. But from the seventies on, young people didn't really speak it.

MARGARITA: In my family we were raised speaking only Spanish. None of my children speak or understand Mixteco.

JORGE: Now my son and daughter, even if they don't study that much, can get a good job if they graduate from high school. I think that they won't go back. It's a different type of life here. We are going to return as soon as the children are grown and they can fend for themselves. When they get jobs, then we can leave in peace. You make a lot more here, but then there's rent to pay, electricity, telephone bills, garbage, and water. It ends up being the same, but you're killing yourself here at work. Money is spent just as fast as you earn it.

MARGARITA: Since we don't own our own home, if we decide to relocate to Santa Maria Tindu we take nothing with us. Whatever we make we spend on bills and end up the same. People in Santa Maria Tindu, like my parents, have their own house, land, animals, and goats. When they decide to sell a goat or two, they get to keep the profit and use it as they'd like. We don't have anything here. We may not have anything there either, but we love our town. Well, maybe our children won't return because they're accustomed to life here, but I think we have to.

3

In Cañon Buenavista, the poverty of migrant Triqui farm workers is not evidence of cultural backwardness or traditional life, as the media often portray it. It is a manifestation of the position they occupy in a reordered global economy. These migrants don't experience globalization as prosperity and modernity, which is the image that maquiladora boosters and free traders promote. Instead, thousands of indigenous families come north from Oaxaca every year to work just a few miles south of the U.S. border. They labor for Baja California's large landowners who, despite land reforms won in the Mexican Revolution, own plantations covering thousands of hectares. These modern industrial farms grow tomatoes, strawberries, and other row crops for export to supermarkets in the United States.

The border region, which has historically occupied the political and social margins of both Mexico and the United States, is moving to center stage. It is a unique area, almost a country unto itself. In this place, where the harsh impact of globalization is most evident, the workforce is made up of migrants from the south.

In the late fall and early spring, almost all the cilantro and green onions on Los Angeles store shelves comes from the Maneadero, San Quintin, and Mexicali valleys. Those who produce these vegetables, however, find that while the border region is dependent on their labor, it provides no place for them to live. Some growers in the San Quintin Valley still operate ramshackle labor camps and barracks. Most farm-worker families, however, like those from Maneadero, don't even have that. They must find land and makeshift places to sleep and eat wherever they can. Land hunger in Baja grows yearly as more families migrate from the south. And increasingly those families decide to remain in Baja year-round instead of making the long trip back and forth from Oaxaca with the seasons.

When people have no fixed place to live and must migrate to earn a living, culture becomes something they carry with them and reproduce wherever they go. Traditional life is not a mystical or romantic past to be left behind but a more complex reality.

Culture binds these communities of indigenous migrants together. Their ability to think and act collectively makes it possible to endure a situation that an individual cannot. Culture is defined by the home you came from, to which you send money every month. The Triqui settlements of San Quintin are named for the towns back home—San Juan Copala in Oaxaca becomes Nuevo San Juan Copala in Baja California. Maintaining culture depends on keeping indigenous languages alive. These communities forced the government to begin setting up bilingual schools so their children would learn the indigenous languages of Oaxaca. For monolingual Mixtec children, bilingual instruction made learning the basic subjects easier while they simultaneously learned Spanish.

Culture includes traditional craft-making skills, which enabled Salomon Alvarado Juarez to leave the fields where he worked as a child and bring in enough money to go to school and eventually the university. Alvarado is a defender of indigenous culture. He went on to law school, at least in part to find the knowledge his community needs to defend its rights.

In the home of the Sandoval family, in a settlement created by land invasions a few miles south of the port of Ensenada, the phone would ring every day at midmorning for almost three years. It was the daily call from the

prison twenty miles away where Julio Sandoval was being held. Sandoval, as his daughter Florentina explains, had a long history of defending Triqui cultural rights. He finally led a land invasion to expand housing for indigenous migrants in his community of Cañon Buenavista. For that, he was arrested and imprisoned.

Communal rights, as defined by Triqui migrants, include more than the right to speak their language and sell their crafts on the streets of Ensenada—they include the right to a place to live. Sandoval, a Triqui, was charged with an offense unique to Baja—*despojo agravado*—instigating others in a land occupation. This was a political offense. According to Beatriz Chavez, a farm-worker leader who was also held in the Cereso prison for the same crime, "the government here is afraid of the poor sections of the population, especially the migrant indigenous people from Oaxaca."

Raul Ramirez, Baja California's human rights prosecutor, says the authorities use the law to stop the land occupations because they're concerned with maintaining an investment climate that is friendly to landowners and industrialists. He points to a crucial human rights debate of this era. While human rights as they apply to individuals are widely recognized, such as the right to free speech and freedom of political beliefs, the inclusion of cultural rights and collective rights within human rights is far more controversial. For Mixtec and Triqui migrants from Oaxaca, two such rights are crucial: the right to culture and the right to housing. Winning these rights is critical to their survival.

As Ramirez defines them, collective rights include economic and social rights, a concept largely absent from the U.S. Constitution but enshrined in basic Mexican law. The situation of migrants in Baja, however, points to a failure to guarantee these rights in life. Tiburcio Perez Castro, a highly respected professor of education at the National Pedagogical University, says that only those provisions of the law which protect private property are enforced. "There's a law guaranteeing people the right to health care, but no one has any," he notes bitterly. "There's a law which protects the right to food, but thousands of people go hungry every day."

The social cost of this policy is that whole families work together—children cutting vegetables alongside the adults. Felix, a twelve-year-old boy picking cilantro in Maneadero, said his parents were making about seventy pesos a day, while he was bringing home half that. "We can't live if we all don't work," he said, in the tone of someone explaining the obvious.

Florentina Sandoval in her home in Cañon Buenavista

FLORENTINA SANDOVAL-GARCIA

WHY MY FATHER WENT TO PRISON

Cañon Buenavista, Maneadero, Baja California, July 2002

At the time of this interview, Florentina's father, Julio Sandoval, had been imprisoned in El Cereso prison in Ensenada since December 2001. She describes how hard life was as the daughter of an indigenous political leader. Sandoval was released in December 2003 as a result of binational pressure by the FIOB and others on the Mexican and Baja California governments.

What my father did was fight to help the people. The people want to know what they can do, and he tries to organize them. That's what he does.

My mother suffered a lot because my dad would often be gone for three or four days. Sometimes there wasn't anything to eat, and she would say, "How can you take care of other people more than your own family?" They would fight, but really my mother always understood my father and supports him to this day. My grandmother did not like what he did, and she would say, "Maybe they'll kill you. It's better if you leave the struggle." But my father never listened.

I remember being hungry, but we had family who were farming. We

would work with them, and that's where we got food. But sometimes one needs a father, and he wasn't there.

We spoke only Triqui, all Triqui, even now. In Oaxaca no one in the family speaks Spanish. I learned to speak Spanish when we got to Baja California. Some of the teachers here are Triquis and they speak the dialect. They tell us not to lose our language.

When I got older I started looking for a boyfriend and left home. During that time my dad was in jail. They accused him of something that wasn't true and incarcerated him for two years and three months. It was very hard.

I didn't get married. We only got together. Since then I've dedicated myself to the home, as they say.

My father struggled to get a street seller's license for selling crafts where we work now in Ensenada. It took a long time, but for the last few years we've been working legally. We make our crafts at home. My mom weaves bags, *rebosos* [shawls], and *huipiles* [blouses]. Sometimes she can sell them, and sometimes not. I make bags, headbands, and necklaces. Now the government wants to charge us more than two thousand pesos, and we don't have it. We sell only enough for food.

My father saw how people suffer and said, "Let's do something for them." Well, what else can we do? we thought. We're not going to suffer the same as we did in our village. We want to change things. We went on marches, organized a tent encampment, and did a lot of things. They tell my dad he's crazy for doing what he does, but he doesn't listen to them.

When the land invasion started and our compañeros moved onto the land, a lot of owners appeared, but false owners, not real ones. They accused my dad of being the leader, but he wasn't even there that day. They put him in jail because they'd wanted to do it for a long time.

We were sleeping at about eleven o'clock at night. The police came, and I don't know if they kicked me or if they hit me with the rifle. I got up and when I saw their guns I knew who they were. They claimed that a thief was inside our house, and I asked them, "And where is he now?" They entered my brother's home and asked me who lived in the house next door. I told them it was my mother's house, but I couldn't deny that my father was there too. They shouted his name and told him to come out. They pointed their rifles at the house, so my father came out. They put handcuffs on him, threw him in the car and took him away.

We were scared, we were very scared! Supposedly they're going to sentence my father to five years in jail, but we still don't know how long he'll be there. We still get worried, especially my mother. She's angry at many of our friends, who speak well when dad's out, but once he's in, no one cares. They don't even bring us a gallon of water—that's what I say. She says, "If he gets out, it would be better if I didn't help him because we're the ones that suffer. The people eat well and live well and we don't."

SALOMON LUIS ALVARADO-JUAREZ
THE LAW STUDENT
Cañon Buena Vista, Baja California, July 2002

Salomon Alvarado, the son of migrant Mixtec farm workers, describes the brutal situation his parents and other indigenous people faced, which convinced him to study law and become a community lawyer.

I was born in Oaxaca in San Geronimo Progresso and came to Baja California when I was six. We came directly to the Maneadero Valley, where my parents worked as farm workers. When I could, I would work with them. I worked for sixteen years in the fields while I was in school. Later I started to sell crafts to the tourists here in Ensenada. I know how to make them, it was a job that I really enjoyed because it's part of my culture, plus I earned a much better wage. We made sombreros, palm hats, bags, baskets, bracelets, hairpieces, and many other things. Everything was made from palm trees. These are crafts that have been made in Oaxaca for a long time, especially the hats and baskets. They are articles we still use.

When I got here I didn't know how to speak Spanish. I speak the Mixteco language. I am a person with a culture, and I want to teach that to my people—my language and the customs or traditions our ancestors left us. I would like to teach them to other people as well, because they are have historical value for Mexico.

I've always wanted to study law, since I saw how the boss treats workers such as my parents. I remember how we, as children, were treated. There was no respect. Workers had no right to a clinic, no right to fair pay, no right to pensions or retirement. They had no right to severance pay, even when they were fired for no reason. They had no right to anything. Why? Because the majority of farm workers in Baja California are indigenous. They don't know the law, and they don't speak Spanish very well. Now I'm studying at the Law School of the Autonomous University of Baja California in Tijuana, and I'll graduate next year.

Salomon Alvarado-Juarez

In the jail there are many indigenous prisoners. They don't speak Spanish, so how were they able to defend themselves? Many never had an interpreter. All of that motivated me. I want to move my people forward, to help them and improve myself.

In Baja California the authorities are against indigenous people. When I started selling crafts, I did not have a permit. I had a very good average in school, so I went to request one at city hall. They always denied it. So I had to work in a hidden way. Sometimes the police would come and take away my things. They wouldn't return them because the fine was so high. I was studying and doing well. I wanted to improve myself. But I would have to run and hide.

We had a strict municipal president who told the police to pick up children. I saw them take children out of the arms of indigenous women. The kids would get scared and cry. Those are moments one does not forget. One time I even went to jail because I didn't want to give up my crafts—it took me a long time to make them. I felt powerless. Now I sometimes run into those people from the past who are still working for the government. When I defend a case they remember me. They say, "You are the child we dealt with back then."

The ideals of social justice can be born in anyone. You don't need to know the law to see that something is wrong. Your heart tells you that you must do something. People make fun of you or they discriminate against you. They call you "Oaxaco," "indigena," "indio." You say to yourself, "No, this can't be. I am the same as them. I have the same capacity, perhaps even more. Neither I nor my people will be an object of discrimination." That's when a social justice fighter is born.

It was a sacrifice for my family to send me to school, especially the university. I had to go to Tijuana and pay rent, electricity, and water, so there was a lot of pressure. Fortunately, I was able to get support from a North American organization, El Montecito Presbiteriano, part of the Presbyterian Church. They helped me move ahead in so many ways, because my family had so little to support me. My father was sick for a long time, and all the money they earned went into his medication and my studies. [*His voice trembles.*]

The formation of Cañon Buena Vista began in 1989, with the taking of fifty hectares of land. Later, a problem developed over the taking of seventy-eight additional hectares. Julio Sandoval was accused of taking these lands illegally. To indigenous organizations, he is a political prisoner. Sandoval made many demands on the government and opened the eyes of indigenous people here in Baja California, especially in the valley of San Quintin. More than twenty-five thousand indigenous people live there, and he criticized the state government for forgetting them. The government set traps for him, and one was in Cañon Buena Vista.

Julio worked for three years to prove that the land there belonged to the federal government. It had been declared national land since 1973, so he asked permission to settle on that property. When the PAN [Mexico's conservative party] came in, all cooperation ceased. Julio's people decided to take the land and tell the federal government they would pay for it. But someone claimed to be an owner and sued. The state government took the side of this person to punish Julio. He was accused of instigating the dispossession of someone's property. That is a unique offense here in Baja California, applied mostly against people who struggle for land. The government of Baja California is interested in this case because we're close to the United States. It wants a good image to make foreign investors feel secure, that they can buy property and invest peacefully.

RAUL RAMIREZ BAENA
THE HUMAN RIGHTS PROSECUTOR
Tijuana, Baja California Norte, July 2002

For Mexican social activists like Raul Ramirez Baena, supporting indigenous people and movements—Zapatistas in Chiapas, Oaxacan migrants in Baja California—is as central an issue as civil rights is for their counterparts in the United States. Ramirez was the human rights prosecutor in Baja California for three years, during which he became one of the most important critics of government policy, which he says protects landowners and foreign investors at the expense of indigenous communities.

I am Raul Ramirez Baena, the human rights prosecuting attorney for Baja California. I was born in Mexico City, and today I turn fifty-three. I was born to a normal middle-class family. My parents have been merchants all their lives.

I was a child of the sixties. I was in high school when the student movement erupted in Mexico, and that's what shook me up. It changed me radically and had a great impact on my generation. Some people have forgotten those ideals, and many are well-off, but some of us continue fighting for them. We are trying to make utopia prevail.

Raul Ramirez Baena

Here in Baja California in 1997 the PRD started a national program in support of immigrants. Jose Luis Perez Canchola, Baja California's first human rights ombudsman, invited me to work in that office in 1998. In May 2000 I was anonymously appointed to the position. I was a member of the PRD, but when I filed my first case I turned in my membership. I feel I have to forget about partisanship and try to be a human rights lawyer for everyone, including those who belong to other political parties.

We have a human rights organization in every state in our republic. These organizations have the objective of promoting and defending human rights against acts by public officials across the country.

We submit resolutions, based on hard work receiving complaints and giving legal advice. But these resolutions are not binding on public officials. Normally, when a court resolves a matter, obeying its order is obligatory. But that is not the case for us. So the strength of our organization is moral authority.

These human rights organizations were created after 1990 and they are part of a developing democracy in Mexico. The institutionalization of human rights is due to social movements, and we should have great respect for them.

The human rights of indigenous migrants, especially agricultural workers, have been one of our targets. People from Oaxaca come with a pretty stable social structure but in vulnerable conditions. They leave Oaxaca to work in Jalisco, Sinaloa, Baja California Sur, Baja California, and then cross into the United States and work almost up to the Canadian border. In 1994, Operation Gatekeeper [a program for increased U.S. border enforcement] began here on the Tijuana–San Diego border and then was extended as far as the Rio Bravo. As a result, this traditional migration of Oaxacans has changed. Those who can establish themselves in the U.S. stay there and then bring the rest of their family.

People used to come and go during the year according to the economic and agricultural cycles. This has changed radically. Oaxacan agricultural workers who can no longer easily cross the border stay here in Baja California. This has created a population explosion and a large need for housing, health care, and education. Instead there is a total lack of resources. The state government here sees Oaxacans as immigrants. It blames their native state for the fact they're here, and complains that Baja California has to pay the cost of the services for them.

We don't agree with this point of view. These migrants create an economic boom with their work. This work is poorly paid, so they create a large profit. Big ranchers become wealthy at the expense of the workers, but they return very little to the state to invest in the needed infrastructure. This creates terrible living conditions for workers' families, particularly for women and children, who lack basic health care and education.

Children begin to work by the age of six or seven in difficult agricultural jobs. The ranchers say these are the customs of indigenous people. This is false. When indigenous children work at home, it is a family job. The family farms a piece of land and wants a child to have a love for the land and work. That does not negatively affect a child's development.

But here it does. Aside from the fact that the child doesn't attend school or have the proper health care or housing, he or she is also exposed to the rough climate, pesticides, and a criminal exploitation. It violates every principle and law, both child labor laws and social norms of every type. Women are also exploited. In addition to the chores and child rearing at home, they also do the work of a laborer. Women who are nursing or pregnant are also exposed to the rough climate and pesticides. This affects their health and that of their children.

One of the most serious conflicts is the land problem in agricultural areas. There are nearly thirty thousand conflicts in Mexico involving land tenancy issues in indigenous communities. Baja California is no exception, but here it's because they don't have a place to live. So, following traditional Mexican customs, they invade what they consider federal territory. Then come lawsuits, and the judicial conflict begins. The easiest thing for the government is to detain and incarcerate the leaders instead of promoting a resolution.

Today two indigenous leaders who are not delinquents or criminals are imprisoned, Beatriz Chavez and Julio Sandoval. Both were accused of invading land that others claimed as their property. Because Sandoval and Chavez are very loud and hard-to-quiet leaders, the state government detained them as a form of social repression. Instead of trying to come up with a solution and negotiate, police enforcement just creates more problems without any resolution.

Because of legal reforms made by Governor Ernesto Ruffo Appel to Baja California's penal code, they are accused of a most serious crime, instigating an invasion, and were denied bail.

This new state and federal government cannot keep leaders behind bars. The law prohibits us from involving ourselves in court cases like those of Beatriz Chavez and Julio Sandoval. In Mexico, as in most underdeveloped countries, economic, social, and cultural rights like the right to decent housing are nonexistent for the poorest people. There is no credit to enable a poor person to buy a home, while large portions of land remain in the hands of individuals. There is a very bad distribution of wealth in our country, horrible. This is also the case in the United States, but here the gap is a lot wider.

Housing, health care, and education are little by little being converted into private services. It's a punishment for poverty. If someone has no housing, the legal authorities will take no action. But if a landowner finds his land invaded, he can present a complaint. The state will then investigate and detain the aggressors. The Baja California state government worries about maintaining an image of stability for investors and therefore protects the right to private property. The border is the key to the manufacturing industry in the north, so all potential conflicts and social movements must be controlled.

This clashes with social reality and the need for housing, for human, labor, and social rights for indigenous people and agricultural workers. The authorities will get involved with land and investment issues only for large owners. Heavy foreign investments and the need for investment security clash with social needs and demands. We fear this will be resolved in an authoritarian manner, and Mexicans don't want to return to those times.

The rule of law is at risk, if we take it to mean not only private property rights but also social rights. Social rights are molded into our constitution, the supreme law of the land, but the government forgets that. What we have is a clash of interests, a problem of social vision, of the government's ideology and politics. This government protects individual rights over social and collective rights.

"Controlling" and "administering" migration are the terms used by the United States, Mexico, and Central American governments when they talk about border issues. They don't talk about stopping immigration, because cheap labor is needed. Without it, there would be an economic crisis in the United States. But there is a discriminatory attitude toward immigrants worldwide, everywhere, not just in America.

4

In the 1990s extreme economic pressure began to produce the migration not just of single men but of whole families. On the border, hundreds of people died every year as they attempted to walk through the intense heat of the Desierto del Diablo, in northwest Sonora. Mexico was electrified when a young Mixtec woman who sought to reunite her family in the United States, traveling north with her baby to find her husband, succumbed to thirst and the desert's heat. She was abandoned by the coyote she paid to be her guide. She died, but miraculously her infant daughter was found at her side, still alive.

The baby was returned to her grandmother in Oaxaca, Paola Angela Galindo. The infant became a symbol of the enormous sacrifice made by families trying to reunite and the terrible dangers that await them on the road north. Three years after her daughter's death, Galindo still couldn't recount the terrible story without weeping.

For an organization like the Frente, mass migration from Oaxaca called for an effort to find new means of survival for the people left behind in the tiny hill towns—the old folks, the women, and the children. In 1993 the FIOB began serious organizing in Oaxaca itself. Some of its first projects involved planting new crops, such as the Chinese pomegranate, the forajero cactus, and strawberries. Beautiful indigenous weaving and craftwork offered another possible means of livelihood.

Centolia Maldonado, an organizer in the Frente office in Santiago Juxtlahuaca, brought together women who sold their handwoven textiles in the city square. The group took advantage of the Frente's binational character by sending craftwork to the office in Fresno, asking members in California to sell it at cultural festivals in the United States. They hoped for a better price in the north. While the cloth is beautiful and attracts immediate admiration, few people in the United States wear the huipil, the garment traditionally made from it. Perhaps the collective will find a way to combine traditional cloth with a more marketable garment style in a new environment.

Maldonado made her own odyssey to the border and became an accountant in a maquiladora. She describes the development of her political consciousness and the way it eventually led her, not north to the United States, but back to Oaxaca.

In the meantime, the Frente has become one of several new political organizations among indigenous people in the state. It eventually opened five offices there, and its membership in seventy towns grew larger than that in the United States. In 1999 the Frente made an alliance with the left-wing Party of the Democratic Revolution (PRD) and elected one of its leaders, Romualdo Juan Gutierrez Cortez, to the Oaxaca Chamber of Deputies in District 21, centered in Santiago de Juxtlahuaca.

Gutierrez is a teacher, and Mexican teachers are often leaders and spokespersons in indigenous communities. Oaxacan teachers especially have a record of battling for political rights. During the 1970s and 1980s, in the long struggle to democratize the National Union of Education Workers, the largest union in Latin America, more than a hundred Oaxacan teachers were assassinated. Gutierrez, who describes his own feelings as an educator, follows in that tradition of political independence and activism.

In 2001 the FIOB experienced an internal division over the actions of one of its founders, Arturo Pimentel. Many members accused Pimentel, who had been the director of the Frente in Oaxaca, of not being accountable to them for the organization's finances and for ignoring their decision that he not run for political office to succeed Gutierrez. Maldonado was a key figure in opposing him. At the FIOB Congress in Tijuana in December 2001, Pimentel was expelled.

The Oaxaca state government then seized on an accusation by Pimentel to arrest and imprison Gutierrez. Here again the Frente demonstrated its ability to use its network of cross-border chapters to pressure Mexican consulates. The Oaxaca governor was flooded with telegrams demanding Gutierrez's release. The campaign succeeded, but the arrest shows that the rights of independent organizations and leaders in the state's indigenous communities are still precarious and endangered.

PAOLA ANGELA GALINDO
HER DAUGHTER DIED IN THE DESERT
San Pedro Chuyo, Oaxaca, November 2002

In 2001 Mexico was electrified by the story of a baby found in the desert next to the body of her mother, who had been abandoned by her coyote and died of dehydration. The baby was taken back to Oaxaca, where she is growing up with her grandmother, Paola Angela Galindo.

My daughter's name was Yolanda Gonzalez Galindo. Her husband, Hermilio Hernandez Velasco, had to go north. He left her with his parents, but she became ill and they didn't have money to take care of her. My daughter and granddaughter came to live with me in San Pedro Chuyo. Then my daughter's husband called for her to join him in the U.S. She didn't want to go, but he called again and again, and sent her the money to cross to the other side. So she had to leave. This man was very jealous of my daughter. She was nineteen years old, and married him at fifteen.

I tried to convince her many times not to go, but she felt pressured by her husband's insistence. I told her the journey was very dangerous. Even though I have never gone, my sons and husband told me many stories of their personal experiences. My son told her many times that there were wild animals, deserts, and very hot temperatures. She decided to join her husband anyway.

When she left the house to go north, I never thought my daughter would lose her life and I would never see her again. She was very excited when she said her good-byes to me at the bus stop. She told me not to cry because she would be back soon. She hugged and kissed me and walked toward the bus, and came back and hugged me again. Every hug she gave me she would tell me that I was in her heart and would return to me soon.

Her husband told her not to leave the child behind, that he would meet them at the border to pick them up. I asked her to leave the child with me, but she said that only death would separate her from her child.

Paola Angela Galindo and her granddaughter

I get very scared whenever other family members journey north. I hope my granddaughter never thinks of leaving this town. If she goes to the U.S., the same thing may happen to her. I want the best for my granddaughter. I want her to study, to go to school here in her country so that she won't have to leave. I feel that I am raising my daughter all over again. She doesn't know I am her grandmother; she thinks I am her mother.

[*She begins to weep and can't go on.*]

CENTOLIA MALDONADO
HOW I BECAME CONSCIOUS
Santiago de Juxtlahuaca, Oaxaca, December 2002

Centolia Maldonado is a leader of the FIOB in Oaxaca. She played an important role in holding a former leader accountable to grassroots members and expelling him when he refused. It was a watershed decision, which preserved the FIOB's democratic character. Here she describes the development of her own political and social consciousness.

She left for Vicente Guerrero in Baja California, where we had family. The last time I heard my daughter's voice was when she arrived. She spent a few days there with my son's wife, who was also going to cross. My son called for her and she left. My daughter had to make the journey later with other people she didn't know.

Her husband paid a man in Vicente Guerrero $1,500 to bring her across to the other side. I don't know when she left because she never called me again. I waited for her call, but there was nothing. When they called me she had already died. They found her in the desert, with the baby still alive beside her.

If my daughter had had money to buy a place of her own, she wouldn't have gone. She wanted a home with her daughter and husband. When she left she said she would return in a year to build a home and live here with her family.

My parents migrated when I was very young. My father had accumulated a large debt, and the lender took possession of our land. My father went to the U.S. as a bracero for five years and then returned to Hermosillo, Sonora. He and my mother sent for me, and I went to the agricultural fields of Hermosillo. They wanted me to study, but I worked in the fields during vacations, thinning cotton and cultivating grapes. The students in my school were almost all children of field-workers. Finally they made enough to go back to Oaxaca.

My family is a mixture of Triqui, Nahua, and Mixteco. In my family no one speaks the language, but I played a lot with Triqui children. The people of my town, Agua Fria, are all mixed like me. The Nagual language is be-

Centolia Maldonado reports to the Juxtlahuaca women weavers' cooperative.

coming lost in Agua Fria—only three people speak it. But there are many families that speak Triqui, so that language is respected and preserved.

Our house was a place to camp for people that came down from the small towns in the hills to the market to sell their products. My father would let them stay in our house.

In those years there were many killings and conflicts among Triqui communities, which were filled with family rivalries. Since the whole community was related, they became attacks against whole towns. My father defended Agua Fria when people from other communities came at night to kill people. My father, my uncle, and grandmother would arm themselves and go out and defend the town. They faced the bullets while my mother ran with the kids to the mountains.

During that time, my father won the respect of the community because he trapped three assassins. People from a community called Tilapa came to stay at our home. After dinner they went to a friend's house and never returned. When my father left to look for them, he found that someone had killed them with a machete. Men from another town, Yutisani, had waited for them in the dark and killed them. My father was filled with rage—my mother says she saw him take his gun and leave the house with my uncle. My uncle trapped one man, and my father got two others.

The whole town of Agua Fria came with sticks, machetes, and torches, saying that these men deserved to burn alive. But my father was opposed to it and sent them to jail instead. I was afraid because I thought they might seek revenge, which was very common. But when I returned from high school to visit my parents, a Triqui woman from Yutisani gave me a bag of guavas the size of oranges from their orchards. She told me, "Give these to your father. My son went to jail, but he's out now. He killed those people, but he's still alive thanks to him."

After high school, I went to stay with my brother. He was in the army in Mexicali, on the border. I needed money and to study—that's why I had to travel so far from my family. But he wasn't earning much and couldn't cover my education. School was expensive and I had to buy all of the supplies. So I began to work in someone's home from 4 p.m. to 7 p.m., and in the morning I went to school. That's how I finished high school.

My brother had been taking drugs, and no one in the family knew. Many soldiers were on drugs, but he fell asleep when he was high and didn't carry out an order. So he was processed out and sent to jail. It was the hardest time in my life. Even though my brother was not supporting me economically, he supported me morally. When he was sent to jail, I lost a lot of hope.

Then I began to work for the maquiladoras, as an accountant, and to develop my own social conscience. My best friend was from Guerrero, also from a migrant family, and she began telling me about domestic violence in her home. Because of it, she never wanted to have a boyfriend. So we started asking questions—Why all of the violence in my home? Why did my brother start taking drugs? We started to reflect about how society affected us, beginning with the family. Everywhere we saw drugged-out young people in gangs—the *bandillas*.

We lived near a repulsive-smelling canal. In the morning I would jog by, and it made me think. Why, on one side, was the property clean and absolutely beautiful? Who are the ones with the beautiful homes? They were wealthy Mexicans or North Americans from the United States. Meanwhile, on our side, the canal was dirty and our neighborhood and homes were falling apart.

Because I was questioning the world around me, I began to see the discrimination in the north against people from Puebla, Oaxaca, Guerrero, and the south. They always belittled us. We were "Oaxaquitas"—Indians. In reality we were also the people who did most of the work. There is terrible discrimination when people migrate. People even discriminate against themselves after a while. People from Oaxaca who've been living on the border for a long time will say, "Oh, those damn Oaxacos!" Because they live well, have a house, and are established, they look down on the people who have just arrived.

Finally, I returned to Oaxaca. A friend returned with me. She said, "I want to know your land," but I had forgotten about the situation there. When I got home I saw what the conditions were really like. I saw the reality. I was so embarrassed because I didn't know my own land. When we arrived at my house it was even worse. We didn't have any furniture, my mother was ill, and there was hardly any food.

So I decided to stay and to change them, not just for my family but for others, too.

ROMUALDO JUAN GUTIERREZ CORTEZ
RUNNING FOR OFFICE AND GETTING ARRESTED
Santiago de Juxtlahuaca, Oaxaca, December 2002

As a high school teacher, Romualdo Juan Gutierrez Cortez sees the social cost of migration in the indigenous towns that have lost much of their population. After being elected to the state legislature as leader of the FIOB in Oaxaca, he was arrested for criticizing government policy and embarrassing Mexico's president. In talking with him, you can't help but admire his complete dedication to the Mexican ideals of education, culture, and democracy.

I am the son of agricultural workers. My father was born in San Miguel Tlacotepec, where I was born. My father told us he didn't have the opportunity to give his first four children an education—the oldest children had to help support the younger ones. The rest of us had an opportunity to go to school, while my older brothers migrated to work during the bracero program. Two brothers who migrated to Sinaloa formed families and never returned. One sister moved to Mexico State and two other brothers migrate back and forth to the U.S.

In 1983 I received my degree as an elementary school teacher, and in 1997 I became a school director. Education is a very noble field, which I love. It means confronting the government, however—you have to be ready to fight for the people and their children, not just in the classroom. You have to be part lawyer and part people's representative. Teachers in Oaxaca are very proud of our independence and our union. We are very strong, but this was not something that was achieved overnight. We have little money but a lot of dignity.

According to the government, illiteracy doesn't exist in Mexico. In reality it is a huge problem. Many people can't even read or write their name. Education has to be linked with development. You can't tell a child to study to be a doctor if there is no work for doctors in Mexico. It is a very daunting task for a Mexican teacher to convince students to get an education and stay

Romualdo Juan Gutierrez Cortez listens while students present an oral report on Mexico's oil industry.

in the country. If a student sees his older brother migrate to the United States, build a house, and buy a car, he will follow that American dream.

It is disheartening to see a student go through many hardships to get an education here in Mexico and become a professional, and then later go to the United States to do manual labor. Sometimes those with an education are working side by side with others who may not even know how to read.

The money brought in by immigrants is Mexico's number-one source of income. But the state government only recognizes the immigrant community when it is convenient. That's the reason that we organized the Federation of Oaxacan Organizations in California and similar organizations in Chicago and New York.

Migration is a necessity, not a choice—there is no work here. But it has disadvantages—there is a break in the family nucleus, and between the family and community, which affects education and morals. When a family leaves there are fewer students. In 1992 I was working in San Mateo Tuluchi, at a school with 8 teachers and 250 students. I just returned to visit and saw the school now has only 2 teachers and 63 students. The students remaining don't receive the education they would if every grade had a different teacher.

But the million migrants from Oaxaca have reactivated the economy of many communities. Migration helps pacify people. Poverty is a ticking time bomb, and as long as there is money coming in from family in the U.S. then there is peace. To curb migration our country has to have a better employment plan. We must push our government to think about the working class.

As a deputy in our state legislature, I was always independent. I represented my constituents fully and never gave in to corruption. After completing my term, I became a leader in the FIOB and demanded that the indigenous people have access to development. Our organization has between seven and eight thousand active members—a danger to the state government because we are not easily manipulated. Indigenous people are tired of government complacency, so we organized peaceful demonstrations to voice our discontent. The government didn't like this.

We joined with the PRD because we felt strongly about their fight for justice for all people in our state. I became the first elected official to go against the ruling party [the PRI] in our region. We started social reform after being elected, and we won legislation for the handicapped. We struggled for legislation for migrants, but since there wasn't backing from the federal government, we couldn't pass it. We also proposed legislation for cultural rights, like legalization of our traditional medicine, for the preservation of our culture.

The PRD has a difficult time nationally because their constituents are very different. They have members who have very liberal views, yet there are other members who come from the PRI, so they haven't been able to achieve unity. A wide array of ideas is a positive thing, but they have difficulty forming one agenda. In Oaxaca, we held meetings with our communities to come up with one.

The government is always claiming that indigenous rights groups are only guerrilla movements and don't help the people. We have always called for peaceful protest. On September 23, 2002, the president of Mexico visited Juxtlahuaca, the birthplace of our organization. They sent in police in advance to prevent our organization from participating in their activities. We weren't looking for confrontation. We simply wanted to voice the concerns of indigenous people. On October 21, 2002, at 8:30 in the morning I was driving to school when several well-armed police officers took me out of my vehicle and arrested me. They charged me because we protested the president that day in September.

Before my arrest I thought we had a decent justice system. I knew it wasn't perfect, but I thought it worked. Our constitution gives us the right to organize and protest peacefully. But I saw that the people in jail weren't the rich or well educated but the poor and those who work hard for a living. I shared a four-by-four-meter space with thirty other men. These unsanitary conditions don't allow any rest or space. If you aren't ill when you arrive, you will be when you leave. I had the opportunity to meet other political prisoners, leaders of a labor union. They were also detained by order of the government, on false charges. There are over two thousand complaints of political oppression in the state that have not been investigated.

During my incarceration, our organization proved to be united and strong. When the community became aware of my arrest they immediately demanded the police release me. They protested here in Juxtlahuaca and all around the state. I even had support from other states and from the U.S. Because of the mounting pressure the government had no other choice but to release me.

In the national Oaxaca indigenous movement our work is the defense of indigenous people and immigrants. Our organization is going to continue it.

PART TWO

TRANSFORMING NEBRASKA

GUATEMALAN AND MEXICAN MEATPACKING WORKERS—
INDIGENOUS CULTURE AND SOCIAL MOVEMENTS IN A
CROSS-BORDER COMMUNITY

Guatemalan workers, mostly from Santa Eulalia and other towns in the highlands of the state of Huehuetenango, cut apart sides of beef in a packinghouse in Schuyler, Nebraska.

Workers cut large pieces of meat into small sizes on a meat disassembly line.

The old Wilson meatpacking plant in South Omaha, which has now been torn down. The homes of the workers, who were always immigrants from somewhere, were built right outside the gates of the plant.

The IBP beef plant in Madison, Nebraska. In the last two decades, meatpacking companies have built newer plants in small midwestern towns rather than concentrating the plants in big cities. As a result, these small towns now have growing barrios of immigrant meatpacking workers, with Mexican stores, Spanish-language radio stations, and a vibrant multicultural life.

Olga Espinoza, a meatpacking worker from Chihuahua living in Omaha, watches her grandson take his first step into his mother's arms.

Juan Valadez arrives home from his job in the ConAgra plant in Omaha.

This meatpacking worker spent years bringing his family from Mexico to Nebraska.

In the elementary school in Madison, Nebraska, the children of Mexican immigrant meatpacking workers are now a majority of the students. Many don't speak English yet.

Madison's elementary school provides some bilingual education to ensure that the children of Mexican and Central American immigrant meatpacking workers can understand what happens in class.

Juan Valadez stands at the gate to the ConAgra meatpacking plant in Omaha on the morning of the union election.

Tiberio Chavez leaflets workers starting the morning shift at the ConAgra beef plant, just before voting begins in the election to decide on whether they'll be represented by a union. Workers voted in favor of the union in a joint campaign by the United Food and Commercial Workers and Omaha Together One Community, a project of the Industrial Areas Foundation.

Eleuterio Valadez and a friend sing to workers as they go through the plant gate on the morning of the union election.

Women organizing the union at the ConAgra plant give the thumbs-up sign the day of the union election.

Bishop Rodolfo Bobadilla of the diocese of Huehuetenango blesses a committee of Guatemalans working in Omaha, Nebraska, at a dinner given in his honor in a local restaurant. The committee brought the bishop to Omaha to strengthen their ties to their hometowns, and to link the Omaha diocese to the diocese of Huehuetenango.

Young Guatemalan immigrants from Santa Eulalia play the marimba during a fiesta in Omaha to honor the visit of Bishop Bobadilla. While the fabrication of marimbas in Santa Eulalia is in danger of dying as people from the town leave for the United States, migrants from Santa Eulalia in Nebraska have a growing interest in preserving the music and culture the marimba symbolizes. Young people learn this traditional music and also integrate it into interpretations of popular music from Guatemala and Mexico.

In his workshop in Santa Eulalia, Guatemala, Juan Mateo makes marimbas.

Old men start drinking and dancing to the marimba outside the church on the day before the fiesta of the Asuncion. Santa Eulalia, Guatemala, is famous for the marimbas made by four of the town's families.

Old men play the marimba on the day of the fiesta of the Asuncion.

Women in front of the church during the fiesta of the Asuncion. In the parish, these women are in charge of the fiesta. Their leader walks across the plaza toward them.

As the marimbas play wild music in the plaza in front of the church, a group of young men dances in masks and tries to terrify the children.

During the fiesta in Santa Eulalia, a mock bullfight features a man carrying a wicker structure shooting off fireworks, symbolizing the bull.

The bullfighter goads the wicker bull while fireworks and sparks streak off on all sides.

Young men sit at the edge of the town plaza of Santa Eulalia, waiting for work. Many have relatives working in the United States and are thinking of going north themselves.

New construction dots the hills above San Pedro Soloma, Guatemala. These homes are being built by families with relatives working in the United States, especially in meatpacking plants in Nebraska.

A woman provides telephone and fax services to residents of rural towns in the highlands who want to communicate with their family members working in the United States.

A boy plays with his electronic game, a present from a family member working in the United States.

A member of the parish council of Santa Eulalia makes a point in a discussion with visitors from Omaha, Nebraska, about possible relations between parishes in both countries. Many families in Santa Eulalia have members living in Omaha, who are active members of the parish there.

A Qanjobal man lives in Paykonob, Guatemala, another community from which many families have emigrated to the United States.

Mateo Francisco and his wife work in her small restaurant near the church in Santa Eulalia, Guatemala.

A young man stands at the back of the church in San Miguel Acatan, Guatemala. He is dressed in the cholo style of Latinos in the United States.

The mayor of San Miguel Acatan describes the bitter experiences of the massacres that took place in the town during the army's campaign against the guerillas.

A mother and her youngest daughter. Her older daughter left San Miguel Acatan to go to Florida.

A woman prays in church in San Miguel Acatan.

1

I first went to Omaha in 1998 to write about Operation Vanguard, a plan by the Immigration and Naturalization Service to enforce employer sanctions in meatpacking plants. Documents were checked for more than sixty thousand workers in over forty plants. When workers whose documents were in question were called in to meet with immigration agents, thousands left their jobs rather than risk deportation to their countries of origin.

Created by the 1986 Immigration Reform and Control Act, employer sanctions make it illegal to hire workers who have no valid immigration documents. On the surface this seems like a law to punish employers, but its real effect is to make the act of working a crime for undocumented people.

Under the Clinton administration, some voices within the INS sought to stop huge meatpacking companies from pushing down wages and undermining working conditions. They reasoned that undocumented workers risk deportation if they protest those conditions. Removing them from the plants, therefore, would make it possible for the remaining workers to push wages back up. Operation Vanguard essentially was an effort to scare undocumented workers out of the plants or get the companies to fire them.

The reality experienced by workers like Manuel Flores and Concepcion Vargas reveals an important truth about U.S. immigration law. Attempts to enforce its anti-immigrant provisions, even in the name of improving conditions for other working families, cause immense suffering to those who become its victims. Flores and Vargas describe the elaborate and difficult stratagems they used to get papers and jobs, and they recount the bitter impact of Operation Vanguard when desperate families were no longer able to work or buy food for their children.

The fear caused by immigration enforcement destroyed the ability of workers to build the organization that actually could have changed conditions. For a time, firings and deportations ended the first efforts to organize unions in the nonunion Omaha meatpacking plants.

Behind those efforts was a remarkable man, Sergio Sosa. A former seminarian and participant in Guatemala's civil war, and a former community organizer among the indigenous Mayan people of the Guatemalan highlands, Sosa used his knowledge of popular education techniques to help Latino meatpacking workers. He was hired by a radical priest, Father Damian Zuerlein, and Tom Holler, head of Omaha Together One Community (OTOC), a project of the Industrial Areas Foundation. Together, they formed an alliance with the United Food and Commercial Workers.

After Operation Vanguard drove members of the first worker committees out of the Omaha plants, Sosa and his coworkers patiently rebuilt them. After a couple of years, they were strong enough to challenge the packing companies directly. They eventually won elections and a union contract at Omaha's largest meat-packer, ConAgra (now Tyson Foods), and organized several smaller plants as well. Unions elsewhere in the United States have carefully examined what happened in Omaha to find techniques and a philosophy of unionism relevant to their experience. The Omaha experience made use of the same immigrant culture that raids and sanctions enforcement effectively target.

The flood of refugees from Central America to the United States has brought with it experienced organizers who have adapted what they learned in war to organize immigrant workers. Sosa is one of the most imaginative, but his experience is not unique. In Los Angeles, Pablo Alvarado uses the popular education philosophy of Paolo Friere he learned in the fury of El Salvador's guerrilla war to organize day labors on street corners. Ana Martinez, who saw her fellow workers dragged by soldiers from the Texas Instruments plant in Ilopango, San Salvador, and shot in the street outside, years later became a strike organizer for the United Electrical Workers in southern California.

Marcela Cervantes went to work with Sosa and OTOC. As a Mexican immigrant, she used her own experience to reinterpret the ideas of a new, more democratic and responsive unionism. She was particularly concerned with organizing women in the plants and overcoming cultural traditions that keep them in the background. But she also saw they share many common obstacles with men, starting with immigration status and fear of firing.

Sosa, Cervantes, and others like them have brought to the United States a culture of social movements and organizations. To them, unions are part of the overall fabric of community life and part of a larger effort to win social justice on issues such as immigration, discrimination, schooling, housing, and culture. These organizers don't see immigrants simply as a vulnerable and easily exploited workforce or just as victims of an unfair system. Immigrant workers are social actors capable of organizing people to change conditions.

In addition, they offer a new understanding of globalization, poverty, and the migration of people and bring a wholly new repertoire of tactics and creative ideas to social movements in the United States in general. If unions and other grassroots organizations in the United States can utilize the organizing energy of leaders like Sosa and Cervantes, they'll be better able to survive.

But change is difficult. Sosa and Cervantes insist that immigrant workers are not content simply to join U.S. unions (or other organizations), pay dues, and keep quiet in the back of the room. They want a voice in how these organizations function. They demand that unions become more effective in protecting workers' rights and achieving a better standard of living. And, most problematic for an entrenched old guard, they intend to fight for the right to lead on an equal basis with anyone else, regardless of where they were born or what language they speak.

Sergio Sosa

SERGIO SOSA
AN IMMIGRANT ORGANIZER
Omaha, Nebraska, January 2002

Sergio Sosa learned the techniques of community organizing and popular education in the middle of Guatemala's civil war. While holding the United States responsible for the death and destruction suffered in that bloody conflict, he nevertheless married an American and migrated to Nebraska. There he has reinvented those techniques and used his experience to organize the immigrant community of South Omaha and workers in the city's packinghouses.

My family has two roots. The Sosas are my father's family. He was from a Mayan town of the Mams and was the second generation that had contact with the European or Ladino culture. He finished the sixth grade of elementary school. First he worked doing house repair—he knew plumbing and electricity. Then he became a tailor. Finally he got a job at the hospital as a janitor and ended up being a nurse.

In the national hospital in Huehuetenango, Guatemala, he met my mother. She was from a family descended from Spaniards. Her parents were very rich and owned several haciendas on land they had expropriated from indigenous people in Calauxte, Nuli, and El Zapote. The relationship between my parents was full of conflict, reflecting that of my country. My father was poor and indigenous, although his generation had forgotten how to speak their native language.

Since my mother was from high society, her family tried to separate my parents after they met. My mother was sent to a convent to study medicine and then to an institute for interns. She escaped and went back to work in the hospital where she had met my father, and they got married. As a result all her inheritance was taken from her.

My first memories consist of all the conflict and violence in my house. I remember seeing my father beat my mother every Saturday when he would get drunk. That's why my brothers left the house early. I stayed to take care of my mother, because I was afraid that if I wasn't there, someday they'd find her dead.

I was very sick as a child. I was forbidden to exercise, and I had to take very large doses of medicine each week until I was sixteen. For that reason I liked books. While everyone was down the block playing soccer I was reading at home. Once I did go out and play soccer with my brothers and friends and wound up organizing four teams and a tournament. The prize was a meal cooked by my mother for the winning team. That was the first thing I ever organized. I would get up at three in the morning to study. It was then that I noticed three people coming at 4:15 a.m. to hand out leaflets at homes. They were flyers distributed by the guerrillas, letting the people know what was happening each day. So I began reading them. That was my first education about what was happening in Guatemala.

One day they caught me taking one of these leaflets, and I asked if I could collaborate with them. From that day on I was the mailbox carrier. They would give me the leaflets, and I would distribute them to the door of every home. During the afternoon I would make sure everyone had read the leaflet. That was my first political activity. Later, they gave me books with a more Marxist slant. I would read and ask questions, and they would explain things such as the class struggle. This way I began learning analysis.

The guerrilleros started identifying leaders, and in my neighborhood there were about four or five of us. I became the leader of a block, part of their larger political strategy of trying to influence people. They would also organize student groups and strikes. Because of the dreams of youth—the romantic dream of the revolution—many of us were affected. In one student strike a student was seriously injured when the army came in. That was a daily thing. No one could be unconscious of what was happening. You would leave your house and every day you would see at least one dead body or someone being executed. If you saw a guerrilla or soldier you knew there would be shots fired. At first the gunfights scared us, but later it began to seem normal.

The revolutionary process started as a Ladino process, of people trained in Cuba and other places. The first guerrilla proposal I remember had a socialist line: Few are rich and many are poor; few have a lot of land and many poor people have little land. But the majority of the indigenous people didn't see their problem as economic. They saw it as cultural.

The language or rhetoric changed from "a few are rich and many are poor" to "a few Ladinos have much and many indigenous people don't have anything." The indigenous people of different cultures and languages identified with this reinterpretation, and the guerrillas became a mass organization. Because the government of Romeo Lucas and General Ríos Montt couldn't tell who was pro-guerrilla and who wasn't, they began a scorched earth policy. They adopted a policy of killing all the people, including pregnant women, because their children would grow up to be guerrillas.

I decided that I couldn't spend the rest of my life taking care of my mother. I began studying agronomy, and I left to enter the seminary. I felt the church could influence the political situation, which was the main reason I wanted to be a priest. I had experienced a lot of family violence, but when I left home I realized that it wasn't as great as the violence in the political system in which we were living. My first natural reaction was to be against violence. We began to organize young people, using nonviolence to re-create our communities. We wanted to offer something from the point of view of faith, something that did not favor violence, because violence creates more violence.

We started among the church youth groups and then with laborers in the urban areas. We organized farm workers and students as well as women who cooked in homes of the wealthy. Our goal was to offer the church as a space for political participation. We would rent a piece of land where everyone could work it. The idea was to teach people to act collectively. We had classes for public speaking and used music and theater to raise people's consciousness.

Because that was the time of repression and scorched earth policies, many of the youth involved were seen as guerrillas, and all our activities were prohibited.

My political philosophy was born from the experience of what I saw and heard, much more than what I studied. My conscience was born like Rigoberta Menchu's, by seeing injustices every day; seeing dead, dead, and more dead.

My neighbor, who was like my brother, was killed. One day the army came and kidnapped him as he left the school where he taught. We found him after four days, by a river, without fingernails. They disfigured his face and cut off his legs and arms . . . and . . . it was hard. We had to put him in the coffin, and I realized this was exactly Guatemala's condition, with the face disfigured and the soul torn in half. All this begins to create something inside that enrages you, and you want to do something.

I decided not to become a priest. I felt better doing what I had been doing before entering the seminary, but with a broader vision and a greater sense of power. The Church gives you power. The minute you are ordained a priest, Pow! you have power. But the majority of the population are indigenes, and the Church was not willing to give up power to them.

After I left the Church I began to visit many indigenous communities. I got married, and the bishop of Huehuetenango did not grant my dispensation, so I was married outside of the Church. My wife is American and was working as a lay missionary. When we got married, I had one condition—that I would never come to the U.S. I held the U.S. government responsible for what we were experiencing in Guatemala. The army was trained in the School of the Americas, and they would come back and kill our people. Add to that all the money that came in, about two million dollars every fifteen days. They used their power, and we buried the dead.

But I found I could see my wife as a person, and with her I began to understand that people are more than any label, title, or ideology. I think the other part is love. I loved her. When our child was born, much of what I thought was transformed. Finally, I decided to come here to Gringolandia.

First I came to the U.S. for a month to see how I felt. I had tuberculosis, and I began to think of my daughter. I wanted to live. My wife had lived almost five years away from her parents and home, and it was no longer just my life. All these things came together, like hunger comes with the desire to eat. I think I am one of those many immigrants who say, "Let's go for a year just to try it out," and then we never go back.

It was a great internal struggle. I came crying the whole way. For the first six months I felt I was nobody. I didn't know anyone. I didn't trust anyone. I started looking for work and the first place I looked in was the Church. Father Damian asked me questions, which now I realize is part of a technique called one-on-one. That evening I was hired as an organizer, and since then I've been organizing for Industrial Areas Foundation.

One-on-one is a technique to create relationships with people, discover their interests, look for talents, and identify leaders in order to begin to organize. This is the same thing we did in Guatemala. I think a lot of Latin Americans do it—it is part of our culture. I began organizing the Latino Soccer League. We started organizing the first committees in seven or eight packinghouses. There are many things Latino immigrants do in common. Once we get to South Omaha, we soon know where the Salvadorans live, where the Guatemalans live, or the people from Chihuahua, or the folks from Oaxaca. We know who the leader is and where they go on Sunday after mass. You drink some beers together and you spend time with people.

The art is to know how to transform these social networks and connect them with African Americans and Anglo-Saxons. I think Latinos can do many things, and this is our moment. But we can't do them alone. We must trust people's political instincts. Many of these instincts don't necessarily come from training but from conscience and experience. When I express my anger, I am most clear about what I want.

Our organization, Omaha Together One Community, is mostly faith based. After working together for a long time, the immigrant meatpacking workers decided to join forces with the union. The Church supported these unions, and people said that if the priest is there, then this must be good. Like anything else, at the beginning it is difficult, like a marriage. Both sides have to be willing to change and learn from the other. They say if a marriage survives the first seven years, chances are it will work. And the results are our children, no? But churches and unions have a tradition of working together, in one way or another.

We are a new generation of immigrants, documented and undocumented—the point of a lance opening the road for the next generation, who will become legal residents and citizens. With the organization we will leave them, they will contribute politically and define this city. With documents or without, we're here to stay. They will try to send us back, but we will return. Globalization opened economic borders, but the people who control it haven't been able to open cultural ones. They haven't been able to absorb and value the culture of immigrants and the people on the other side of the global divide. For that they need us, to place a value on human beings that goes beyond just making money.

CONCEPCION VARGAS
A MEATPACKING WORKER
Madison, Nebraska, June 1999

Concepcion Vargas came from the border to work in a meatpacking plant in the small Nebraska town of Madison. Migrants get jobs through family networks like hers. She describes the danger and bitter sacrifice she was willing to make for her daughter, and the disastrous impact of Operation Vanguard, a huge immigration enforcement action in the meatpacking industry.

I went to college in Reynosa, right across the border from Texas, and studied business administration. I only had a year and a half to go to get my certificate when I had to leave to find a job. I found work at the Delnosa maquiladora, which belongs to General Motors. I was a trainer and crew leader helping other workers learn their jobs. The company paid about $20–$30 a week.

After a year, when I got married, Doroteo didn't want me to work, so I left. It was very hard for us to survive, though, and we had a daughter, Guadalupe. After a while, we decided to come to the U.S. I don't mean just for a while. This was a much bigger decision. We decided to go and get jobs.

Doroteo's sister was living in Madison, Nebraska, where she worked at the IBP plant. Her brother-in-law, Alfredo, had been living in Los Angeles when he got his legal papers through the amnesty. He went to Madison because he heard there were jobs at IBP. At first he slept in the parks and in cars. Finally he made enough to rent an apartment.

So Alfredo brought his sister-in-law, and she brought Doroteo. It's like a chain. First one person comes, and they bring someone else. And we are all looking for something better because the economic situation at home is so bad we can't survive. Three months after Doroteo left for Madison, he came back and got my daughter and me. She was four then.

At first, we couldn't get jobs at IBP because we couldn't find any papers to show them. Doroteo was working general labor and fixing cars—whatever he could find. Guadalupe began to get sick because she couldn't get accustomed to the cold here. It was October, and she would cough all night. We didn't have any money to take her to the doctor.

Doroteo still didn't want me to get a job, but we made an agreement. We would both try to get papers, and whoever got them first would go to work. And in the end, that was me.

If you're Mexican here and you have family, they know who to go to for papers. So a woman we knew finally got me a birth certificate and a Social Security card. I paid her $650. But that wasn't enough to get into IBP. You needed another ID as well, one with a picture on it. So she took me to the county building, where they give driver's licenses. But when we got to the counter, my friend suddenly told me to leave quickly. I ran away, and when my friend came out, she told me that the true person whose papers I was using had already gotten a license from that office. Her description didn't match me, and the woman at the counter got suspicious.

My friend finally took me to the next county, where I tried again to get the ID. When you have kids, you're willing to risk a lot, and my daughter was sick. The day my ID came in the mail, I went down to IBP and applied for a job. They accepted me right away.

They gave me a job in a building behind the main plant, called SPS, which makes ham and bacon and cooked meat. I was hired on the evening shift, which starts at noon. On my first day, I showed up at 11:15. They put me to work in a freezing cold room. I had to strip plastic bags off big legs of meat. They were frozen and hard as rocks. I had to put them in a big vat, and after there were a hundred or so in there, we filled the vat with water to thaw them. I just brought a light sweater with me, and I was very cold. The work was hard, and I felt denigrated and humiliated. Finally, I got so cold I asked permission from the supervisor to go to the bathroom. When I left the line, I wasn't going to come back.

I went up the stairs to where the bathrooms are. And then my daughter's face appeared before me. I saw her eyes looking at me, and I remembered how she had been coughing all night. I remembered how much we needed the money. I didn't go to the bathroom, and I didn't leave either. I just stood there, crying. Finally, I went back to work.

Every few minutes I'd ask someone if it was time to go home yet. I even cut myself that day with a knife. When I got home, my back and hands hurt so much that I couldn't lie down. I kept remembering going to school for that business administration certificate. But after the first day, I just tried not to think about it any more.

IBP has lots of work during the season before Thanksgiving and Christmas. After that, the work really drops off. I was a temp, and they moved me then from job to job. Some days I'd just scrape paint off the walls and re-paint them. Since I was a temp, they only paid me six dollars per hour. The wages in the main plant were eight dollars, so I asked my supervisor for a transfer over there, but he wouldn't give me one. I was a good worker, he said, and he didn't want to lose me. After the next season, I asked him again, really nicely. This time he said the only position open over there was washing and hosing down the machinery every night. No women had ever worked on that crew.

But I kept asking, and eventually six of us became the first women to do that job. It's very hard—you have to hold a thick hose and nozzle. The pressure of the water is so great that it can kill you if you let go and the hose gets out of control and hits you. My hands are small, and it was hard for me to hold on. When I came home from work after I began that job, my hands were so cramped and my fingers were so curled that I couldn't unclench them. Eventually I had to see a doctor. But I stayed in that job.

Finally, I got pregnant again and left the plant. When I was ready to go back, someone in the office told me not to go down to IBP again. They said the person whose papers I had was working in the IBP plant in West Point. If the company saw two people using the same Social Security number, they'd investigate. So I couldn't get my job back. Everyone in IBP has had their own experience like this.

I have two brothers, two in-laws, and two other family members all working in the plant. Some of them have legal papers and others don't. The company knows there are a lot of people working here without good papers. If you ask anyone, they'll tell you the same thing. There was even a man in the human relations office for a time who was charging people three hundred dollars for a job. I heard they fired him for that.

I think the company likes having people there who don't have papers because we have to work like animals and we can't defend ourselves. They ask you to do something and you just do it. In the plant it makes an enormous difference if you have papers or not. I've seen people when they get their papers, and they suddenly begin demanding their breaks or saying they have to leave the line to go to the bathroom. In our plant, we have this rule that says you can only leave the line to go to the bathroom twice in a week. More times than I can count, I've heard people ask the supervisor if they can leave the line and hear them being told to hold it until they get their break. There aren't very many bathrooms, so only a few can go on their breaks.

There's no union at the plant, no one to support us. The company fires people without any consideration for the time they've put in there. What IBP wants is cheap labor.

When Operation Vanguard came along, many people got letters telling them there were problems with their papers and to report to be interviewed. IBP put out a list of the people who were being called. Alfredo had brought other people from his hometown, and when four of them got the letters they just quit.

Another one—he was really brave—went to the interview. He knew that the person whose papers he had was sick in Mexico and wasn't working. They asked him a lot of questions in the interview and even called the schools he said he'd gone to in Texas. But finally they let him go back to work.

I heard there were over 250 people who got the letters and only 6 who went to the interviews. I think we have about a thousand people in the plant. Doroteo never got a letter. I was very relieved, since I don't know what we would do if he lost his job. Some people just didn't go to work on the day of the interviews and then just went on working after that.

I think Operation Vanguard was very unjust. I know the U.S. has its laws, like any country. But we're not here to break the law. We just have to work, especially if we have children. The company goes to California looking for people like us. IBP even advertises and interviews people down at the border.

The days after the raid, there was no one drinking in the bars or shopping in the stores here. So many people didn't have paychecks. And there's no other work now for people to go to—it's not the season yet in the corn, and that's the worst work of all.

There's a lot of racism against us here, inside the plant and outside, too. In Madison, it's almost unheard of that a Mexican lives here and doesn't work for IBP. There are no white people in the heavy production jobs—just Mexicans. If you look at the people standing around at break—rubbing their shoulders, warming their hands up in hot water, and taking pills for the pain—they're all Mexican. The white people here are supervisors or have better jobs. Even in town there are bars where Doroteo says they won't wait on him. He's gone in there with Mexicans who speak English, and even who are citizens, and they still won't serve them. At Food Pride there's a clerk who treats us really mean because we're Mexican and then speaks nicely to the white people.

But the thing is, they need us. Maybe that's why they're angry.

MANUEL FLORES
CHASED FROM WORK BY THE *MIGRA*
Madison, Nebraska, June 1999

Manuel Flores describes the economic desperation of a working-class family in Hidalgo, unable in Mexico to earn enough to live. After getting a job in a Nebraska meatpacking plant, however, Flores was caught up in Operation Vanguard and lost his job. There seems no way for his family to free themselves from hunger and poverty.

Before I came here to work at IBP in Madison, I lived in Tulancingo, in Hidalgo. My home was in a *colonia* [neighborhood] called Paradise, where there was no electricity and no water. Now there are whole new neighborhoods there—hills of Paradise, lower Paradise, upper Paradise, and so on. People are coming in from the countryside where they can't make enough to eat anymore.

I was a truck driver delivering supplies to building sites. I was making about 130 pesos a week in 1992. That was just enough to buy a kilo of beans, a gallon of milk, some rice, and a little more. It just wasn't enough for us to live.

Eight of us, friends from Tulancingo, went to El Monte in Los Angeles to look for jobs. But I couldn't find any steady work there. I went out onto the street every day. There was a place next to a building supply store where many of us would stand, hoping that a contractor coming by would pick us up. Sometimes I would get one or two days of work a week there, but other times I'd go a couple of weeks without any work at all.

We were all living in an apartment, and at first I didn't have to pay rent because I couldn't find a job. But after a while the landlord said I had to pay fifty dollars a week. I asked him, How can I pay if I'm not working? But he just said that if I wanted to keep living there, I had to find the money. Another friend from Michoacan came to El Monte. He said his brother-in-law was working in Nebraska and that there was a lot of work there. I had no idea where Nebraska was or what kind of work I could find there, but I was desperate. So I said, let's go.

It turned out this man was working at IBP. I got a job working at another meatpacking plant in Norfolk, Beef America. I used the papers belonging to someone I knew who was working at IBP. But at Beef America I eventually got fired because they found out my papers were no good. Then a friend told me he could get me other papers. So I paid him two hundred dollars, and he gave me a birth certificate and Social Security card. I've been using these same papers ever since. Today they'd cost about a thousand dollars.

With those papers I got a job at IBP. But after only a few weeks, I had to go back to Hidalgo because my daughter was sick. I wound up staying in Mexico for a year and a half. But eventually, the same problems caused me to leave again. This time I brought my wife, Lydia. For days we walked through the desert north of Reynosa. She was already four months pregnant, and it was very hard for her.

When we got to Madison, I got a job at the Beef America plant again, this time using my new papers. They were only paying six dollars an hour though, and as soon as I could I got a job at IBP, where they were paying a little more. I didn't like the treatment at Beef America either. The supervisors would shout obscenities at us to make us work faster. They never trained me for any job. They just put me to work next to someone who would show me a couple of times how to cut the meat, and then just leave me to it. There were a lot of injuries, and the line ran really fast—about a thousand animals an hour.

While I worked in the plant, Lydia stayed at home and took care of our kids and those of other workers, too. She had about seven or eight kids every day. We'd left one of our children in Mexico, though, our son Mario. He was five years old. He got sick, so we had to rush back. But when we got to Paradise, there was nothing we could do, and he died. It hurt us a lot. We still have pictures of him, dressed up in a cowboy costume, getting ready for a party.

I went back to work driving a truck, but it was no good. I was making 250 pesos a week, but by this time, in 1995, everything cost a lot more, too. We still had hardly enough for food. In 1997 we came back again, and once again I went to work at IBP. For a while I was working on the washing crew, but I wanted to change jobs. We had four of our kids with us finally, and I couldn't even see them because of the shift I was working, so late at night. It was very wet work and very cold. So I got a job cutting, which paid better.

In May I got a letter from the *migra* [the INS] saying my papers were bad. They told me to come for an interview. Then my supervisor came to me at work and said I was on the list they'd gotten from the migra. She didn't care if my papers were good or not, she said. She just wanted to know if I was going to continue working. I told her I could do that if the company would help me. But she just said I had ten days to fix my papers or I'd have to leave. So I told her if they couldn't help me, I'd work until the fifteenth. And that's what I did. That was my last day at IBP.

There were a lot of people on the list—even the supervisor herself. I know a lot of those people had papers that were as bad as mine, and a lot of them are still there. Others who also had bad papers didn't even have their names on the list.

After I lost my job at IBP I got a couple of weeks of work on a truck selling tools in Mississippi. When the job was over, they didn't even pay me my last paycheck. Other than that, I've been looking for other work, but I can't find it. I feel really scared. I was making $460 a week at IBP. We're paying $330 a month rent, our food bill is $160 a week, and I still have to send money home for my children there. We have nothing left to fall back on.

One of our children, Socorro, was born here, and we've applied for food stamps and medical care for her, but that's not enough. I feel really desperate. I don't want to go back to Mexico, but maybe we'll have to. I don't know how we'll live there either.

I don't think Operation Vanguard is fair. We weren't doing anything bad to anyone. I'm just trying to support my family. I don't want them to suffer. I especially don't want my kids to live like this. If I don't work with bad documents, how can I work? We can't get green cards—if we could, we would.

I really believe if the company wanted to, it could do something to help me. But I don't think they care. IBP just wants our work. That's the first thing you hear when you get a job here—the supervisors tell you that if you don't want the job they have, there are three or four people like us at the door looking for work.

Marcela Cervantes

MARCELA CERVANTES
ORGANIZING WOMEN IN THE MEATPACKING PLANTS
Omaha, Nebraska, May 2002

With Sergio Sosa, Marcela Cervantes was part of a unique collaboration between community organizers and the union for meatpacking workers, the United Food and Commercial Workers. Cervantes had to learn everything at once—to organize, to speak English, and especially how to bring women into union drives.

I left my town at the age of eleven to go to the state of Coahuila to study at a Catholic college. It was an opportunity, a privilege. Only two cousins and I went from our family. I went three years without seeing my mother and siblings. At fifteen I had to start to work, because as the only person to

graduate from school in my family, I had to help them out economically. I felt committed but at the same time frustrated because many things didn't turn out the way I wanted.

I graduated as a public accountant and typist and started working as a secretary in a law firm. I immigrated to the United Stares because I got married and my husband was already over here. He'd come to Omaha, and a year after his arrival he had the opportunity to legalize his immigration status under the amnesty for field workers. Then he went back to Mexico in '88 or '89, and we were married. When my son was born I made the decision to come, because I didn't want to see my family divided or my son live without his father.

I attempted to cross five times. Four times I was deported with my son in my arms, and I made it the fifth time, so here I am.

When I came we lived in the house where my husband lived with other people from our same town. It's commonplace among immigrant families to do this. You rent an apartment or house and many families share the space. In our house we had my husband and myself, my sister-in-law and her husband, and about six single men who were my husband's cousins. There were four bedrooms and the single men lived in the basement. I didn't like it. I had put myself in danger in search of a better future, but this was not good for me or for my son.

I began working at a Mexican restaurant, but I didn't have any papers. After that I worked at IBP, where my husband worked, also as an undocumented worker. I was shocked when I looked around and didn't see any blacks or whites, only Hispanics. I didn't like the way they treated us. In the beginning I was afraid they'd report me to immigration, and that frustrated me. I wanted to expose the mistreatment and shout it out, but I was afraid because of my legal status. You had to work and that was it. You just had to work. That made me angry.

I obtained my legal status because my husband applied for citizenship. Then I felt I had a little more freedom. It was like a liberation, and I felt the need to demand my rights as a person first, and then as a citizen.

I became involved with Omaha Together One Community [OTOC] almost from the time I arrived in '92, because of school issues. When I enrolled my son in school, there were things that I didn't like. He was sent to a school far away. He had to walk three or four blocks to catch the bus and be there half an hour before it came. Why, I wondered, should my son have to go so far, when we live two blocks from a school?

I attended mass at Guadalupe Church, and one Sunday the priest said that if we wanted to do something about the things we didn't like about our community, we should go to a meeting. I hesitated at first because of the language barrier. I didn't feel I was a part of the community. I went but left frustrated because the meeting was in English and I didn't understand anything.

Nevertheless, I continued and began getting involved. OTOC had an alliance with the United Food and Commercial Workers and was looking for an organizer. That's how I began organizing workers for the union.

I didn't know much at the beginning. I knew about unions in Mexico because my father was always fighting for workers' rights. He was a *cetemista* [a supporter of the Confederation of Mexican Workers, CTM]. Little by little I learned more about how a union works. A lot of times I went to talk to workers, and their questions were similar to ones I had. I was learning and teaching them at the same time.

When I began working, the first election campaign was already in progress at ConAgra. I knew all of the workers because I used to work there. I also got involved in the election at Nebraska Beef. By then I was feeling more confident in that I could teach workers how to organize themselves.

I'm doing this work because I like it. I feel like it's my calling—more than a job. Learning about our rights and understanding how power works has helped my own growth and development as a person. What's really beautiful is to be able to show this to others. I also do it for my children. I feel that we are building a future for them.

As workers we have the responsibility of making sure unions do what they are supposed to. We can do this only by organizing. Unions see workers just as members. I think that this should change. We should try to think of it as relationships. The workers are the union. When I talk with someone about unions, I'm not selling anything. I'm trying to educate people so that they can make their own decisions and see what can be beneficial for them.

The union should really be concerned with what people think. What are their concerns in relation to their work, and what are their fears? Unions have to understand fear about their legal status, for instance. They have to really know the person. Men, for the most part, are here alone, and their families are back in their native countries. They have to work double so to speak, to support their family there and support themselves here.

It has been difficult doing this job as a woman because I was always working with men. When I went to visit workers, the majority were men. Many times it's cultural. The Hispanic woman has always been viewed as a servant. In the Nebraska Beef campaign, I tried to organize a committee of women. Most believed that men are the ones who make the decisions in regard to politics and all of those things.

I tried to solve this problem through the church, and I use the relationship with the school. For the most part it is the women who worry. I'm not saying that the men don't, but it's more common that the women know where their kids go to school and what their children are going though. They are mothers first. So when I started to conduct individual meetings, mainly with women, I would talk not only about work issues or about unions but also about what they thought of their communities, their children's schools, or about church. I began to investigate what churches they attended. Our culture is very rooted in our religion. You trust in your church and your beliefs. Connecting with them is one of the strongest tactics.

Once I went to visit a Nebraska Beef worker. She had seen me before outside the plant. She immediately recognized me as a union organizer and didn't want to talk to me because her husband was there. I didn't talk to her about the union. I started to ask her what she thought of the schools, and her children, and she began to talk about everything that was going on with her children in their schools. She began to come to the meetings because she saw that her job was just as important as her children's schools and her community.

I like my job, but I have a lot to learn. I think that this is something you learn along the way.

I don't want my children to forget their roots. I want them to know their culture, to grow from their parents' roots and not to forget who they are. My children are perfect bilinguals. We made a rule that during the week we speak Spanish, because there are many things that I can't pronounce. On the weekends—Friday, Saturday, and Sunday—we speak only English. My children at first didn't understand me. When I spoke to them in English they would tell me to speak to them in Spanish, but I continued. Now I'm learning more.

We read books with them, and I try to tell them about the history of Mexico through stories. I know they're learning about different cultures, but I would like them to also know their own.

2

Omaha's meatpacking organizing drives were successful because workers had high expectations. Many Mexican and Central American immigrants are veterans of social struggles in their communities of origin, struggles which define for them the ideals of social justice. Tiberio Chavez as a young man participated in Mexico's great struggle for land reform, invading an old hacienda and helping to break it up into smaller plots for farmers. The Zapatista ideal that "the land belongs to those who work it" became transformed in his experience as an immigrant in the United States, where it reinforced the idea that all people deserve equal status and fair treatment.

The denial of that fairness and the stratification of the workforce in the United States by race and nationality fuels an explosive anger among millions of immigrants like Chavez. Chavez points repeatedly to the willingness of immigrants to do the worst jobs at the lowest pay. Why, he asks, do they then suffer discrimination and a second-class social status as a result? When he describes racist attacks and beatings in the plant, he makes it clear that people have to be willing to fight to enforce any degree of equality. These experiences became the bedrock of his activism.

Olga Espinoza also became a courageous advocate for the union in ConAgra's meatpacking plant. Her willingness to confront this powerful corporation came not from participation in a social struggle in Mexico but from her dogged personal fight to reunite her family and support them under the most difficult conditions. Espinoza had to negotiate the dangers of the border, where men have all the essential wealth and power. Then she used the strength she gained there to stand up to the foreman on the meatpacking lines. When she met her husband, Eleuterio, he supported her activism. Twenty-two years on the skin line (where animal carcasses are skinned) had given him an intimate knowledge of discrimination and injustice, along with the anger needed to speak out against it.

Of course people don't always react heroically to adversity. Some try to escape oppressive conditions through alcoholism and other self-destructive devices. Antonio Hernandez offers a devastatingly honest account of his own personal journey through these demons and his eventual personal salvation and that of his family.

Almost all immigrants offer stories of the enormous difficulties and dangers incurred on their journey to the United States. They testify to its great expense—at least a thousand dollars just to cross the border. Many die on the perilous trip through the desert. Others suffer the humiliation of being hidden in anonymous houses, packed into truck trailers and car trunks, and finally being caught and sent back to start all over again. These sacrifices are part of the life experience and family histories for millions of people. Their inventiveness and determination to find ways to cross and then to remain in the United States should inspire admiration and respect.

Yet once they are here, their lack of legal immigration status becomes a means of control, and people are forced to work under often oppressive conditions. Whole industries are built on this system, from farms to garment shops to construction sites. But nowhere is it more extensive and systematic than in meatpacking plants. In recent years large corporations and their managers have been charged with maintaining elaborate recruitment schemes, gathering workers once they cross the border, and funneling them into plants in the Midwest. Some companies have been accused of supplying the immigration documents themselves, although in most cases they leave it up to the workers to arrange documentation on their own.

For those workers, the ultimate disaster arrives in the form of the immigration raid. Gustavo and Jose Guzman both went through one of the worst raids when working for Nebraska Beef in 2000. The Immigration and Naturalization Service said it had evidence that a Nebraska Beef recruiter in Mexico was offering jobs at $8.50 per hour along with a hundred-dollar signing bonus, free housing, and a fake Social Security card. But the INS deported the very people who could have testified about how they were hired, so a federal judge dismissed the charges against the company in April 2002, and the company walked.

As a result of the raid, two hundred and twelve of Gustavo and Guzman's coworkers were deported. Gustavo and Guzman survived and tell the story.

TIBERIO CHAVEZ
ALWAYS LOOK FOR SOMETHING BETTER
Omaha, Nebraska, January 2002

Tiberio Chavez participated in a land reform struggle as a young man and took the ideas he learned into the packing plants. The biggest idea, he says, was that by getting organized, people could stand up for their rights.

My mother was a nurse who worked in lumber camps. We never suffered from hunger, but we had no land. This was the time of land redistribution. New towns were being formed, and my mother moved our family to these places, always looking for work. We came to Benito Juarez, where the Pejuanez estate was located, when the redistribution was happening. In the Mexican constitution, the land belongs to the nation, and to Mexicans who want to work it. Since we were Mexicans who wanted to work the land, we invaded the estate. We organized a caravan and camped out, sleeping and eating there for six months.

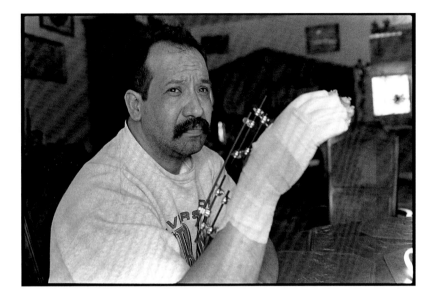

Tiberio Chavez, with the bones of his arm held in place after they were broken in a fall at the plant

Our family received a piece of land, but because it was a small piece and my family was large, there wasn't enough for everyone. I saw that when I wanted to start my own family, I wouldn't be able to provide for them. This was what made me leave.

But our land invasion was one of the most beautiful memories I have of my country. It gave us opportunity, and our rights were respected. It showed me that with unity, a group of people could achieve something an individual never could alone. Indeed, it gave me the idea that social justice is possible, although often people must work to win it. Otherwise justice is nothing more than words written on paper, and there are many people, especially politicians, who would like it to remain that way. It is up to us to put justice into practice.

But I couldn't be content. A friend told me to come to Omaha because it was a nice place, a big city with wide streets, and calm. There was a lot of work in packinghouses. I came here in 1977, and I've been in Omaha ever since.

Union Pack gave me a job in the hardest section they had, where they folded the skins of cattle. It was a cold, dirty, tough job, and poorly paid. The skins were filled with worms, and we had to get them out with our bare hands. You've never seen such dirty work! The job started at four in the morning and ended at six or seven in the evening, for $3.50 an hour. Since I wanted to work, I was ready to deal with those things.

I was never beaten, since I used a knife at work, but on one occasion someone tried. They didn't fire me, perhaps because it was a very hard job that no one wanted to do. I went into the office with the steward and the supervisor, still with a knife in my hand. I said that if I ever heard that anyone beat a Mexican, someone would have to kill someone, that we were here to work, not to be beaten. As I told my friends, we're illegal in this country, but we aren't doing anything wrong, so if they attack us, we have to fight back. And it stopped there, that same day.

We had been working there for a long time and could see that our salaries were never increased. So we went to Frank Johnson at the union hall. I didn't even think that as illegals we could organize, but he said we could. Frank was black and a union organizer. So we started to invite people to meetings, and a lot of people came—blacks, Mexicans, and even the Americans. The company began to reduce salaries, saying it was facing bankruptcy. After 1980 they closed the plant. It was the first contact I had with the union, and I thought it must have been the union's fault that the company shut down. Today I understand that at the end of the seventies a lot of packing companies were doing poorly.

With my wife's help I obtained legal residence and then U.S. citizenship. I learned how to live a little more in the American way, where you always look for something better. The culture of the North Americans taught me to look for progress. I began to realize that I had rights here, like everyone else.

Finally I got a job at the Northern States packing plant, now called ConAgra, as a welder. When the union organizers began to speak to me, I was not in agreement. I had seen a lot of plants shut down, and everyone said it was on account of the unions. But as the days passed, I saw the poor treatment of the people in production. Once a man on the line asked me to go with him to the nurse. He had a piece of metal from one of the machines in his eye, and, not speaking English, he couldn't explain what had happened. They washed his eye out, but an hour later he came to me again, and by then his eye was inflamed, because the piece of metal was still there. This time the foreman yelled at him, saying he was just a complainer. It was too much for me, and I got angry. But that's what life on the line is like. They want you to work as fast as possible, there are lots of accidents, and no one cares about the price we pay.

Then they began to take away our benefits in the maintenance department, as if they had never existed, without explanation. They told us that if we didn't like it, we could go home. A plant engineer said to me, "Listen, we consider minorities the labor force, nothing more." We won the election and negotiated our contract. I was on the negotiation committee. Now I see the great benefit of being connected with others and the support we can give to the community. I am totally new to this, but I am growing in my ideas.

Later they were doing construction on a new part of the plant. There were no catwalks, and I had a harness, but I had to undo it to move to another place. I never thought I would have an accident, but I lost my equilibrium and fell. Now they have taken advantage of this to get rid of me. They know that by getting rid of me, it's very probable that confidence in the union could disappear and my coworkers would be demoralized.

My vision of social justice is respect for human rights, in whatever part of the world we find ourselves. In the United States, Hispanics are always accused of not belonging here. But I believe that if we contribute to the community we are entitled to the same rights. We are always viewed as the labor force, and the only right we have is the right to work. Often what would take two or three men to produce, one Mexican can do, and at a lower salary. This disturbs me and gives me strength to find a way to organize, because I know we can change it. The day we organize a strong united effort we will force them to grant us the rights we are entitled to, because all human beings have rights.

Whether on this side of the border or the other, life is a continuous struggle. The powerful will always try to take away the rights of everyone. The companies want more money, and if one day they can make us work without pay, then they will. I don't see any other solution than to try to stop this by fighting against it.

But if a worker in one place benefits, everyone benefits. It is contagious—the idea that we have the right to organize. Even though I lost my job, if the people where I worked get organized, it will give me the satisfaction of knowing that I contributed to something positive. I won't be feeling miserable—"Oh, poor Tiberio!"—because I did what I could to improve things. If we just leave it, the world will deteriorate and become so hostile it won't be worth living in.

OLGA ESPINOZA
I SAY I CAN DO EVERYTHING
Omaha, Nebraska, January 2002

Olga Espinoza did almost everything a woman can do to keep her family together and finally found a stable situation for them in Omaha. She became the leader of the effort to organize a union at the meatpacking plant where she works—just one more way of fighting for her daughters.

I was born in a very small town. It had only about fifteen families, and that was it. I wanted to learn about other places and know some other kind of life. I wanted to get out of there. I left to look for work in the city of Chihuahua.

Olga Espinoza and Eleuterio Valadez

I had a daughter, but I left her with my parents so that I could go work in the city. Every two months, I would bring her clothes and money. I suffered a lot being so far away from her. I was only eighteen. I decided to find work where I could see my daughter more easily, so I went to Juarez. I cleaned people's houses and lived where I worked. Then a man hired me to take care of his father. The son owned a factory that made coupons. I worked there for another three years, taking care of the old man at night.

You must always believe in your mind that you're doing something for the future. I was working so I could have my daughter with me. That's the only thing that ran through my mind—to work and find a way to be a family again. Thank God I was able to accomplish that. Every night on the news on the television, there would be reports of women getting murdered. Juarez was very dangerous. My mother said that every time she watched TV she would ask God that the dead girl wasn't her daughter.

I met someone who I thought I was going to marry and start my life with, who would help me bring my daughter to live with me, but again I misjudged. He was a liar and had a wife in Zacatecas. So I was left with one more daughter.

Then I met an American, nineteen years older. It didn't matter to me. I needed a place, a marriage, to form a family where I could have my daughters. He offered me that, and I took it. He looked like a good person. But my main interest was bringing my daughters and me together.

After two years he offered to bring me here to the United States. He helped me get documented and my girls, too, but when I brought my oldest daughter, problems began. She was already twelve, and he felt uncomfortable. I cried at night, and he said he wasn't happy either. He suggested we get separated.

I had a brother here in Omaha and went to live with him until I found a job. It only took me a week, and I've been here seven years now.

I work at ConAgra, where I met Eleuterio. In El Paso I felt like I was caged. When I got here with all the people, I felt very happy. I felt free. I spoke to everyone. When I started working, Eleuterio worked next to me. We just talked and talked. I told him my story, and he told me his. He started singing me pretty songs. That's how he conquered me. We dated for two months and got married in Chihuahua with my family, five years ago. My parents were very happy.

The work was hard. My first job was putting plastic on the legs of the cows so they wouldn't get dirty from the grease on the machines. It was a very fast job. The days went by so slowly, and my back hurt really badly. It was always the same movement.

I have a job now that requires me to change what I do. One week I do one job, and the next day I'll do something different. Right now part of my hand is swollen, where I have to put a lot of pressure on it. It hurts, and the work is fast. In the job I was doing before, this fingernail fell off, but now it's growing back. I'm constantly doing different work.

I am a very ambitious woman. I never like to say that I can't do something. I say I can do everything. I feel very strong, and I can do many jobs. There are about twenty-five women where I work, and we get along fine.

When I first got there, there were very few. Men were disrespectful in their language, but now there isn't a whole lot of that.

There are jobs that, honestly, a woman cannot do, but I'm seeing women performing jobs that men usually did. I feel bad for some who can't do it, but there are also a lot who can. Right now I'm earning $10.75 per hour. Men and women earn the same. They've made me fill, weigh, tie, and lift boxes weighing seventy-five pounds. At night, I couldn't even get my arms comfortable enough to sleep. I told the manager, "I have to strain too much on this job, and I can't do it. You need a man to do it." He said, "What are you trying to say? Are you trying to suggest that there is only work for men and not women? No, the work here is work." We're always fighting.

Last year the representatives from the union started talking to us as we walked out of work after we finished our shift. I was very interested because I had seen all the mistreatment. I told Jose, "El Sapo," who was working next to me, about a meeting. The foreman walked by and yelled, "Shut up, stop talking, you can't do the job well if you're talking." "See?" I told Jose, "The only thing left is for them to whip our backs so we work faster." Later he walked by and told me, "If you continue talking, I'm going to tape your mouth." He was playing, but at the same time they say things like that to make an impression.

I told him, "I have my hands covered in blood. I'm really thirsty and hot. I don't even have time to wash my hands or to remove my gloves. When can I even get a drink of water? Break time's still another hour away." The guy just laughed.

There are a lot of things that can change with the union, even as simple as having a place to drink water. We come from Mexico very poor. We work very hard over there, too, and we come here and act like we're in heaven because we have a job. We have enough to buy food, and we're happy because in Mexico we hardly had that. So people don't stop to think and fight to get things better. We don't even feel like we deserve better.

It's difficult to convince people that we need a change. I wonder if I should keep talking to them. I told Sapo, "Here there will be a union. Someday there will be a union."

The company has the right to tell us that we have to work eight hours, but there is a limit. They don't want that. Why can't I say, "My body can only handle so much"? Like Eleuterio. He's been working there for twenty-five years, and none of us understands how he's done it so long. Look at him now—the work's made him sick, but they'll never admit it.

My oldest daughter is nineteen years old, and she's going to the university. She wants to get her diploma and study medicine. She has good ideas. That's why I'm taking care of my granddaughter. That way she'll be able to improve herself. I don't think our children will go back to Mexico to live. Life is more difficult there. But we keep distancing ourselves from our family. When you come as an adult, the dream is to work, to improve your life, and, if God permits, to grow old in Mexico. That's the dream. But our children were brought here when they were very young, and their dream is not the same.

The only thing that's left for us in life is to fight. If things improve at work, we'll be able to improve the lives of our children.

ELEUTERIO VALADEZ
TWENTY-FIVE YEARS ON THE SKIN LINE
Omaha, Nebraska, January 2002

Eleuterio Valadez voices the rage of meatpacking workers trapped in low-paying jobs on a production line that always runs faster and faster. That's why he wants a union.

The first time I crossed the border I did it in Tijuana. With the help of a coyote, we began walking through the mountains, a whole night and part of the next day. He had twenty-five people and couldn't take us all, so he left fifteen of us hidden in the mountains. For two days we had no food or water, and when he returned he said immigration caught the first group and put him in jail. They deported him, and he came to get us. We all got in his van, lying on top of each other to fit. That night immigration got us, too.

They took us back to Tijuana. I waited two days to rest and attempted to cross again. Well, they got us again, in the same spot, and took us back to Tijuana again. I rested another two days and the next time we did pass, going through the mountains the same way. Friends from my hometown put me on a plane in Los Angeles, and I flew to here to Omaha. That was in 1977, and I've been here ever since.

I started working at the ConAgra packing plant when it was called Northern States Beef. I've worked there for twenty-five years.

In 1980 we wanted to join the union, but the company fought it. We were on strike for a year. Then they said we had lost and the company had won. The governor of Nebraska convinced the owners to give us our jobs back, but only after the workers who replaced us left. During the year before I returned to work I didn't have enough to live on. The union gave us fifty dollars a week to go on the picket line. I had to spend all my savings—nearly three thousand dollars—to keep living. Finally, I returned to work.

I've always wanted the union. That time the union could not win because the company fought it. I never blamed the union, and when they came again, I still wanted it. I don't care if the same thing happens. I want to keep fighting for better benefits and better wages.

Other places that have unions have things way better than we do. I earn eleven dollars an hour, but I still don't think this is fair. Other people earn much less, and I don't think that's fair either. I think a fair wage would be eighteen dollars an hour.

I've been on the skin line for more than twenty-four years, and it's one of the most labor-intensive jobs. My wage was frozen for many years at $8.15 an hour. There weren't any pay increases until all of a sudden ten positions opened up and they were offering to pay $12.50 an hour in those position, if we could do more than 97 percent good work. They did not want the meat to be torn, the skin to be torn, the meat to get dirty. It was very difficult to earn the $12.50. When they saw that we were getting the 97 percent good work, they said it wasn't enough and we wouldn't get the $12.50.

That's how it was for a long time. We always did a good job, so that we could earn the $12.50, but for a long time they'd give it to us one week and not the next. Finally they left it at $12.50.

Then they opened a new line and increased the speed of the chain. The people could not do the same work at that velocity. Jobs got harder. They demanded that I do the same operation, and I couldn't. It was too much. "But you were doing it before," they'd say. They threatened to decrease my wage, and I told them that the chain was too fast, which they denied. They gave me two options. Jesse Esparza, the foreman, told me, "Do the work how it was done before at $12.50 an hour or part of the work at $9.50." I told him I wouldn't work for $9.50, and I got angry and left.

The company asked me what I wanted. They told me they wouldn't pay $12.50. I told them that a knife sharpener job was going to open up, but the company said that job paid $9.50. Finally one of the managers said that he would pay $11 for that $9.50-per-hour job, so I accepted it. Now I sharpen the knives, and I fix the guns they use to kill the cows and the tools and razors used for skinning. It's a lot of work for less money than I earned before.

I'm ready to walk out again. I can't stand them. I don't know what they want, because I try to do the best work I can. I hurry to try to meet their deadlines and they're still not happy. If they wanted to fire me, then I don't know why they called me back when I walked out. I don't understand them. I've worked long and hard for that company and I think they owe me a lot. I don't think that I'll last much longer.

That's why I would like to get the union in. It's my only hope to make some changes.

I have five children, and none of them works for a packinghouse. I don't want them to go through the same experiences I went through. I don't want them to kill themselves for little pay.

The company treats us this way because we're Mexicans—that's what I think. We come from other countries, and they know that we don't know anything and take advantage of us. Each week they steal an hour from our paycheck. Nobody gets full pay for the hours they've worked, and no one says anything because they fear losing their jobs. They're afraid the foreman will say, "Well, if you don't like it, there's the door."

We want to work, but we want to be treated justly, like humans. We are people. We're a different race, but we're humans not animals.

GUSTAVO
THE STORY OF A RAID
Omaha, Nebraska, May 2002

Gustavo survived a famous immigration raid at Nebraska Beef when the company was charged with smuggling workers from Mexico and giving them false documents. The charges were later dropped after the workers who could have been witnesses were deported. Following the raid, workers tried to organize a union but were defeated, as he explains.

People said we should come to Omaha because we could make more money here. It was easy to get a job in a meatpacking plant because I had a friend who was a foreman. At the beginning, they gave us normal work, but after a while they started increasing the speed of the line until it burst. They'd hire people in Mexico and bring them here. I heard that there was a lady who would make them a fake passport in Mexico, and with that they could pass. After they started working, it would be payback time.

On the day of the big immigration raid, half an hour after our break, the supervisors said the migra was here. They stopped the line and told people to go upstairs. Lots of people went up, and that's where they were taken. They closed all the doors after they were in the dining room and checked people one by one. It seemed they were after the ones who came from El Paso, the people who were brought here.

Some people got into the combos, the containers where the meat falls after being cut on the line; other people covered the tops, and that's where they hid. With my coworkers I went downstairs into the cooler and never went up. Our supervisors told us that the ones who didn't have papers should hide in there. Some people stayed there for five hours or more without the special suit for the cold. They almost froze to death.

A supervisor had the idea of taking us to a trailer. He put us inside and that's how we escaped. The truck was full of broken shovels. When agents arrived they opened the doors and asked what was inside. The supervisors said, only shovels. The agent looked with a flashlight, but he didn't see us, thank God. And he left.

Afterwards, a truck driver drove the trailer to Lincoln. Then secretaries and supervisors came from the factory to pick us up. They took us home in their own cars. That night the foreman told us to go to work the next day, that there would be no problem. Many didn't come, though, because they thought that immigration would be there. They lost their jobs.

When I arrived in the U.S. I got all the documents I need to be safe. I could pass as an American. If they asked me whether I was a citizen, I said yes. Once when I flew to L.A. from Omaha, immigration stopped me when I arrived. I said I was an American citizen, so he asked for my ID and my Social Security number. I know it by heart, and I have all the documents, so he let me pass. If you're nervous or don't give your personal information correctly, they'd take you. More than anything else, you had to give them your Social Security number by heart.

But what happened with the terrorists [on Sept. 11] changed everything. Now you can't take a plane. Before with an ID you could. Now if you're undocumented they take you down.

After the raid, some women upstairs demanded a raise, and they were fired. They said the line goes too fast, and it does. What should be done in ten hours they do in eight and a half, and then give us a day a week to rest. And the wages are at the bottom. That's why I still support the union. My supervisor told me that I shouldn't vote for it because it would take money from us and reduce the hours in the workday. I said I didn't think the union could steal more from us than the company already does, and that I'd rather be robbed by the union than by you. He got mad at me.

He walked around with a little notebook, writing down the names of those who were voting for the company and those who were voting for the union. We got mad at him and told him he was invading our rights. Let us decide for ourselves, we told him. Unfortunately, they know we don't have any papers. They said the union was going to call immigration, to scare us. And they did scare a lot of people. They also promised fifty cents more per hour if we didn't vote for it.

When we had the union election they brought in people who had never worked in a factory before. One told me he was the son of a supervisor. It was obvious who the new people were; even a blind person could recognize them. They all came down with new helmets, overalls that didn't even have a stain on them, brand new shoes—just in order to vote. And the rest of us lost. Lots of people who had voted for the union went back to Mexico, and when they came back to work the factory didn't give them their jobs back.

Afterwards they never gave us the fifty cents. Not even a pair of pants.

JOSE GUZMAN
HIDING IN THE AIR-CONDITIONING DUCT
Omaha, Nebraska, February 2002

Jose Guzman, who was also caught up in the immigration raid at the Nebraska Beef plant, tells a story of spending hours hiding in an air-conditioning duct. People without papers, he says, have to put up with almost anything.

If they treat you poorly at work, you have to take it, because you don't have any documents. You have to keep working because if you lose that job,

finding another one is difficult. From the moment you start working at the packinghouse you have to move. The machines run by the second, so we have to perform the work in seconds.

At first you don't know the tools or how to sharpen the knives, so you can hardly eat because your hands hurt so bad. You have to get used to it and learn how to use the knives and how to sharpen them. Work starts at 5 a.m., and you have to get used to a totally different rhythm.

When you first get here, your friends and family usually have connections and let you borrow money. They help you find people who sell their identification cards to others who look like them. Once you find work, little by little you start paying people back for the papers. I bought a Social Security card, which back then was enough to start work anywhere. I was able to get one for ten years, so for nine years I didn't have a problem finding a job. Now it's much more difficult. You can't do that anymore.

Once you have your papers, you go to the plant office and fill out the application. Then you get an interview. People say that at this point they call immigration, who might pick you up. So you go with a little fear the first time you get a job.

I started at a company called National Beef, where I worked for four years. Then I went to Oklahoma as a pig caretaker. If you don't move around, you have problems, because year after year, you're not filing your income tax. You have to move to keep working.

In Omaha in 1996 I started working for Nebraska Beef. The plant was a lot smaller then. There's more technology at the bigger packinghouses, and people kill themselves less. At the smaller one you have to do everything by hand.

At Nebraska Beef, there are thirty-five steps from the bottom to the top where the restrooms are, so during the first break it's fine. But people walking up the stairs to use the restroom later on sometimes fall, because we're working with fatty meat and the fat makes the stairs slippery. The supervisors tell those who complain, "There's the door, and go home because we don't need you here. Those who want to work, then work." We can only work and work and work.

When you don't have papers, you're always being threatened by the people who do. They tell you the migra is coming. That happens daily, so people don't believe it after a while. The day of the immigration raid, we got our break before the regular break time and went down to work again. We'd only been working fifteen minutes when the chain stopped and they rang the break bell again. Everyone began climbing the stairs. The migra was waiting for them in the lunchroom, but the people at the top couldn't turn around. Once they climbed up, they never came down.

Our boss came down to tell us the migra was in the lunchroom. I didn't believe him at first, but I finished the job I was doing and went to the cooler. When I got there, the migra was taking people out. A foreman was calling everyone, helping the migra, because people were trying to find places to hide. He was taking us out, telling people to go upstairs. In the back where the trucks are, another foreman put all of the people near the cooler in an empty truck. He drove off with all of the people inside, as if he had meat in the truck. A lot of people were spared because of him.

I left the cooler and walked up to the lunchroom. Halfway up the stairs is a door that leads to the offices and the men's bathrooms. I went that way. I stayed a while in a locker room for people who clean at night, but the migra came and told us to go up to the lunchroom. I took a turn into the women's bathroom and got to a place where all of the pipes lead to the roof. On one side I looked and I saw the migra rounding up more people. On the other I looked at the roof and saw that there was a hole in the insulation. I thought that if I climbed in there I wouldn't have any problems, so I moved a bench and climbed up into an air-conditioning duct.

Every time they opened the door, I felt sure they were going to find me. I couldn't move or make any noise. I was like that from 10 a.m. until evening. It was very noisy, and the water from the air-conditioning system was right behind me. During those hours I thought about my wife and my family. I had filled out my application to get all of them documents. If the migra had taken me, I would have ruined all of that. I couldn't urinate because that was my last place to go. I couldn't go anywhere else. I thought of all of my hopes and dreams ending there. From the moment I saw the migra, I thought, "Everything is over." Thank God I escaped.

I didn't get out until 7:30 that evening. I don't know what happened to the rest of the people. When I climbed out the plant was empty, and the migra was gone.

People blamed the company for the raid and asked for more money. They asked them to lower the speed of the chain. It was mostly women doing the talking. One by one, they started to fire them. There's no respect for anything there. No one has any rights. Whoever talks is fired, especially if they talk about the union.

I worked nine years butchering at Nebraska Beef. Butchering is tough. The body never gets used to it. Outside the plant, you see someone who is well respected, but inside you see them crying because they can't do the work. People have to feed their family, so they put up with it. They have to work no matter how they're treated. It's going to be tough to change that.

ANTONIO HERNANDEZ
THE STRUGGLE TO GET PAPERS
Omaha, Nebraska, January 2002

Antonio Hernandez describes what it was like to work for years without papers, doing hard, painful jobs in a meatpacking plant. He recalls two attempts to organize a union where he worked, both of which failed, but a year after he was interviewed workers finally succeeded in their organizing efforts.

I've been a packinghouse worker in Omaha since 1978. First I worked in the slaughterhouse and then later in the fabrication section, where the animals are cut up.

Everything a person does, according to my way of thinking, is for the good of the family—whether it's to live better in Mexico or here. Even if you

Antonio Hernandez

have to leave your mother or wife and children, you do it in order to live better. I came from a small ranch. Even though we had a way of earning money as farmers, there wasn't enough to eat. We were children of a very strict father who kept everything that was harvested or received from its sale. We got food and clothing, but we couldn't keep any of the money. When we worked other land with my father's tractor, the money he was paid would go to maintenance or diesel fuel. We didn't get any. We were like employees.

My mother would give us an allowance and clothes, shoes, and food. Meanwhile my father was here in the U.S., but even while he was there, all the money made from the farm and the tractor was his. All of it.

The first time I came north was in 1978. My brother got me a job at Northern States Beef in Omaha. The day I began I started fine, but by the afternoon I was exhausted and even had a fever. I had to lift thirty-two-gallon barrels filled with legs and feet and dump them in a hole. When I left I was in a lot of pain, especially my fingers. That happens to everyone who comes into the plant without knowing what to expect.

But I never thought of quitting. Earning money to bring my family gave me the strength to continue. Anyone can stay in an easy job. But in the difficult ones, that's how you work hard and not quit. Sometimes in the slaughterhouse I would go in on Saturdays, even after having gone drinking on Friday. I only missed work twice in all that time, even though sometimes I was a little drunk. But that's dangerous, especially when you work with a knife. I started drinking right after I got here. For years I wasted a lot of money on beer or in bars with friends. My wife and children never lacked food, clothing, or shelter, but I wasn't able to save anything. I could barely make it with what I was earning. But in 1984 I stopped drinking once and for all. When I started working in the fabrication department, I felt I couldn't work after drinking all night. So I stopped, cold turkey, and haven't had a drink since then.

I was here without documents for a long time. None of us had legal residence until '86 when the amnesty program began. In 1982 I was held in jail for fifteen days and then deported to Mexico. After four days on the border I came back, and a week later our daughter was born. That is something I don't wish on anyone, to leave a pregnant wife like that. Since we were illegal we had no support from government programs like Medicare. Fortunately, as soon as I returned I got my job back at the slaughterhouse. I began making money and paid the hospital bills.

In 1983 my wife and I were caught in the laundromat. The INS wanted us to come downtown, so they could write up a file on us to send us to Mexico. I told my wife it wasn't a good idea for us to present ourselves because they would deport us if we did. We decided to go to California and lived six months there.

Two years later the INS waited for me to come out of the house in the morning. It seems someone told them I was an illegal. They took my wife and me downtown and started deportation proceedings. But during this time the amnesty began and we filed our papers. For my wife and children things worked out right away. In fact, we were among the first who regularized our status.

But I couldn't get legal residence until 1995 because of my problems with the law. Drinking was the principal reason they didn't want to give it to me. Finally, in 1995 I got residency status under family reunification.

In 1980 there was a strike at Northern States Beef. When we went to other meat packinghouses, we were denied work, despite the fact we knew how to do it. I think they did that because the company we were striking probably called all the other packinghouses and told them not to give us jobs because they wanted us to go back to work.

Union organizers pulled us out on strike, but I don't think they were well trained because they didn't have a plan to win. A lot of new people came in—blacks, whites, and Mexicans. People who did not go on strike began bringing in their families. Even though it took time, little by little they were learning the work. The company got some production out, and these people learned in the process. Finally, the bosses said that if we wanted to return we could have our jobs back. Some went back with their seniority and others didn't. I was able to return in time and continued working with my same seniority. No, I did not like that strike.

When we started organizing the union again, our reasons had to do with the way we were treated. They always want you to do more work than you can. And the more work you do, the more they want.

I was working in the chucks department. There are five ribs in this piece of meat and all the bones in the neck. We cut all the meat from the bone. You have to make several cuts. The neck has many little bones, and you have to cut around all of them. And you have to cut up about twenty pieces per hour, about three minutes for each piece, more or less.

After a ten-hour shift your fingers are inflamed and you can hardly move your hands. You only get feeling in them when you wet them. Sometimes they fall asleep on you, and at midnight you wake up with inflamed fingers and pain all through your hands. My whole arm would hurt from the shoulders to the tip of my fingers. Sometimes I would take aspirin, but I did not want my body to get used to antibiotics or painkillers. I would let my arm hang off the side of the bed to diminish the pain and go back to sleep.

If you accomplished a certain quantity, for example 100 per hour, the next day it would be 102 per hour. They would increase the number of pieces per hour each day. For them, that works better. We get paid less, and they get more production.

So friends who worked there started talking with me. Other people came to my house and explained the benefits and why we should get organized. I began thinking about it and got involved in organizing at the worksite, talking with the people. When the supervisors and the antiunion people would talk, I would tell them that I was in favor of the union. I wasn't afraid of telling them. The company had a meeting and showed us antiunion videos, but I felt they should give us the chance to express our opinion freely.

Our vote was pretty low, compared to what we expected, because the vice-president of the company promised the situation would improve. But as a matter of fact, it did not improve. I was very disillusioned because after seeing with their own eyes what was being done to them, people still voted against the union. One day they'll experience what I experienced, where they fire you just like that, and they'll find they are not indispensable. We are people that can be replaced.

Since my hand was already injured, they had me on light duty before the election. Then they fired me afterwards because I did not bring a paper from the doctor. But I am sure I lost my job because I was organizing with other workers. I can no longer work deboning because I can't cut the way I did before. I spent five years in the slaughterhouse and seventeen cutting. That's twenty-two years.

I don't want my children to suffer what I did. I don't want them to end up there. Any job is a dignified job, but I don't want them to get hurt the way I did and then not be able to work or do another job. I have been looking for work all of last year without any results.

I couldn't go back to Mexico until 1988 because of my papers. But when I got the first permit, as soon as the kids got out of school I bought a cheap flight on credit. For the first time in almost ten years I set foot again in my dear Mexico and we could see all the family we left behind. We go back regularly now every other year.

My kids, though, do not want to go back. They say they have made their life here. I believe the children are free to decide whether to live in Mexico or not. I can't force them if they don't want to, although I would like it if they did. Last year we went to build a house in our hometown. It is big enough for everyone. But I won't force them to go. I want them to live well, more than anything.

I am waiting for my appointment to become a U.S. citizen. They are demanding it in order to qualify for Social Security, but I also want to be able to vote and express my desires about how we should be governed. You can be both Mexican and a U.S. citizen. And I see that U.S. citizens are treated much better, even in Mexico. The authorities have more fear of you, instead of your being afraid of them.

3

Indigenous Guatemalan immigrants in Nebraska, like those from Oaxaca in California, face difficulty preserving their culture in the United States. Trying to hold on to traditional music and dance and pass on their language to their children, Qanjobal and Mam communities began organizing networks in the late 1990s and the first years of this new century.

Their first groups were often given the name "Ixim," after the word for corn in Guatemala's twenty-three indigenous languages, according to Sergio Sosa, because in an ear of corn all the kernels are bound tightly together. These networks were based on people from the same town or region. In Omaha and the surrounding Nebraska meatpacking towns, the Ixim group consists of migrants from the highland towns just north of Huehuetenango.

The townspeople of Santa Eulalia, San Miguel Acatan, San Pedro Soloma, and other places were caught up in Guatemala's civil war of the 1980s and 1990s. Thousands of people fled the military, which, as Sosa says, couldn't distinguish between guerilla fighters and the indigenous population on whom guerillas depended for support. The army carried out genocidal campaigns against entire indigenous communities. The guerrilla fighters also sought to punish those who cooperated with the soldiers by supplying names of families and even communities with pro-guerilla sympathies. Many Guatemalans living today in the United States remember the almost daily discovery of bodies dumped on the roads during those years.

Those who fled went north, first to refugee camps in Mexico. They then undertook the arduous journey to the United States. Following the massacre in San Miguel Acatan in 1982, the concentration of San Miguel residents in Los Angeles and Florida grew so high that their communities became known as Little San Miguels.

In the Midwest many migrants came from Santa Eulalia and its neighboring *aldeas*, or villages. Jesus Martinez and Domingo Cristobal describe efforts to bring these migrants together to form the Ixim chapter of Santa Eulalia residents living in the United States. For a while it was named, appropriately, Citizens of the World. One intention of that effort is to funnel the remittances of migrants living in the States into community projects back home, such as public works and church reconstruction. But Martinez also mentions a new goal—the desire to influence the political process there as well, by ensuring that Guatemala continues to follow a course away from the military violence and dictatorships of the past.

Cultural preservation is another link bringing Guatemalan migrants together. For decades Santa Eulalia has been famous for making marimbas, and now the marimba has become a cultural symbol for Santa Eulalia residents living in the States. Francisco Gaspar bought two marimbas from

Santa Eulalia master craftsman Juan Mateo, and they are played at the fiestas that periodically bring together Santa Eulalians in exile.

Nostalgia for home is a common thread in the immigrant experience of most people. But now even young people with few, if any, memories of Santa Eulalia play the marimba, too. Often they were either born in the United States or came so young that they had no chance to hear anyone play the instrument in Guatemala. So they learned in Omaha to play the traditional Qanjobal music heard in the fiestas back home. But as the Nebraska night grows later and the older folks leave, these young musicians begin playing new combinations of the old Guatemalan tunes and the *banda* music popular among Mexican immigrants.

Migrants reinvent and mix cultures to make them relevant to their new experience.

Jesus Martinez presents the draft of a letter about the Guatemalan elections to community activists at the fiesta welcoming Bishop Rodolfo Bobadilla.

JESUS MARTINEZ
WE MUST NOT FORGET THE PEOPLE OF GUATEMALA
Omaha, Nebraska, August 2003

At a fiesta in Omaha to welcome Bishop Rodolfo Bobadilla from Huehuetenango, Jesus Martinez and Sergio Sosa brought a letter urging Guatemalans not to support candidates who were responsible for massacres during the civil war. They were concerned that General Efrain Ríos Montt, who launched a scorched-earth war against indigenous communities, was a candidate of the largest right-wing party.

During the war in Guatemala, indigenous people like us were the ones most affected. The heaviest concentration of fighting was in the west, in Huehuetenango and the areas around us. My uncles both died in the war.

I went to a school in Santa Eulalia, run by the brothers of Maryknoll, and got a scholarship to study in Huehuetenango. The war derailed my dreams of getting an education and having a career. The fruits of war are hunger, the lack of opportunities, and oppression. What resources did I have to study with? If there was no work for adults, there was even less for a youth like me.

My father expected me to stay at home and farm, but our small piece of land wasn't enough for those dreams, so I went to the U.S. It was not my intention to stay. I thought I would come and work for three years and then return to Guatemala to study. But once you start living in another country, where you don't speak the language, it takes a while to assimilate. The time went by so fast that to this day I still haven't returned. I have been here sixteen or seventeen years—I don't even remember exactly how many. Maybe because of my age, I don't remember anymore the dreams I had as a child.

I began working in Arizona on a cattle ranch in a Native American reservation. I then moved to Florida, Arkansas, and other parts of the U.S. I was always looking for a job, and I was fortunate to find work everywhere. I arrived in Nebraska in 1995, and I've been in Schuyler for eight years.

I was amazed at how many animals they butcher there, and how many people work in the plant. It is a difficult job, but you get paid for it. Every job is hard in the beginning because you have to get accustomed to it. Once you get the hang of it, you're fine. Thank God I am in a country of many opportunities, and I have to take advantage of them. Now I train the new employees how to do their jobs.

Father David Lopez came from Santa Eulalia to Nebraska and called on us to organize and help our people. In Schuyler we formed an indigenous organization, and groups were organized in Omaha, Sioux City, and other parts of the country where we Guatemalans reside. Our purpose is to strengthen our culture and pass it on to our children, and to support each other. For example, if a fellow countryman were to pass away, we would quickly mobilize to gather money and send the body to Guatemala. It is important to know where we came from and assimilate into this country at the same time.

I bought a marimba for my son when I went to Guatemala and brought it to Schuyler, but it is only about a foot long. Francisco Gaspar has two big ones in Omaha and an excellent group called Percusión Guatemala. It is a symbol of Santa Eulalia—I think that's what it's about. My son likes to dance to the marimba. My wife danced marimba when she was pregnant, so I think that he hasn't forgotten. We are passing that on to our future. I also speak Qanjobal very well—I hardly speak Spanish. I am teaching it to my son. He says a few words already.

We also want to continue to play a role in the life of our country. At the fiesta everyone was discussing a letter to be sent to Guatemala with the bishop, about the elections. As citizens of our country, it is our obligation to take an active role in who becomes president. We have no affiliation with a political party, but we want to make the people aware. The church has been our voice, and I hope people elect a good leader.

I don't think it is a political move. It is just a call to consciousness, the first opportunity of its kind. We must not forget the people in Guatemala.

DOMINGO CRISTOBAL DIEGO
WE ARE CITIZENS OF THE WORLD
Omaha, Nebraska, August 2003

Domingo Cristobal Diego believes that Guatemalans living in the United States have to actively preserve their culture, so he helped form a new organization, Citizens of the World, to do that. But that name has a larger meaning.

I work in a ham and bacon factory called Plumproast in Council Bluffs, Iowa. There are about ten of us Guatemaltecos working there. Some are from Santa Eulalia like me, others are from San Miguel Acatan, and some are from San Juan Barillas—all towns close to each other in Huehuetenango.

My parents were very poor, and I had no way of obtaining an education. I was in the army, and there was a lot of persecution during those times by the communists and by the government. A farmer had no way out. A person simply needed to point you out and you were killed. I came to this country to escape that.

I came in 1989 with a group of friends and found work in a Los Angeles garment factory. It was the easiest job to find and you were quickly hired. The first days were hard, and I was not used to this work. I lacked agility, but I like adapting and learning new skills, and with time you learn.

After six years I moved to Omaha with my brother. We heard that there was better work with better pay. He got married here, and I am still single, and we both have a better life. I've managed to buy two houses here. In Los Angeles I didn't advance much.

Domingo Cristobal

We are also trying to preserve our culture here in the U.S. Our fiestas have marimba music, which is authentic music that touches each of us. It reminds us of home. We are so bombarded with rap, salsa, and other types of music here, it is easy to forget our native music and its origin. Through the marimba, our past comes to life and makes us want to return to our native land. It reminds us of our family, children, and homeland.

As parents it is our responsibility to teach our children about our culture. If one day I have children I will teach them everything. I want children here to learn to play the marimba so that the culture doesn't fade away. Before our group started, no community leaders thought of taking that on.

In our organization we believe that borders don't exist that divide our culture here from that at home. By helping one another we can preserve our cultural values that matter most to us. We are all citizens of the world.

The people at my plant are Latinos. In every factory I've worked, I have found Guatemaltecos. Some are from Huehuetenango, and others are from other parts of the country. I just joined the Guatemalan Coordinating Committee—Citizens of the World. Their meetings motivated me so much that I wanted to belong. My vision aligns with theirs—we all want to help others. Along with the Catholic Church we will do that.

When I was a child, I could not attend school because my family lacked the money. I wanted to be a doctor or lawyer, but that was not possible. Through this organization I can help other children in my hometown to attain that goal. That's why I'm so excited and committed about working with this group. We are going to raise money here and send it to the church in Guatemala. It will be their responsibility to give it to the people and rural schools that need it most.

FRANCISCO GASPAR
BRINGING MARIMBAS TO NEBRASKA
Omaha, Nebraska, August 2003

Francisco Gaspar was one of the first Guatemalans to bring marimbas to the Midwest. He plays the instrument in fiestas almost every weekend, part of a renaissance of Guatemalan music and culture among migrants in the United States.

When the war started in 1980, I came to the U.S. There were a lot of people killed, including people in my family. In many places in Guatemala people were killed by both sides, and their bodies were just left on the roadside. If you didn't go with the guerrilla, then they killed you. The same thing happened if you didn't side with the military. I was a farm worker. I didn't have any weapons. I saw so many bodies on the road that I got scared and

Francisco Gaspar and his family brought this marimba from Santa Eulalia to Omaha and play it at Guatemalan fiestas in the midwest.

came to the U.S. When I decided to leave, my father cried. I am his only son. But I told him that if I stayed with him I would be forced into the military or be killed. I was trying my best to save myself.

We had a teacher in school who knew Spanish and Qanjobal. He would speak in our dialect most of the time. I only learned to speak Spanish when I was older and traveled from town to town looking for work. I learned more Spanish when I crossed Mexico en route to the U.S. I still speak my dialect with my wife, but my children, who were born here, speak Spanish and English.

I came through Chiapas, where I bought Mexican clothes. When we got to the Mexican border we said we were from Oaxaca. We got to the U.S.-Mexico border in Sonora and guided ourselves by walking toward a mine

on the U.S. side that bellowed a lot of smoke. We walked through miles of desert until we got to an Indian reservation, and they drove us to Phoenix.

When I started looking for work, I lived under a tree for three months, gathering wood to make a fire for warmth. I didn't have a house or friends. I ate tangerines and oranges or anything else I could find. I couldn't start buying food and clothing until I got a job.

After I found work, I joined the farm workers' union because the farmers weren't paying enough. I belonged to the union for two years and helped organize strikes. We struck one company where we'd been picking oranges and lemons. For three months we slept on the side of the road and ate what the United Farm Workers provided. The company gave in and raised the wages.

I came to Omaha to work in a meatpacking plant. My daughter told me there was a lot of work and that they paid well. At Nebraska Beef I work ten hours a day, six days a week, and my checks come up to five hundred dollars. I close the boxes of hamburger meat and put the boxes on the pallets. I think I'm going to stay there, because I like my supervisor. There must be two thousand workers at Nebraska Beef—African Americans, Mexicans, and Guatemaltecos. It's an impressive sight.

I brought a marimba five years ago when I was in Arizona, where I worked with a lot of people from Guatemala. The first one was small, but people knew how to play it. They told me to bring a bigger one. I spoke with Mateo Juandiego from Santa Eulalia and he built it. He has been doing this for so long that he has the finest wood and does good work. I've had it for five years and it still looks the same. I spent a lot of money, about $3,700, for that marimba and for shipping it to Arizona. The price is getting high because the wood is becoming expensive. But it was important that we don't forget our culture, so I collected donations. A few people pitched in twenty dollars here and there. I bought drums and speakers in the U.S. so in the end I spent more than seven thousand dollars.

I like the marimba, and I spend a lot of good times at family events with it. The marimba is the heart of our culture, and when we say there is going to be one at a fiesta, people come from far away. We don't charge a lot so that people can come. It is not really a business, because I hardly receive any money for playing it, usually only enough to cover the gasoline. But we have a lot of fun, and at the same time we show Americans a little bit of who we are.

In Santa Eulalia the old men who play have been doing it for so long they know the songs by heart. But those old men don't emigrate, so here young men are learning the tradition. Mateo tells me that people from various states in the U.S. have begun to order marimbas. But I think the tradition is going to slowly die, because their sons don't want to keep it going. Lots of young people only listen to Mexican music now.

4

In one of the ironies of Guatemalan migration, while residents of Santa Eulalia in Nebraska pine for home and order marimbas to keep alive their music and culture, in Santa Eulalia the manufacture of the instruments is in danger. Young people of the highlands not only see little economic future in this traditional industry, they see little advantage in education itself. Why go to school, they ask, when a high school teacher in Santa Eulalia with a university degree earns less than an unskilled and uneducated migrant on the line in a Nebraska meatpacking plant?

The dream of the north has become powerful, and life in Santa Eulalia is changing drastically under its impact. Land prices rise, because people with relatives sending money home can afford to buy it and build new homes. Those with no access to remittances, or to migration itself, go to work for those who have it. A new class division is becoming apparent, dividing those who can migrate from those who can't.

Sometimes the dream of wealth in the north does not come true. The

son of the marimba maker Juan Mateo, Mateo Juandiego, returned home disgusted after a decade in Los Angeles garment sweatshops, with little to show for years of toil. Yet even on his return, he didn't take his father's place in the marimba factory but instead opened a store with his wife in the center of town.

The people who make out the best are the coyotes. Both Omar and Nicolas Francisco describe the money to be made taking people north, whether strangers or family members. Francisco today owns Santa Eulalia's only hotel, and he raised money to rebuild the church after it burned.

Omar describes the thriving networks that take people from Santa Eulalia to Nebraska. It is expensive, five or six thousand dollars for the trip. Given their low incomes in Guatemala, whole families pool their resources, going into debt to come up with the money. Any family member who goes is under enormous pressure to begin sending money home immediately to pay back the loans and raise the living standard of those who sent them. When that doesn't happen, as was the case with the sons of Alonso Pedro, the bitterness is intense. And someone who dies soon after arrival, having sent back little or nothing, brings disaster down on the heads of those left behind.

Still, people look at coyotes generally with admiration and respect, even if they are exploiting the desperate need of people to go north. After all, they are doing nothing illegal in Guatemala, as Omar says, and even provide a service people need, and for which they're willing to pay dearly. Coyotes obey the law of the market religiously.

For families divided by migration, survival is not easy. Emilia Juanantonio and Lorenzo Francisco describe, from opposite ends of the journey, why they decided to live apart for twelve years. They had to find ways to raise their children with the values they hold dear, and to build a house depending mostly on Emilia's labor. For Lorenzo, this meant enduring acute loneliness and separation and a life made up almost entirely of work. For Emilia, it meant doing double duty raising children and adding her income to what Lorenzo sent home. As her children grew older, she began practicing midwifery and assumed an important role in Santa Eulalia.

Lorenzo still expects to make a little more money and then go home. This is the dream for most who migrate, but few, in the end, are able, or want, to return.

JUAN MATEO JUANDIEGO
THE MARIMBA MAKER
Santa Eulalia, Guatemala, August 2002

Juan Mateo is one of the four old men in Santa Eulalia who make marimbas. Their knowledge may not survive, though, because young people leave for the United States instead of going into the workshops. But now Guatemalans in the United States have started to order the instruments for use up north.

Juan Mateo Juandiego in his marimba workshop

I was born here in Santa Eulalia sixty-nine years ago. My father made marimbas long before I was born. He died when I was four, so my brother taught me to make these marimbas the same way I make them today. I was fourteen years old when I learned this work. At that time they sold very well. But now people don't come to my factory to buy them as much.

In my family this job was like an inheritance my father left me. He was very dedicated to making marimbas. We don't have much land, just this house, where we've always lived, so instead he left us this knowledge. I'm sorry because now I think the inheritance is going to be wasted.

I wanted my children to learn, but I only have one boy. I have daughters, but it's not the custom for women to make marimbas—only men. My son, Mateo, decided that he didn't like doing this. He was still a child when he told me that he wanted to go to the U.S. to work. That's what happens to the young men of his age. They all go to work somewhere else and leave Santa

Eulalia. What can I do? Everyone has his own idea about what he wants to do with his life.

When Mateo was a child I didn't dream he'd do anything other than make marimbas. Even when he came back from the U.S. he began to work in his store instead of here. He thinks that job is better than this one.

Occasionally other people come and work with me. Sometimes, if I need to make a marimba to fill an urgent order, I look for someone to help. But I leave it up to them whether they want to go on learning or not. Since I'm not interested in making a lot of instruments and a lot of money, it's difficult for them. Sometimes they go to another factory. But what can I do? My son didn't want to learn. It's better if I work here by myself.

All my granddaughters and grandsons work in Mateo's store. I'm still happy, though, because I live in my own house. If I want to rest for a while,

I can go outdoors and warm up in the sun. Afterwards I can come back and work some more. I'm very satisfied with my work, and I know I've earned my pay for the day.

There are other people who make marimbas here in Santa Eulalia: Don Juan Antonio Díaz and Don Pascual Mateo. There's also another family member who makes marimbas, Valentín, my brother's son. So right now there are four factories here making marimbas.

Santa Eulalia is famous for its marimbas. People come here from everywhere, even from the U.S. People who leave the mountains and go to the coast also come back here for them. There are no factories like ours in other villages. Santa Eulalia is the only town that makes marimbas, the only one. It's not that it's forbidden or that others are prohibited from making them. Nobody can forbid making marimbas. There's no point in smuggling them, because the knowledge of how to make them is free. But it's a knowledge that belonged to our ancestors. It's our fathers' culture. Until now, it's never been in danger of being lost. But in the future, I'm not sure how it will go. I don't know whether making marimbas is going to continue or it's going to end, because the only ones working at this are the four of us, and we're all old.

Some of them have sons, but sometimes they also go to work on the other side, in the U.S. One is in the U.S. now, and another just came home for a few days. I'm not sure whether they're going to learn to make instruments or going to go back to the U.S. because they're used to the money there. Valentín has four sons, and they're going to learn to make marimbas. Juan Antonio Díaz also has sons learning this.

It would be much better if all our boys had learned to do this work. They would have stayed at home in our village. A lot of people go to the other side, and sometimes it works fine for them, but other times it doesn't. I don't think it's good to go, but if they don't go, they'd be dead, too. Before people started leaving, there was no money here, there was nothing. We were poor. Our homes were not like now. It's changed now because of the money people made in the U.S.

And now, because of money coming, there are more people buying marimbas. People come from the U.S. to buy them and take them back.

This has helped us. But not everyone with a family member in the U.S. buys a marimba. Sometimes they buy land or a car instead.

MATEO JUANDIEGO
THE SON WHO DIDN'T MAKE MARIMBAS
Santa Eulalia, Guatemala, August 2002

Mateo Juandiego decided not to follow his father into the marimba workshop. While he had dreams of having his own business, he went instead into the garment factories of Los Angeles. After a decade he returned to Guatemala, with no more money than when he left.

I was born here in Santa Eulalia in 1973. My father is a carpenter, a maker of marimbas. Ever since he was thirteen years old that is how he has made a living, and now he is almost seventy. Once in a while, when work would start to pile up, I would help him. When I was a child, I would work with him, but then I left Santa Eulalia for a few years. When I came back, I decided to work in another business.

I thought of becoming a musician, because we have that history in our family. As a child I liked my dad's work and the music. I can make a marimba, but I can play it very little. I did fail in that aspect.

Making marimbas here, our family had to struggle economically. That's the reason I had to leave the town and search for a better future. The work wasn't enough to allow me to get a better education. I wanted to have a career in medicine or become an attorney, but I realized that I shouldn't be dreaming about that because I would never make it. I had really hoped to continue my education, but he couldn't help me.

When I grew older I recognized the effort that my father made for me, and that he wanted me to continue. He too felt the pain when I couldn't. He

Mateo Juandiego in the family's store near the plaza in Santa Eulalia

said, "One day we will talk, son. I really did want to give you a better future, make it possible for you to study, but you know that my pockets were empty. I couldn't give you that." I understand how he felt, so I told him, "Don't feel bad. You gave me the best that you could, and I thank you, and God bless you, dad."

I had to leave my village to look for my future and to make my own my destiny. There were two ideas in my family. On one side, my mother agreed with me. She would say, "My son, you have to look for a better future, so take my blessing and go find work in the north." On the other side my father felt that when you have a child, he should stay with you. He said, "Look, son, you have to take the occupation that I have—carpentry in the marimba factory. You have to stay with me, and with that you will earn enough to live." So he didn't agree with my leaving.

I got the strength to leave from my mother. She told me, "Although our souls ache, we can't give you a better education or a better future. Maybe if you look for it yourself, you can find it. We can't make you stay here with us by force."

I left when I was fourteen years old, when I finished primary school. I arrived in Guatemala City and stayed there four or five years. With a friend's help I started my own business at fourteen. By the time I was sixteen I had already three people working for me. At the end of 1985 I left Guatemala with forty quetzales, and with that I barely got to the bus station in Tabasco. I looked for work, and I got a little more money and went to Mexico City. Finally I got enough money to get to the border. I didn't know where I was going. I just navigated with a map, like the Americans do. That's how I went, a little at a time, working from place to place. I got to Tijuana and from there I crossed, going along with other people.

I stayed with the people I met along the way. Together we lived in the mountains near Encinitas for four or five months. Now at my age, I would maybe not go. But back then I didn't know what fear was. I felt strong—full of energy. In Encinitas the work I got was cleaning yards. We would go out in the streets and wait for work. The Americans would come in their cars, and we would signal each other by signs. We would hold up one finger and they'd hold up two meaning that they need two workers. You had to be fast, because immigration would come around a lot.

In five or six months I crossed back into the U.S. fifteen or twenty times. Not speaking English, I would get bored and sad. Sometimes I would just go out in the streets looking for the migra so that they could get me and send me back to Tijuana. The trip was free, and I would hang out in Tijuana for a while before coming back.

But I got tired of all of that. In the U.S. they look at you like a little animal—you don't have any rights and you're not worth anything. You start to think, "What evil am I doing? I just want to live and improve myself. I am just a person, a child of God."

I got to Los Angeles, and there I learned how to use a sewing machine and became a garment worker, which I was for many years. I worked on the overlock machine from 1986 to 1995. The work in Los Angeles is not very secure. At any time the companies can stop sending work to the factories. When that happened, we had to go from factory to factory looking for a job. Sometimes the factories would close due to bankruptcy, owing workers their salaries. We would wait for days, and what we saved helped us survive without work.

My wife and I knew each other for ten years during that time in Guatemala City, and were already friends. She told me about her studies and I would tell her about my business selling candy and gum. I liked her because her goal was to be a business owner and that's what my goal was too. I left for the United States, and when I returned we were still just good friends. I never thought that she was going to be my wife. Then all of a sudden it happened. She looked at me with huntress eyes. [*They both laugh.*] I hypnotized her. [*Even stronger laughter.*]

After I got married, I still went by myself to Los Angeles for three or four years. Then I took my wife. We have two children who were born there. But we both wanted to go back to Guatemala and start a little business.

She worked at the sewing factory, too. She didn't like it, because you work under a lot of pressure. They don't pay overtime. You have to work eight to ten hours for the same rate and sometimes even below minimum wage.

They would pay us by piece rate. If the owners saw in one week you earned a good paycheck, the next week they'd lower your wage. A piece of sewing that used to pay ten cents would be paid at seven cents. All the contractors did that. In the time I was there, almost ten years, I hardly ever saw an Anglo doing that kind of work. It was mostly Latinos. I don't think an American would work even two hours for the wages we earned. It is true that the United States helped us tremendously, but we were still undocumented.

In the end we decided that we were going to go struggle somewhere else. My wife came back to Santa Eulalia with both children. I stayed a little longer because there wasn't enough money for all of us to go back. To get established in Santa Eulalia, you need at least one good paycheck. We didn't even have a house then. I thought maybe I could save a little money without the whole family living with me. Alone, if I earned two hundred dollars a week, I'd try to send a hundred.

My sister had already started a store. When my wife returned from the United States she took it over. She knows more about the business than I do. She is the head of the business.

After my wife left Los Angeles, I stayed for three years, always thinking of improving the small business. After a time there was no work and I was desperate. I said to myself, "What am I doing here without work? Without any money and without my family? I should go back to Santa Eulalia at least to see my kids." That's when I returned. I came back with hardly any money.

I did go to the United States again, to Georgia and then Omaha. But I always had problems because I had no Social Security number or work permit. I couldn't buy a car because I didn't have a driver's license. So I went again to Los Angeles. They don't ask for documents there. They don't care if you have them or not. You go to a factory, and if there's work you go to work that instant. They put the machine in front of you and have you sew something. That's how they hire you. I stayed for a year and four months in Los Angeles and came home again. I had to see my family.

A large percentage of Guatemalans are working in the United States, and many from Santa Eulalia. Out of all the people who left when I did, maybe only ten or fifteen have returned. Most have stayed. In all the neighborhoods here people speak of the U.S. Many people have illusions about what life is like there. But I have been there personally, and I don't have any urgency to return. I thank God a lot that people do go to the United States. The country has helped Santa Eulalia immensely, and I see money circulating in the town. However, this also hurts us. When I see a neighbor repairing his house, I say, "Bless him, Lord," because I know what sacrifice has been made.

It hurts me that I didn't learn my father's skill. But my people don't forget their roots. No matter how long they stay anywhere, they remember the marimba. So the U.S. is another market that has opened up. Before, we sold them throughout Guatemala but not in the United States. But lately we have had orders. I'm very happy because I think it means that my people haven't become lost in some other culture.

I had two children born in the United States, and one is already thinking about going there. I think that will always be part of the future of Santa Eulalia and my family. They will go over there on their own. My son can cross the U.S. border whenever he wants. He doesn't have to go undocumented—he can go legally. So it's possible that in the future he'll have part of his family living over there and another part here in Santa Eulalia. He can decide where he wants to live because he was born there. If he wants to live in the United States, then he should. I think that for the most part he will.

OMAR
THE STORY OF A COYOTE
Huehuetenango, Guatemala, August 2002

Omar, a former teacher, explains the business system of coyotes and polleros, *those who take people from Guatemala across the borders to the United States. His sophisticated analysis sees it simply as another form of economic activity, fulfilling a social need.*

The coyotes are the real winners. Eight or ten years ago, they were paid eight or nine thousand quetzales for the trip to the U.S. Nowadays, they charge up to forty-five thousand [more than five thousand dollars]. In Guatemala this is enough money to start a serious business. In order to come up with it, people have to give their houses as security and sell their land.

There are usually two ways people travel. One is overland, in a van or car. They take groups of sixty or seventy, and it's a good business, but sometimes this has terrible consequences. People have died because the vans are completely closed. The majority of people leaving Guatemala come from the high plateau, where it's very cold. For them, crossing the border through the desert alone is a sure death. Sometimes the coyotes leave them there and they get lost.

Today coyotes also take people by air. They rent a plane in Mexico and take eight or ten. They make several stops on the way, since you have to refuel to reach the border. In Tijuana they turn the people over to a Mexican pollero, who brings them across. There must always be a relative on the other side waiting, because that's where the coyote receives part of his payment.

This is an open business. Anyone can point out someone they think is safe to take you to the border. I worked for the government in a national education program for many years. Sometimes people ask me for a safe contact. I give them a telephone number, and they make the call. Before you even notice, they've flown away. People do recruitment as a job, just like a real estate agent. It's a free market, and many people need this service. I don't feel guilty because I'm not causing harm to anyone. On the contrary, I'm helping people leave a bad economic situation. As a result of the armed conflict in the 1980s, poverty got worse in our country. That's the basic reason people immigrate to the U.S.

Some coyotes make what we call dirty papers to cross Mexico. If Mexican immigration asks questions there's no problem. The bigger problem is to pass the U.S. border. Each coyote or pollero has his or her own way. Latinos in general are very creative. Not long ago, I saw on TV that there are even tunnels five or six kilometers long that cross the border.

The recruiter can tell you what the trip costs, the travel conditions, and if they're traveling by land or air. They tell you to take a change of underwear for the journey. There's no time to take a bath or change clothes, and you eat whatever and whenever you can. You're taken to hotels, perhaps not of very good quality, but you survive. They give you telephone numbers to call wherever you are and tell you who to make arrangements with.

After people know that a certain coyote can produce results, he gradually increases the price, raising it by a thousand quetzales, and then another thousand, and then another. They communicate and decide on it. When it's more difficult to cross, they ask for more. Nowadays, it's very hard to get a visa. Perhaps out of a thousand people only twenty get one. So this is the law of the market: when there's more demand, the prices rise. Some people in Guatemala look for Mexican polleros because they think it will cost less, but in the long run the price is the same. There are always a lot of people who need to go north, so they keep raising the prices.

Here in Guatemala the coyote charges fifteen thousand quetzales to cover all the expenses from Guatemala to the U.S. border. At the other end, another payment of $2,000 to $2,500 is made in dollars. That's where the profit comes from, and everybody gets some of that—the coyote, the recruiter, and the guide who travels with the people. When the work of the coyote ends, he just takes a plane back to Guatemala and prepares another trip.

In fifteen days a coyote can make five thousand quetzales per person, which is fifty thousand quetzales for taking ten people. For the average person here, it takes more than a year of work to earn such an amount. When people see that a coyote has a two- or three-story hotel, good cars, and lives in luxury, they want the same things. So they take the road to the U.S.

A coyote is a businessman, simply doing a job. Nothing illegal is taking place in Guatemala. What's illegal is to cross the border—inside our country no laws are being broken. There's no need for him to buy the authorities in order to be able to operate freely. Nevertheless, his money does give him power in his own community. Some coyotes even finance political groups so that nobody bothers them. That's like any other business.

It's very different from drug trafficking, which is illegal everywhere. It's like buying cigarettes. Any boy here in Guatemala can buy one and smoke it. In other countries it's prohibited to sell tobacco to a boy under eighteen. A coyote's business might be illegal abroad, but in Guatemala it's not. If terrible things happen to the emigrants, like the recent case of seventeen people who drowned while traveling through Mexico, there's no applicable law to sanction him in Guatemala. If he's caught outside Guatemala, he has to accept what the law in that country stipulates.

People who leave without papers must take a risk, the way the coyote does. They have to accept what happens. That's why the journey is so expensive. How many people never make it, never reach their destination?

In the long run, the immigrant in the U.S. is solving a problem for the Guatemalan government, which is happy about it. The price for what it takes for a family to survive has been increasing sharply, and nobody says anything. Certainly nobody regulates the increase of prices. A normal salary here is 2,000 quetzales per month, or about $250. With $250 a person in the U.S. cannot live—you would be homeless.

The government says that people are remitting 500 million quetzales a year. So for the state, immigration is beneficial. There are close to a million Guatemalans already in the U.S., and people keep leaving.

The migrants earn less for their work in the U.S. than people living there, but for us here it's a lot. An immigrant getting five dollars an hour for five hours a day earns the equivalent of two hundred quetzales. Here in Guatemala, many people earn twenty-five quetzales per day, working from 7 a.m. until 5 p.m. Here people work twice the hours and earn eight times less. This is the reality of economic necessity. Of course, for people living in the U.S., this can be harmful because they get displaced.

People look for the opportunity to go north and make the American dream come true. But sometimes the dream collapses. A lot of people come back and say that they couldn't get used to being away from their family. But it's not only that. It's that the pace of work is hard. And everything is relative—people earn more, but they spend more, and everything is more expensive. Some even work three different jobs in the same day, or three different shifts.

Going north and having a chance to earn some centavos is a dream people cherish for a long time. They are not doing anything bad. People are in need since the Guatemalan economy can't provide for them. Our current government has been a complete economic failure. Poverty is everywhere. In Guatemala some people don't have anything to eat, while others have three cars parked in front of their house.

Money from the north has changed us. People start forgetting their roots. They stop listening to the national musical instrument of Guatemala, the marimba, and listen instead to the Mexican music that's become popular because of all the movement north. The youngsters want to form the famous *maras*, or gangs.

Now money means much more to us, and people have adopted a consumer mentality. They talk all the time about how much they'll earn in the north. The price of land has increased. In many places now a small piece costs two hundred thousand quetzales, the equivalent of a lifetime of work. If people don't sell their land so someone can go north, it's not possible for them to survive with what they earn here. So going north has become a necessity, not a luxury.

NICOLAS FRANCISCO
THE HOTEL OWNER
Santa Eulalia, Guatemala, August 2002

While many migrants don't realize their dreams of prosperity, Nicolas Francisco did. He started as a labor contractor on Guatemala's coffee fincas and then brought his family to work with him in the United States. He returned to Santa Eulalia, built the town's only hotel, and collected money from other migrants to rebuild its church.

I worked as a contractor in the fields for about twenty years. I took people out to harvest coffee. Over there you get ten cents for every shift people work. So, if the workers do about twenty to thirty thousand shifts a year, then you will make about eight to ten thousand quetzals. At the end of every year you keep a tally called *corte cuenta*, to see how many shifts were completed by the workers.

If workers owe money, then there was no money for them. Before you hire anyone they must be given an advance. First, we were giving five quetzales. With time we increased it to ten, then twenty, and finally a hundred quetzales per worker. If people don't pay their debts, then it's taken out of their salary from working the fields, and they're left with nothing.

Where I worked the landowners were North American. They were giving twenty to forty thousand, depending on whether you're bringing a good worker. If you bring them the people they want, you get a better cut.

In '82 the guerrilla arrived, and the massacres happened. Most North Americans were unable to give us money because they were afraid of the assaults. At that time neither the military nor the guerrilla would help us. They were involved in a battle with no beginning and no end. Since the workers were not getting paid they didn't want to work. People were also afraid because we went to work in buses, and sometimes the guerrilla would burn them. That's how we lost our work in Guatemala. We began to look for another life, and I eventually went to the United States.

For me it's very bitter to remember. I went as an illegal immigrant because I had no papers. In '87 North American employers began to ask for papers, and I didn't have any. In Colorado I filled out the application for amnesty and found a job in the mushroom sheds.

I feel bitter because I had no money or friends and I was hungry. My family stayed here. My wife had to collect firewood and do hard work with the hoe, the work of a man. She went to harvest coffee, loaded up the animals, and brought it all back. Then she washed and dried it to get it ready for sale. She learned to do all the work that I did.

My friends would go to the bar and leave with the women they'd find there. I decided that if I did the same thing, there was no way I would prosper. So I sent for my wife and two daughters. Then I brought my entire family. I wanted her companionship, and she worked in the mushroom shed too, for twelve years. Three of my kids are still working there, one at a hospital and the other in a restaurant.

The church in Santa Eulalia burned during the war. Everyone wanted to rebuild it, but there was no money. They started a collection, and some gave one or two hundred quetzales, some gave ten quetzales or five quetzales. But there still wasn't enough. We began to think of how many people from Santa Eulalia live in the United States. We began to connect with people in Los Angeles and Florida, North Carolina, South Carolina, Pennsylvania.

When I saw someone with family in the north I'd ask them for their phone number. We began to rebuild the church.

From Colorado we first collected five thousand dollars, and then another seven thousand and then another four thousand. Florida sent twelve thousand dollars and Los Angeles twenty thousand. Our organization still exists in Colorado, and in Los Angeles it's called Ixim.

I started building a hotel in 1996. That's when I bought the land. Since they know me at First National Bank in Colorado, they gave me a loan for twelve thousand dollars. This hotel has helped my entire family. I work six months in the United States and return home for six months, so that when I reach retirement age Social Security will help me, since I already gave them a lot of my money.

I have seen men that go to the U.S. and begin buying boots worth ninety dollars and pants that cost eighty dollars. When I first arrived in the United States, I bought pants at thrift stores for ten or fifteen cents. I began to save money that way, and that is why I have what I have now.

In Colorado we have a marimba from Santa Eulalia. I wear my clothes from Santa Eulalia driving my car or walking around in the U.S., and Americans make me feel welcome. They approach me and ask me where I'm from. They like it when I show my culture.

ALONSO DE ALONSO PEDRO AND OCTAVIO ANDRES ESTEBAN
TWO BROTHERS
Paykonob, Guatemala, August 2002

Two brothers have a dialogue about their children. Some are in the United States and don't send money home. Others want to go. Families who don't get money from the north work for those who do.

Octavio Andres Esteban and Alonso de Alonso Pedro

ALONSO: I have two sons, Alonso and Enrique, working in Omaha, Nebraska. One has been there ten years, but neither sends money back home. Maybe they waste it on bad habits. I have a third son here, Efrain, who has a house and a piece of land. My oldest son also went to the United States, where he fell from the third floor of a house and died. He had a wife, and she sends me money when she can. He was buried here about ten years ago. One brother brought his body home and then left again.

OCTAVIO: Maybe they're spending all their money. Alonso has a wife already, and she may not want him to send money back home. I feel bad for my brother. I thought it was good that his sons went to the U.S. because they did not have work here. But they seem not to remember their families, because we are barely making it here. Our small piece of land is not enough to grow corn, potatoes, or vegetables. I hope they realize this. There is land we could buy, but we need money to buy it.

My brother's third son did well. He bought a piece of land and built a house here. But we don't know even where the other two are.

ALONSO: Enrique was drinking a lot, they say. He sent me two hundred dollars when he first got there, and I bought two bulls. That's all he sent me. The other day Alonso sent me a hundred dollars. I needed money to pay a fine, but that isn't enough, so they'll put me in jail. When his mother was sick I called him. I told him I would sell our piece of land to take his mother to the doctor. He told me not to, but he still didn't send me money. Sometimes I call him and he doesn't answer. Sometimes he gets mad and says he has a lot of bills to pay.

My last son, Efrain, wants to go to the U.S. again to earn more money. He was there four years and returned three months ago. But there is no money, and they charge a lot to take someone to the U.S. I told him he had to stay here. We would like to go, too, but there is no money for this. The coyote charges twelve thousand quetzales to take somebody to the border, and another two thousand dollars when they get a job.

Now we have cars in Paykonob, and there's work for us because of those who have children in the U.S. We work for them. They build their homes and pay us twenty or thirty quetzales a day. People are always needed to carry sand or bring wood. That's what we do. Our own houses are made of adobe. We can't build concrete houses like those new ones, and sheet metal is very expensive.

Because Efrain went to the U.S., we're able to build his home. He made money over there and sent me two thousand dollars. With this I bought cement, iron, and sand and paid people to haul them. I bought him a bit of land.

Efrain drinks, too, but he sent money, unlike the others. Perhaps they'll live over there and never return. What would they do if they did come back? Alonso says he has money in the bank over there and two cars. Maybe this is where all his money goes. He hasn't explained things to me, so who knows what he's thinking?

OCTAVIO: Some people are selling their land to pay for their transportation costs. Like my brother says, we all want to go, even me. I say that I won't go because I feel too old, but I'm told that men older than me who go become more youthful in the U.S. This is because you aren't going to be killing yourself at work. Over there you'll find work that is fairly easy. I know how to work—I work hard here.

The U.S. gives life. Some people use their five senses wisely and they succeed. Those who lose do not leave. The aldea [village] is beautiful now because our people go the U.S. to work. I have two sons who want to leave, but I can't help them. Perhaps I could borrow the money—otherwise I don't know where we would get twelve thousand quetzales. But I'd rather not go into debt, so I think I won't send them. We are poor and have no savings, but we always have food. We're not starving to death. Even if it's just vegetables, it's food. So it doesn't matter. That's what I think.

EMILIA JUANANTONIO
WOMEN ARE WORTH MORE THAN MEN
Santa Eulalia, Guatemala, August 2002

You feel Emilia Juanantonio can do almost anything. She tends births, built her house, and raised her children while her husband Lorenzo sent back money from Omaha. Emilia seeks fairness and equality in relationships between men and women, and she respects her cultural traditions, despite the great gulfs of time and distance that separate families divided by migration.

When we were brought up, we were very poor. Our dad worked in the fields, and it is there we grew up. When my siblings got older they left one by one for the United States. Since there were ten of us, dad had no way to clothe and feed us all. My brothers first started going north when very few people did. Now all my brothers and sisters are there. Since the majority of the people from Santa Eulalia have gone, the town has changed. Houses are being built, people are able to clothe their children better, and some have even purchased a car. Almost all of my family have built their own house,

Emilia Juanantonio

bought their own cars, and even purchased cattle and land. Most families in town now have someone in the U.S.

I started working when I was thirteen years old. I don't have much education. I was eight years old when I started school, but I only stayed for about six months. I grew up in the fields until I was married and left. I could work with a hoe, machete, or axe. Even today, I leave the house at eight in the morning, and by eleven I'm back with two horses loaded with wood I chopped. In the afternoon during the harvest we bring back a hundred bushels of wheat a day. Thank God I've always been able to work.

When I was a child we spoke Qanjobal. Now many young children speak Spanish, and our Qanjobal culture is almost nonexistent. Kids are even embarrassed to speak it. I don't speak Spanish with my children. In school their teachers give one class in Spanish and the other in Qanjobal, because those who come from the U.S. don't want to speak Qanjobal, or even Spanish for that matter. They only want to speak English. The teachers say they have to give Qanjobal

classes in order for the culture to live on. So in Santa Eulalia we have Qanjobal classes now. Children have one exam on Qanjobal and one on Spanish. If we are going to be embarrassed to speak our language, our culture will end.

Growing up I paid close attention to how people talk, read, and write. I made an effort to learn, and my mom sent me to work in Guatemala City, at the Colegio Saleciano in the kitchen and as a chambermaid. Then I moved to the laundry room, and I cooked for the seminary students. After I learned a little Spanish I began working for Father Carlos Quintana, and that's how I met Lorenzo.

He was in the choir. When we saw each other we would talk, and we agreed we wanted to have a good life. We didn't know what life had in store. But when I came to live with him what awaited me was physical violence. I told him if he didn't want me to live with him, I would leave. He made an effort, and we stopped fighting.

We decided to build a good life and educate our children. Even if we were not able to get an education, we should try to educate them. What good is it, even if we are good people and well liked by others, if our children are not well mannered and have no respect? You'll never hear my children say that they're leaving and not coming home at night.

Lorenzo had to migrate because here we had no money and he had no job. We thought he'd be able to send money back to us and we'd build a home. When he left we only had two children, no house, and no job. I have a family of seven now. We built our house and bought a car.

When he left we owed a lot of money at 15 percent interest. Farm workers here only earn twenty quetzales a day, and we were never able to save money. He went to Mexico to work, but he was robbed twice, and our debt increased to seventy-five thousand quetzales. So he went to Los Angeles, but he wasn't sending much money at first. There were times when I didn't have enough to buy necessities for my children. So he went to Nebraska, where he was able to save money for the house and car. During the first ten years we had some sad times, but lately we've been able to enjoy life more.

Omaha is really helping us. Now we only owe 10,000 quetzales. God has allowed us this. Six children are in school—only the small one is here at home. Almost every week we spend two or three hundred quetzales. Before they didn't have much homework, but now we have to pay for books and school supplies.

It's sad because our men are very far away, and we are here with the children. When they get sick or we do, who helps us go to the doctor? Thank God Lorenzo and I really understand each other. He cares about me and I care for him. Some people abandon their families and never think about them again. Their children turn to gangs and don't respect anyone. When men leave they tell their families not to worry, but when they get there they forget. Some women also leave their families for another man. When the man finds out he returns to fight, and sometimes even kills. The man is at fault though, because he is the one who leaves.

When he was in Los Angeles, Lorenzo would send me two or three hundred dollars—not for my expenses but to pay off our debts. Only leftover money was for me, so how was I supposed to buy sugar, soap, or medicine? When my children had a headache, I would pick a handful of herbs and boil them.

When we built our house, it was very sad-looking at first. First I bought blocks and then wood boards. The children were very small, but they hauled sand. After I finished working at the clinic, I came home and turned dirt with a hoe. Sometimes we wouldn't finish work until 11 p.m. But I know how to work. I built the house on my own and didn't wait for my husband to do it.

Lorenzo says if he doesn't leave, we will not have a very good life. There is nowhere here he can make enough money. I know he has to leave. It's true. Sometimes I ask God why I have to live like this. Maybe it's just our destiny. Sometimes my husband will be with me and sometimes he won't. Maybe this is how we'll live our lives. But I pray to God that Lorenzo will return well and we'll live together.

I hope this will be the last year, and he'll come to live here for good. Like I said, my children and I have to do our part. If I waste the money he sends, or I don't treat him well when he comes home, then he won't want to be here with us. However, if we understand each other and I obey him, then we'll be okay.

My mom was a midwife, and she told Lorenzo that she wanted me to take her place. Lorenzo said I could do whatever I wanted, and he would stay with the kids if I decided to do it. So I started to assist in births after I had my second child, and now I'm working with the community. Here in Santa Eulalia birth is always at home unless there's a complication. A well-trained midwife will know what to do. People give me something according to what they have. I tell Lorenzo that here in Santa Eulalia there's no money, so how can I ask? People would have to borrow it. I let everyone decide how much they can give.

Midwives charge less for a girl because she will grow up to live in another home, while the man is the one who will make money, stay with his parents, and support them. So they're more expensive. These are people's attitudes, but none of that was mentioned when we were taught.

A woman does all the housework and still does the work of a man. She cultivates the land and carries wood on her head while holding her babies under her arm. The man works, but when he gets home he gets fed and sits around. Some may help with the children while the woman cooks, but many never bother to help their wives. Forgive me for saying this, but that's why the woman is worth more than the man.

LORENZO FRANCISCO
MY CHILDREN NEED MY PRESENCE
Omaha, Nebraska, August 2003

Lorenzo Francisco married Emilia Juanantonio and for many years has maintained a family separated by huge distances, absent for months and even years at a time. Like his wife, he hopes that eventually he'll be able to return for good, but in the meantime he and other Guatemaltecos are organizing to defend their rights.

The life of a young single man is very different from that of a young married man with a family. When I married Emilia, I began to need a steady stream of money coming in. My country was living through a state of war. The economy was bad, and I was married with two kids. It was a hard decision to make, but we had to face the situation. The U.S. is the place that one thinks of when trying to make a better life.

Deciding to come was not a discussion of two or three days. It took a long time. My wife stayed with the children, and leaving the family was very difficult for me. But I could see they needed an education and food, and there is no source of work in our country. I didn't come out of curiosity.

The first time, I paid the person who brought me four hundred quetzales. In that time it was a lot of money. I had to work until I paid off the debt. I went to Los Angeles because there was a lot of work there, but it began to diminish. Everyone started to leave in search of jobs, and I came to Omaha. There are a lot of people from Santa Eulalia here.

I would love to bring my wife and kids, but that is not possible because of the difficulty in immigrating. One always needs one's mate. Who can I tell my problems to? I must keep it bottled up inside. This leads some to alcoholism and drug addiction. I am in constant communication with my family, but that gets expensive too.

I admire my wife and her work a lot. She is an intelligent and strong woman. She has been a midwife for four or five years, and when she first told me about it, I supported her. But her job is difficult, and she is starting to have health problems because of stress. I have thought about returning more frequently so I can help her out at home. I wish I could bring her here, but I can't. I'm willing to risk my life for my wife and children, but I'm not willing to risk their lives.

I wish I didn't have to come back to the U.S., because I am tired of working. I even forget how old my children are. Let's see. My oldest is seventeen, my second is fifteen, the third is thirteen, the fourth is eleven, the fifth is nine, and one is seven. My youngest is two years old. Many children want to come and work in the U.S. because that is what they see their fathers do, but I want mine to get an education. I have no permanent future here. I will never work for myself in this country. I will always be at the mercy of my employer.

One son that tells me he wants to come to the U.S. Of course it scares me. Once he comes here and starts earning dollars he won't want to study anymore. Money is very important, but there is nothing like family. I cannot stay away from mine for long periods of time. My children need my presence.

In Omaha we are organizing ourselves to support our hometowns in Guatemala—not just Santa Eulalia but all of Huehuetenango. I know we cannot take all our people out of poverty, but we can help. It would be great if this organization could join every Guatemalteco together. We invited the bishop to come from Huehuetenango, so we can work together. The bishop knows the needs of his people and he can help us. We are Christians and need to help our brothers in need. With his visit the Catholic Church here in Omaha will see us more clearly as well.

In the U.S. we are a large community but not very visible. While we are here we are going to work as hard as we can. I think that we can earn respect through our work ethic. If we work hard there is no reason anyone should discriminate against us. Whether we are here legally or illegally, we are still paying taxes. We pay our bills. Most of the money we make stays here in the payments we make. It is only a little of our money that we send to our country. No one should look down on us, because we are helping the country.

Nevertheless, there is a lot of discrimination toward immigrants by authorities and employers. The government doesn't realize that workers are the motor that drives these huge corporations. It is therefore up to the church to defend us and our rights. There are no authorities who come out in defense of our people.

If we could organize ourselves as Guatemaltecos we could petition the government for changes in the immigration law. Right now we are not sure what we will do, as we are barely starting. In the long run, though, I think we can do a lot.

5

Looking at the migration process from a Guatemalan perspective, Bishop Rodolfo Bobadilla finds it a mixture of benefits and disadvantages. He worries about the ability of the community of Santa Eulalia to survive the onslaught of new values and styles, especially among young people. And he also worries about those who have gone. He traveled to Omaha and Schuyler to see what life was like for them.

The bishop's visit was an unprecedented event for the Guatemalan community in Nebraska. It gave people an opportunity to celebrate in the traditional ways of their hometown—a mass, a fiesta, a baptism, the blessing of a house. Bobadilla even took a tour of a meatpacking plant to see the impact of the work on the migrants who perform it.

Some assimilation, he says, is not only inevitable but desirable. Remaining an outcast community, at the fringes of social and political life in the United States, is dangerous. Yet he believes it is important to not only hold on to many traditional values but also to try to impart them to North American society itself. He finds the throwaway culture of the United States offensive, for instance, along with the way work turns people into automatons enslaved by the need for money.

Together with Sergio Sosa and Father Damian in Nebraska, Bishop Bobadilla began a cross-border project to link the diocese of Huehuetenango with the one in Omaha. First a few activists traveled to Santa Eulalia to pave the way, and then other larger groups of Nebraska parishioners made similar trips. Integrating churches and congregations is difficult, however, and requires both Guatemalans and North Americans to cross wide gulfs of race, culture, and economic status. Can an immigrant meatpacking worker speaking Spanish or Qanjobal find the language to speak with a white middle-class professional from the Omaha suburbs? It is a brave and hopeful experiment. The Ixim group in Omaha, committed to the idea, took the unprecedented step of asking white people to join Guatemalans as members.

The migration of people is creating new communities, and the very definition of community is changing as a result. The migrants of Santa Eulalia living in Nebraska, or the Triquis and Mixtecs in Oaxaca, Baja California, and California, belong to organic communities that exist simultaneously in more than one place. People are tied to each other by culture, economic status, and their place of origin. And despite the ferocious enforcement of the border, which results in hundreds of deaths every year, people still move back and forth in these larger networks in a fluid way.

There's no reason to believe that the flow of people across the border will stop or can be stopped by draconian enforcement. Migration is a permanent fact of life according to Mexico's National Population Council, which concludes that by 2030 the Mexican-born U.S. population will double, reaching sixteen to eighteen million. "Migration between Mexico and the United States is a permanent, structural phenomenon," it reports. "It is built on real factors, ranging from geography, economic inequality and integration, and the intense relationship between the two countries, that make it inevitable."

This conclusion is no less true for migration from Guatemala, El Salvador, Honduras, or other countries of Central America and the Caribbean, or for that matter, countries even farther away. Networks of transnational working communities are having a profound impact on people's lives—on their work, their families, and their cultural practices. And these communities are changing life and culture in the United States as well, where the traditions of the social movements in communities of origin are being used to strengthen and reinvent social movements in the north.

Migration has complicated social costs and benefits. It threatens cultural practices and indigenous languages. Emigration often seems, especially to the young, a more profitable alternative to education. It exacerbates social and economic divisions. But it has become an economic necessity in the absence of any other path of opportunity. The families of those who take the road to the north often do benefit, although they must endure danger, debt, and separation to receive its rewards.

MATEO PEDRO BARTOLO
THE CHURCH COUNCIL PRESIDENT
Santa Eulalia, Guatemala, August 2002

Mateo Pedro Bartolo is one of those who went to the United States and then returned. He finds the system unfair, and although he is president of Santa Eulalia's church council, he wants to know what God thinks about this.

I went north to find work five and a half years ago, to Rancho Bernardo in San Diego County in California. We always used to go to Mexico, but then the Mexican peso lost its value. We went to the coast of Guatemala to work in the fields, but the wage was always low. We heard from Mexicans who went to the U.S. that there was money there. So we left this poverty to look for it.

The war brought us poverty. We couldn't have a good home, a job, or clothes. We couldn't take care of our families. Disease and illness were everywhere. Children or family members could die from lack of money needed to take them to the clinic or hospital or to buy medicine. That's why we decided to go to the U.S.

When we arrived Father David helped us organize the church of San Rafael in Rancho Bernardo. Later, North Americans formed an alliance with us so we could work together. People from Santa Eulalia also started churches in Escondido and Fallbrook.

When we arrived we were afraid of immigration. We didn't know where to find houses or apartments for rent, so we lived in the fields. Later we or-

ganized, and they gave us political asylum. That's when we were able to live in the North American community. People from Santa Eulalia and San Pedro Soloma arrived throughout '89 and reunited in Rancho Bernardo. The majority of Santa Eulalia's men and women have gone to the U.S.

When I was in the United States I worked as a gardener, cleaned homes, and picked grapefruit, apples, and other fruit. Other Guatemalans worked in construction, landscaping, or restaurants. I decided to return to Santa Eulalia because you are always alone over there and my family was alone here. We keep in touch by telephone, cassettes, or photos, but it's not the same as being able to come home to them.

My way of thinking is that God has us here on earth to work. I feel that God is inside each person. But sometimes people don't understand. When some church leaders go to the U.S. they think only about money and forget their obligations. They begin to find another lifestyle, and when they return here they no longer want to be church leaders. Youth who have an education think they are going to make a lot of money in the U.S. When they return they are different, but they don't understand how. Money makes them change.

It is good to search for a better life. If you remain at home you don't advance. But sometimes there are a lot of problems because people are leaving. The coyotes ask for twelve or fifteen thousand quetzales to get from here to the Mexican border, and to enter the U.S. they want another two thousand dollars. So when someone leaves the village, they already owe thirty or thirty-five thousand quetzales.

Who makes the most of that money? The coyotes. It's not like before. The first time I went, we took the train from here to Mexico and then all the way to the border in Tijuana. Now coyotes take us through the mountains, the rivers, and hills. We have to walk at night. And it's a lot of money. In order to earn this you have to work for a year, or a year and a half. If you get there without a job, where are you going to earn it? What if there's no work?

Banks here don't lend money to immigrants to go to the U.S. The money comes from people who are already there, or people sell their land and their possessions, or they go to moneylenders. This week, a man who went to the

U.S. died in an accident in San Diego County a week after he got there, when he went to look for a job. According to the family all the money he took was borrowed. How will they pay it? They're very worried.

I'd like to know what God thinks, what governments think. There's no permit to work there, and afterwards what do we get back to? I'd like to know what they think about that.

BISHOP RODOLFO BOBADILLA
THE BISHOP OF HUEHUETENANGO
Omaha, Nebraska, August 2003

As a young man, Rodolfo Bobadilla worked in El Salvador with Archbishop Oscar Arnulfo Romero. When right-wing soldiers assassinated Romero, Bobadilla wept. Today Bobadilla sees that his charge includes not only the indigenous communities of the Huehuetenango highlands but also the people who have migrated from there to the United States. In 2003 he visited his parishioners in exile to see how they live and work.

Today in Guatemala we are living with the legacy of violence. Guatemala signed a peace treaty in December 31, 1999. The military and the guerrilla were supposed to comply, but only some men returned their arms; others didn't. A young man eighteen years old at the start of the war would have been forty-eight by the time the treaty was signed. He would only know how to kill, how to work with a gun, and not how to work farm equipment.

In Nebraska it is easy to see the economic difference. Schools in the U.S. have computers and great supplies. Rural schools in Guatemala have no computers. But we must be responsible for our own development. We must not envy others but build from what we have. We must not lose our human values.

Bishop Bobadilla blesses children after mass in Omaha.

Watching the meticulous butchering of the animal in the meatpacking plants makes you think about the workers. They are using their intelligence, but making the same movements for hours seems robotic. The human being becomes a slave to technology.

In today's world slavery still exists. In Guatemala people on their farms are in a sense enslaved by their work. They are forced to eat only what they grow. They don't have medicine and are subject to third-world conditions.

People can also be enslaved in other ways, for instance, in their desire to earn more and more money to send to their families. They have heard of the golden opportunity in the U.S. and in desperation use all the money they have or go into debt to get there. It costs an average Guatemalteco about six thousand dollars to immigrate to the U.S. I see the suffering that people endure as a result but also their desperation to be free of those conditions.

The families that stay home benefit from the money sent their way, but they do not see the sacrifice and hard work that goes into earning it. With the money sent, many families live well back in Guatemala. Some have enough to build their own homes, and I have seen improvement in the quality of housing. The house is better, but family warmth is missing because the father is absent.

People from Guatemala here in Nebraska are very organized and support one another. If they decide to stay here in the United States, they should keep their own culture, but they should begin to integrate themselves into U.S. culture as well. Otherwise they will always live separately. It will take a lot of years for immigrants to integrate themselves into this country. People must reside here and plant their roots.

They should try to put forward their own values and ideas. For example, Americans have the practice of throwing away lots of things. Food is sacred in Guatemala, and here it is thrown out like it is nothing. That's not a good idea.

When people return to Guatemala, they often bring back these negative aspects of American culture. There is more drug and alcohol addiction. They return without wanting to work because the Guatemalan salary is so low compared with American standards. The family nucleus is broken when the head of the family leaves and the wife and children stay behind. Some men come here to the U.S. and start a new family, even though they have a family back in Guatemala. Many times the husband never returns, and the children grow up without a father.

In the church we have a commission dedicated to immigrants. For those traveling to the U.S. to find their golden opportunities, we have committees in place to help them on their way. Bishops from this committee in the U.S. traveled to Central America to speak with us. They asked us to send priests to the U.S. to serve the needs of migrants. As a result, Father David Lopez in Arizona is holding religious workshops for Guatemalans and serves as a means of communication between families in Guatemala and immigrants here in the U.S.

Our two governments must do things differently. The U.S. needs these workers, and there should be a system to allow them to come to this country in a legal manner. But when only men come to the U.S. on a less-than-permanent basis, we have family disintegration. Indigenous people are very family oriented, and governments should focus more on strengthening families and the community. Both governments also need to set guidelines so that our men no longer face such danger when crossing the border.

PART THREE

MINERS AND MAYOS

GOLD AND COPPER MINING TOWNS AND INDIGENOUS MAYO
COMMUNITIES IN NORTHERN SONORA

Guillermo Bovey and his son Samuel Othon are *gambusinos*—placer gold miners. Othon comes to La Cienega, Sonora, to stay with his father, who is one of only a handful of people who still make a living from mining gold in this way. Othon lives in Pitiquito, a large town near Caborca, Sonora, where he works in a maquiladora.

Guillermo Bovey turns the crank on the *polveadora*, a centuries-old apparatus invented by the Spaniards to sift gold from dirt in the desert, where water is not available.

Jesus Heberto Bejerano Vingochea socializes with other customers of the grocery store in Trincheras, Sonora.

The front of the mission church in Caborca, Sonora, built by Padre Kino. Still visible are bullet holes from the attempt by William Henry Crabb to take Caborca and northern Sonora from Mexico and incorporate them into the United States just after the Mexican War and the Treaty of Guadalupe Hidalgo in 1848. The town's residents took shelter in the church, defeated Crabb, chopped his head off, and displayed it in the church tower.

Maria Martinez and her sister stand in front of their house in the middle of the Sonoran Desert. The fence around their yard is made of dried ocotillo cactus.

Maria Martinez's hands show the effects of arthritis and a lifetime of work taking care of a rural household and family in La Cienega, Sonora. Up until the 1930s La Cienega was a center of gold mining and sometimes had thousands of working claims. Today only a handful of inhabitants remain—mostly the very old and very young. The rest have gone to Caborca or to the United States.

A tin headstone marks a *gambusino*'s grave in the middle of the Sonoran Desert.

Alfredo Murrieta, at ninety-two years old, is the oldest living descendent of Joaquin Murrieta, the famous insurrectionist, who tried to return California to Mexico after the treaty of 1848 and the killing of Sonoran miners in the California gold fields. Murrieta lives alone on a ranch outside of Trincheras, Sonora, where many residents are also Murrieta descendants. He says he sleeps with a pistol under his pillow.

A traditional fence for horses on the ranch of Alfredo Murrieta. When Joaquin Murrieta gathered horses for his cavalry to fight the California Rangers, he kept them in corrals like this in Trincheras and La Cienega.

A copper miner works in the mine at Cananea, Sonora, one of the world's largest.

Cananea is the site of the miners' uprising of 1906, one of the events that launched the Mexican Revolution. This is the only barrio left of the old town. After the mine was converted from shaft to open pit production, mountains of slag were dumped in the canyons where the other old parts of the town were located.

Copper miners take a bus from the mine to the center of town at the end of their shift.

The family of a copper miner waits for him to come out of the mine at the end of his shift.

A Mayo woman gleans beans from a harvested field in Rancho Camargo, Sonora. The Mayo are extremely poor, and after the government dissolved the ejido system, many families with no land of their own went hungry.

Señora Angela is a curandera in the small Mayo community of Rancho Camargo.

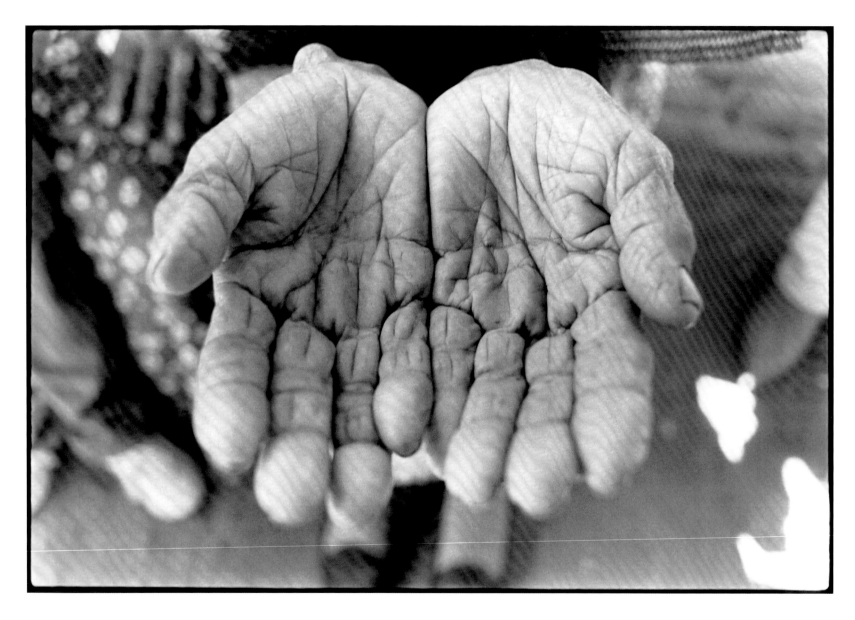

People believe the hands of Señora Angela can cure them.

A man carries his boot-shining brushes and polishes at the
fiesta for Joaquin Murrieta's birth in Trincheras, Sonora.

A dancer from the El Quinto school in the Mayo community of Etchojoa, Sonora, performs the role of the principle of good in the Pascola, a traditional indigenous Mayo dance. The performance take place at the fiesta in Trincheras celebrating the birth of the hero Joaquin Murrieta, who was probably of Mayo descent.

The young women in the role of the three Marias go from one station of the cross to the next, carrying water to give to
Christ, during the Mayo celebration of Easter in Rancho Camargo, Sonora.

A young boy in Rancho Camargo dances as the deer for the first time at the Easter celebration, a syncretist combination of Catholic and pre-Columbian rituals.

Traditional dancers, *fariseos*, enliven the Mayo celebration of Easter in Rancho Camargo.

At the end of the four-day Easter fiesta, the whole community of Rancho Camargo walks in a procession to the church, led by traditional musicians and the deer dancers.

1

The migration of people to the United States is not new. In its earliest moments the movement of people from present-day Mexico to present-day California was not a migration from one country to another at all. Before 1848, the states that today receive the most migrants from Mexico were part of Mexico—California, Arizona, New Mexico, Nevada, Texas, Colorado, Utah, and parts of others. Mexicans coming north today as immigrants are returning to a land from which most Mexicans were expelled a century and a half ago. The slogan on T-shirts commonly worn in today's immigrant rights demonstrations that protests "We didn't cross the border, the border crossed us!" is simply stating a historical fact, in language that requires one to rethink the question, Who is an immigrant?

One good place to consider this question is Trincheras, Sonora, where every year the town holds a fiesta celebrating the birth of Joaquin Murrieta. In the heyday of the Chicano movement in the 1960s and '70s, Corky Gonzalez wrote a famous poem, "Yo soy Joaquin!" It was a call to pride in Mexican identity and also a call for recognition of the real facts of the history of Mexicans in the United States.

It is a history of dispossession. In 1848 the Treaty of Guadalupe Hidalgo added the states of the Southwest to the United States, almost doubling its territory. While taking this land from Mexico, the treaty guaranteed the security of the people living there and their rights to continue using their language and culture and the right to cross the new border freely. The life history of Murrieta shows how short-lived those guarantees were. Today migrants return to this land as immigrants. When their children are denied bilingual classes in California schools or hundreds die in the desert crossing, it is clear that the guarantees of 1848 remain unenforced.

In California schools students in fifth grade are introduced to the state's history for the first time. The schools themselves often bear Spanish names, some even of the original land-grant families dispossessed in 1848. But what they often learn of this history turns it on its head. Murrieta's treatment is the means for hiding dispossession and its consequences. Since modern migration is based on dispossession, both that of 1848 and more recent forms, it is easy for students to come away thinking Mexicans are as foreign in California as Martians, with as little right to live there.

Textbooks tell students that a white storekeeper discovered gold at Sutter's mill, near Sacramento. They present Murrieta as a murderer and leader of Mexican bandits who terrorized the hardworking miners of the gold country until, in their righteous anger, they formed a posse to chase him away.

The truth is that Sonorans began coming to California when the gold country was still part of Sonora, crossing the Altar Desert in the spring and returning to what was then southern Sonora in the fall. They dug the first mines at Santa Clarita, near Los Angeles. After the 1848 war, word spread east that gold could be mined in California, and white people began coming west. Their heads were filled with gold fever but empty of any knowledge of mining techniques.

They learned to mine from Mexicans—the Sonoran miners already there. Then white miners organized vigilante gangs to drive the Mexicans out, using as their pretext a new law requiring foreigners (that is, Mexicans) to pay a special tax. As Alfredo Figueroa points out, the people hung by vigilantes in Placerville in those years, when it was known as Hangtown, all had Spanish surnames. While the California Rangers lasted only a couple of years, its sister bands, the Texas and Arizona Rangers, lasted longer. They all had the same roots in the effort to establish the dominance of white settlers over the Mexicans who lived in these states before them.

Perhaps Murrieta, as a patriot and nationalist, had dreams that the treaty itself could be undone and California returned to Mexico. In any event, the Sonoran miners fought to keep their claims and resisted the terror campaign to drive them out. Murrieta led them but ultimately had to flee south to his original home in Trincheras.

The Murrieta name continued to frighten U.S. authorities for over a century after his death. Alfredo Figueroa's grandfathers were jailed for singing the "Corrido de Joaquin Murrieta" in the 1920s. Antonio Murrieta recalls that family members, living just a few miles south of the border in the 1940s, were still unable to get visas to return to the land whose mines their great-grandparents had developed.

The Murrietas and the Sonoran miners were one of the first communities to exist on both sides of the U.S.-Mexico border, along with the native people whose land the border still divides. In the spirit of our times, over the last decade descendents of those miners have formed a cross-border organization to clear the historical record and provide needed material help to the small town where so many still share the Murrieta name.

Alfredo Figueroa describes the meaning of Murrieta's life for the Chicano and Mexicano mining families who live just north of the border. He talks about the vision of social justice they forged as they fought for a place in a land where, despite their historical roots, they were never secure. Antonio Rivera Murrieta looks at the roots of this famous family from the Mexican perspective and connects the historical struggle of Joaquin Murrieta to the current efforts to win political rights in Mexico and social equality for immigrants in the United States.

Antonio Rivera Murrieta

ANTONIO RIVERA MURRIETA

I AM TRANSNATIONAL

Phoenix, Arizona, December 2001

Antonio Murrieta is the president of the International Association of the Descendents of Joaquin Murrieta. They want to rectify the historical record of the treatment of Sonorans in California 150 years ago and win respect for Mexicans working there today.

I was born at a very beautiful place in the state of Sonora—in Trincheras, on the land of Joaquin Murrieta. I call it Joaquin Murrieta's land because that's what my great-grandfather told me, and he was Murrieta's cousin.

I have always been a social fighter. I participated in politics in Mexico for sixteen years, from the time I was sixteen years old. I was the president of the PRI [Mexico's old ruling party] in Caborca and the secretary to the municipal president. I was the secretary for civic participation in the town of Benjamin Hill. The government did not want to accept change or to support social struggles. People used power to fill their pockets while the town they were governing became marginalized.

They'd tell farmers to plant a certain variety of peach even though it was designed for a climate like Kentucky. How could it grow in Caborca? Or a grape variety that grows well in northern Italy but cannot function in the desert here. They got country people to take out loans they would never be able to repay because they were never going to produce.

So I changed parties. I started the National Action Party in Sonora because that was the only way to fight the government. I went on a hunger strike of nine days in Caborca after I ran for deputy and my election was totally stolen. Two days later the state police and Caborca's municipal police beat us with sticks. They left me with two broken ribs. One of my brothers was beaten and others as well. Because the government was following me, I came to work illegally in California.

I worked as a tractor driver in Ripon, Manteca, Stockton, Lodi, Modesto, and Turlock. I lived in Manteca and Escalon—Joaquin Murrieta's area in the San Joaquin Valley. It should be called Joaquin's Valley, not San [Saint] Joaquin Valley, because there, at the foot of Yosemite is Sonora, a town founded by the people of Sonora. There are still people working the gold there after 150 years.

Joaquin Murrieta was one of the Sonorans who went to California to mine gold. Murrieta himself had indigenous blood because his last name was Orozco, which is associated with the Otum and Pima. I think the principal blood the Murrietas have is Mayo blood because they came from Alamo, Sonora, which was the Mayos' area then.

They spoke about Murrieta as the guide who would take the others to and from Sonora. There were 10,300 Sonorans living in California then. In the United States there weren't many gold mines, only one in North Carolina. So the Anglos who arrived in California didn't know how to mine the gold. It was the country people from Sonora who showed them.

The textbooks in the primary schools in Arizona and California say he was a "gringo hater," that he killed people in knife fights. They call him a bandit. But Joaquin Murrieta was a social fighter. He wanted to retrieve the part of Mexico lost in 1848 in the Treaty of Guadalupe Hidalgo. Mexico was mutilated, and he loved his country. The Mexican federal government didn't support his effort, so the only thing left was to defend himself and the rights of the Mexicans still living there.

People from Sonora living in California, Arizona, New Mexico, and Texas were the last ones to realize that the land wasn't part of Mexico anymore and that they were no longer Mexicans. There wasn't mail in those days or anything that could have told them what happened. They started to realize it when Anglos came and wanted to take away their mines, their farms, their cattle, their way of living, and the little they had. They were assaulted and killed. There were many Joaquin Murrietas. Many Mexicans were angry and fought, but Joaquin Murrieta lasted the longest because he was more organized.

After they returned to Mexico, these people faced persecution and were afraid to speak about Joaquin Murrieta. They feared that the people who persecuted him would follow them all the way to Trincheras. People from our family, the Murrietas, couldn't come to the United States. In 1946 Juan Murrieta, whose brother today is the president of the association of Murrieta's descendents in Trincheras, was passing through Nogales. They asked him, "Are you related to Joaquin Murrieta?" When he said he was, they told him that he no longer had a passport, and ripped it up.

It took the U.S. government more than three years to give me a visa. They asked me if I was in the Communist Party or an activist against the Mexican government. But I knew what the problem was. My last name is Murrieta. The name still bothered them.

We want North Americans to understand the fundamental value that Mexicans contributed to the development of California. The gold fever was the foundation that created California, and people from Sonora taught the Anglos how to mine the gold. Joaquin Murrieta was not a bandit or a killer. As I said, he was a social fighter, and that's why Mexicans call him a patriot.

I would like North Americans to understand Mexicans better because we come to work here. We come to develop this country, to work in industry, the restaurants, the cleaning, in the warehouses, and the fields. Without Mexicans, the crops wouldn't be harvested. Let's be honest—the majority of North Americans don't want to work as farm workers. We do. Maybe we're used to hard work.

In 1988 we started to fight to clear Joaquin Murrieta's name and formed the International Association of the Descendents of Joaquin Murrieta. We want mutual understanding between North Americans and Mexicans about who he was, to show he wasn't a gringo killer, a bandit, or a *pistolero* [gunman]. We want people to understand that he fought to recover part of his fatherland and that he defended the Mexicans of that time.

Today we fight for our people here who can't get driver's licenses and whose car insurance costs them triple that of a North American. Just because someone is illegal doesn't mean that he doesn't know how to drive. We have to fight for the undocumented, against the abuse they suffer. We have more than three million people right now in the United States, and we have no way to get them legal status. We want an agreement that these people have rights, that they should get paid better, get a green card, a driver's license, car insurance, and a house to live in.

Since we started, we've helped the clinic in Trincheras, where Joaquin Murrieta lived. We have taken them medication, medical instruments, and an ambulance. We are in the process of getting them a school bus and two computers for the high school. We want to pave the main road to the state highway.

I am transnational. I have both roots. I have learned to care a lot about North Americans, to love this town [Phoenix] because it is a fighting and working town, with all of its vices. There are rules that don't sit well with us, and racism is deeply rooted here. But I want people here to understand that we did not come here to take. We came to contribute the little that we have, so that this country develops.

Alfredo Figueroa, with the banner of the Association of the Descendents of Joaquin Murrieta in Trincheras, Sonora

ALFREDO FIGUEROA
FORMING A CHICANO IDENTITY
Caborca, Sonora, November 2001

Alfredo Figueroa was a hero of the Chicano movement in the 1960s and has spent the decades since rectifying the historical record of Joaquin Murrieta, the first Mexican rebel against racism in California. Figueroa's personal history is the story of the way that rebellion lives on.

Joaquin Murrieta was a *gambusino*, a placer miner, from Sonora. Sonorans made the first big gold strike in California in 1841 at Santa Clarita Canyon north of today's Los Angeles. They lived right south of there. They were migrants. They'd cross the Desierto del Diablo from Sonora in the early spring before it got hot and come back to Sonora in the late fall. They continued moving north through California, pursuing the gold, prior to 1849.

That stopped in Joaquin Murrieta's times—1852, 1854. The people were forced from the gold fields. The Foreign Miners Tax Act was enacted in 1850, approved by Governor John Bigler and enforced by the vigilante committees in Tuolumne and Calaveras counties. The Anglos just wanted them to get the hell out. The Sonoran miners were very dissatisfied, and the law broke the camel's back. If it hadn't been for that, the merging of the two cultures would have been a lot easier.

The miners tried to defend what was theirs, but to do that they had to organize a clandestine movement. Murrieta tried to raise an army and take over California again. Every Sonoran knew him. They harbored him and protected him, up and down the state. Eventually, the great bulk of them went back to Sonora, because they would have been killed otherwise. The names on the lists of the people hung by vigilantes in the goldfields are all Spanish. The first woman hung in California, in 1853, was named Juanita. According to the last California Ranger, William Howard, her last words were "Viva Joaquin Murrieta!" So when they killed these people, the rest left voluntarily. That was the agreement. If you left voluntarily, you could leave freely.

My great-great-grandmother, Teodosa Martinez Murrieta, was born in La Cienega, a little mining town in northwest Sonora in the Desierto de Altar. Most of the gold miners were family. She was a cousin of Joaquin Murrieta and a very strong woman, one of those hard ladies. When they went north, she went with all the Sonorenses, ten thousand of them, and died at the age of 107 in 1931.

My mother's family were all Chimahuevos, one of the Colorado River Indian tribes. My father was from the Rio Yaqui in Sonora. He used to speak Yaqui and dance the Pascola and the Matachin. He worked in all the mines around Trincheras and Caborca. My grandfather worked in Cananea and was involved in the strike there in 1906.

My father used to tell us that your biggest enemy is your boss. When he saw any injustices he would intervene and protest. He came to the U.S. in 1918 during the Bisbee strike. The Wobblies had a big strike there, and a lot of the miners that came from Mexico were deported—any foreign miner that had anything to do with the union. And my father joined the union—he got involved because everybody struck. After that he worked in Jerome, Ruby, Globe-Miami, and Sonora Rey in Arizona, called that because Rey was the Anglo town and Sonora was the Mexican town. They had a big strike there, too. My father died of silicosis, his lungs full of clots. Blood would come out when he spat.

He never wanted us to work in the big mines. We were gambusinos,

small mine operators. The average life of a miner is not that long. My father liked to be on the surface, placer mining and panning for gold. He was very successful because he was a connoisseur of minerals. In Mojave County he would always win the blue ribbons for knowing, just by looking, what kind of minerals a rock contained.

I was born in Blythe, but when the mines opened up we went to Oatman. When they closed again, we came back to Blythe. Racism was rampant. We always fought gringos, and always won. My brothers were fighters, and we were a big family. We weren't pushovers. They used to have Americanization schools just to retard you, like the Indian boarding schools. They should have called them brainwashing schools. When kids got out of school after sixth or seventh grade, they had to pick cotton. I barely picked cotton one day in my life—we were always in the mines. When I entered Blythe high school in 1947, only four Chicanos had graduated since 1916. When I graduated, just five Chicanos graduated with me out of a hundred students, and Chicanos were the majority of people in town. More blacks graduated than we did, and they didn't come to school—they worked for the grower. He would say how many pounds each picked that week, and that was how they were graded.

We had to fight for everything. My other brother, Gilbert, was *el asote*—the guy with the big blow. My brother never lost a fight in Blythe. You didn't mess with the Figueroas.

In third grade we were starting geography, and the teacher pointed to a map on the wall and said, "Now this is the United States that we all love so much." I got up like an Indian and raised my hand and said, "Well, I don't love it too much. My father says they stole this land from us." They took me to the principal's office, where he had a big old paddle that they used to call the "board of education," and they paddled and whipped me.

They kept me away for two weeks. They made a play named after Philip Nolan's book, *Man without a Country*, and showed it at school, just to intimidate the Mexicans. They named it *Boy without a Country*. My mother negotiated with the principal, and I had to write "I love the United States" a hundred times on the blackboard in front of all the kids. I was just telling them, "This is my land." Can you imagine, nine years old? But that's why they had the Americanization schools, to brainwash all those young Mexicans and Chimahuevos living in Blythe.

Mining gave us a lot of independence. But the workers who worked for the big mines were not so independent. We had a big mine in Blythe, the United States Gypsum Company. The company owned all the houses and stores. The people were just like property of the mine, too. The Mine Mill union [Mine, Mill and Smelter Workers Union] was being organized all over Arizona, but my father used to say the miners there were just dominated by the bosses. They paid a lot better then for work in the fields, so the miners thought it was a damn good job.

People would go to Caborca [across the border in Mexico] whenever there were big happenings. The dollar and the peso were two to one. After the war it got to I don't know how many hundreds to one. You needed a wheelbarrow to exchange it. But before, there was more difference between Sonora and southern Mexico than Sonora and Arizona.

The miners were the elite. A miner always had a damn good shoe and a damn good hat. On the commercial farms, workers were always domestic slaves. At that time we had five thousand braceros in Palo Verde. The contractor would charge them for everything, so when they got their check it was zero, zero, zero, zero. If the grower needed a hundred workers they'd send two hundred to do the job, and the people would only be able to work half the time.

In 1960 the Agricultural Workers Organizing Committee started a big strike in Calexico, so we went to Imperial Valley to get involved. We'd meet right at the border. We couldn't win the strike because of the braceros. When we would try to advise them about their rights, they were deported. I didn't stay too long 'cause it was too damn rough. When we came back, the growers already knew we'd been in the Imperial Valley. They took us to the Farmers Merchant Bank, and you should have seen the third degree they gave us.

There was a lot of animosity against the braceros because the growers wouldn't give jobs to the local Mexicans. They passed a law that growers first had to deplete the sources of local workers, but you know, they never did that. Finally, the braceros all were returned in 1964. If it hadn't been for the Mexican American Political Association and Bert Corona, Public Law

78 would have been extended. We were able to stop that damn law, and as soon as that happened, in 1965, AWOC and the Filipinos struck. If the Filipinos hadn't started that strike, Cesar Chavez wouldn't have joined them, and there wouldn't be any United Farm Workers.

Joaquin Murrieta is the grandfather of our Chicano movement. All my life I knew about him. In the early 1900s my grandfathers were thrown in jail in Arizona because they sang the "Corrido of Joaquin Murrieta." They were very proud of being his descendents, so they would get drunk and start singing it. The sheriff arrested them because the song was outlawed in California and Arizona, even on the radio.

During the height of the Chicano movement in the 1960s, people started to recognize Joaquin Murrieta as one of our heroes. People were seeking a way not to be so ashamed about being Mexican. He was the symbol of liberation, our true identity.

Murrieta didn't succeed in achieving his ultimate goal, but he succeeded in organizing his people to fight for justice, and that's what we wanted in the sixties. We were fighting not to go into that damn army and to Vietnam. We have a saying in our Association of the Descendents of Joaquin Murrieta. We have to know who we are, to know where we're going. Once you're on solid ground, nothing will stop you. Joaquin Murrieta is the symbol of that spirit.

I've invested years of organizing these fiestas in Las Trincheras, where he lived and the Murrietas still live. The thing was to make people understand. There *was* Murrieta. We *did* fight. Today people are very proud. Everywhere you go in Trincheras they'll say, "Viva Joaquin Murrieta!" The teachers in the schools have more information, and students make plays about him. They named the main street Calle Joaquin Murrieta. Up north in California they've started Joaquin Murrieta Day in Mendota, in the San Joaquin Valley, where his group was ambushed on July 25, 1853. Avenue 63 there was changed to Joaquin Murrieta Avenue.

We want to rescue our history from the lies our governments have told us for so long. Our history isn't just something from an academic publication but traditions taught from early childhood that help us understand what life means.

The other day we had a ceremony in Holtville, remembering the six hundred undocumented people who died last year trying to cross the border. Many are buried there, and no one knows their names. Can you imagine? They were trying to cross the desert, just like the miners did from Sonora 150 years ago. So things haven't changed so much after all. These things were happening in 1848 and they're still happening right now in 2001.

2

The oldest form of mining in Sonora is still practiced today by a few people called *gambusinos*, who use *polveadoras* to separate gold from the dirt. Despite the more recent introduction of hand-held metal detectors, the solitary miners of La Cienega and El Voludo work with techniques that have changed very little from those brought by the Spaniards. Not many of these old gambusinos are left, and the kind of mining they practice will eventually disappear.

Mining, however, still provides work for thousands of Sonoran families. More than a century ago, huge industrial copper mines replaced the labor-intensive, small-scale methods of the gambusinos. The border runs through the vast copper belt of northern Sonora and southern Arizona and New Mexico. Today, the enormous open pits of Nacozari and Cananea in Sonora are two of the world's largest. Open pit mining itself replaced the original methods, in which miners extracted ore from deep underground shafts. Pit mining made huge changes in the physical landscape. Behind the Cananea mine and its now-closed smelter rise huge mountains of discarded rock excavated from the new pits after the old shafts were closed. Man-made hills of tailings now cover the original homes and barrios where mining families lived in the early 1900s.

Cananea was the site of the uprising of 1906, when miners, inspired by the words of the Flores Magon brothers, fought the armed militia of Colonel Greene, then the U.S. owner of the mine. The brothers planned the rising, now viewed as the first battle of the Mexican Revolution of 1910–20, in the barrios of Mexican railroad workers from East St. Louis to Los Angeles, a true cross-border effort. For their temerity in defying the economic elite of both countries, the two were pursued by J. Edgar Hoover, at the urging of Mexican president Porfirio Diaz, and imprisoned in the federal penitentiary at Leavenworth, Kansas, where Ricardo died. The Flores Magon brothers were early transnational labor activists. They launched the Mexican Liberal Party, which started the revolution, and belonged to the Industrial Workers of the World, advocating industrial unionism, racial equality, and radical social change.

In U.S. copper mines, miners also challenged the existing social order. Mexican and Chicano miners fought a decades-long struggle to eliminate the "Mexican wage," a lower salary paid to Mexicans doing the same jobs performed by whites. The Mine, Mill and Smelter Workers, one of the few unions of the 1940s and 1950s in which Mexican workers became leaders, finally defeated that discriminatory institution in the United States. The Mexican miners' union did the same in Cananea, as Jesus Morales Tapia remembers.

The eloquent film *Salt of the Earth* tells the history of one of those bitter battles, the strike at the Empire Zinc mine in Arizona. Written by blacklisted Hollywood screenwriters in the early 1950s, it starred Mexican actress Rosario Revueltas, a role that earned her deportation from the United States afterwards. The movie itself was suppressed for many years.

The border runs through the communities of copper miners. Families who work in the great pits of Nacozari and Cananea frequently have members working north of the border as well, in the mines at Ajo and Clifton/Morenci. People move back and forth from mines on one side to mines on the other, although this movement has been curtailed by the closure of many U.S. mines and by the militarization of the border itself.

Solidarity and mutual support across the border didn't end with the imprisonment of the Flores Magon brothers. In the 1950s the Mine, Mill and Smelter Workers Union supported Mexican strikes in Cananea, partly because of the family relationships described by Moises Espinoza. Mexican miners did the same when U.S. miners went on strike. Miners in Cananea struck again in 1998, and once more those family relationships sparked support efforts by Arizona unionists. Jerry Acosta, a U.S. union leader, and his uncle, Genaro Sanchez, a retired Cananea miner, describe the caravans that took food to the strikers.

The bitter 1998 strike was caused by the neoliberal economic reforms that accompanied the North American Free Trade Agreement, especially privatization. The Cananea mine, nationalized in the early 1980s, was then sold to one of the wealthiest families in Mexico, the Larreas, in the mid-nineties. Jorge Larrea's Grupo Mexico sought to cut labor costs by no longer providing water service to the tiny mountain town and by laying off workers in many mine departments. Miners lost the strike. Javier Canizares, Juan Gonzales (another of Jerry Acosta's relatives), and Gabriel Parra all describe the strike's consequences from different perspectives.

Gonzales also relates his own history of forced migration to Arizona as an undocumented worker. His experience is an example of the way globalization and its accompanying economic reforms uproot families and lead to migration both inside Mexico and across the border.

JUAN GONZALES
A BLACKLISTED MINER
Phoenix, Arizona, December 2001

Juan Gonzales was a union activist in the huge copper mine in Cananea, Sonora. After the union there lost a big strike in 1998, he was blacklisted and forced to cross the border to Arizona to survive.

I lived all my life in Cananea, Sonora, until I came to the U.S. I started at the copper mine in 1981 when I was eighteen. My father was a miner before me, and his father before him. We could live a decent life then. The money they paid was enough to live on. It was also like a school, in which we learned how to work. I learned many jobs—welding, driving heavy equipment, administration in the warehouse. I became a mechanic, and after three years I was in charge of the shop.

I was a member of Section 65 of the Mexican Miners' Union. I participated in all the movements because I wanted to help people. But the company opposed us and wouldn't let us move forward. And then they threw us out.

The movement of 1998 had its origin in the struggle over our union contract. The people who bought the mine didn't want to pay our bonuses. I was making about 750 pesos a week, with a family and three kids by then. When the company refused to pay, it hurt because the bonus was between 250 and 300 pesos of the 750 we were bringing home each week. It was the same as cutting our salary, and it didn't leave us enough to maintain our families.

The first place they tried to implement it was the First Metallurgical Department, one of the smallest ones, to see how we would react. We sent a commission of workers to Mexico City, but the government wouldn't listen to us. And when they came back, the company retaliated by assigning them to jobs they didn't know how to do, to set them up to be fired. After that, many people didn't want to get involved.

We discovered that getting rid of the bonus was permitted under the contract, the famous productivity agreement negotiated by Elias Morales, who was in charge of negotiations for the national union. He told us one thing at the meeting where it was adopted, but the company later interpreted it their own way. When Morales presented the contract, people didn't agree at first. Then he began to tell us that we would make a lot of money. It got late and people began to leave the meeting. At the end, there weren't even fifty people left when they took the vote, and over two thousand of us were working in the mine at that time.

When the contract came up for negotiations again, we decided to stop work. I was on the committee, and I went out to try to get support for the strike. I came here to Phoenix once, and I went to Mexico City, too. I went to all the meetings. We had a lot of support from the U.S. during the strike.

Caravans arrived from Arizona, which lifted our spirits and made us even more determined to keep on fighting. We didn't want the union to fail.

But unfortunately, we were getting more support from the U.S. than we were from Mexico. We never really had the support of our national leaders. They lied to us, and they didn't respect the decisions we made in the meetings when they went to talk with the company.

People finally went back to work because they couldn't survive without an income. We had been out of work for four months. We had no alternative but to accept what the company demanded, because there are no other jobs in Cananea.

The company began by shutting down the smelter. Then they shut down the waterworks. The people who were working in those areas weren't allowed to return. The company posted lists for each department of the people they were accepting back. When I went to look at the list for my department, my name wasn't on it—I was out. In my department, the two people they didn't take back were the two of us who participated in the movement.

Section 183 of our contract says when they close a department, they have to give you severance pay, but I wasn't in any list to get that pay either. I went to the company office, and the coordinator for labor relations told me it was because I was such a *grillero*, a person who always spoke out, who was always involved in the union. I had always had a lot of problems with him because he was always trying to violate the contract. That's why the company didn't want me back. He told me they'd put me on a blacklist and I'd never get a job anywhere in Mexico after that. They'd put my name on a flyer and send it to other employers. The ironic part of it all is that they finally fired this labor relations coordinator, too, even though he talked to me as though he was an owner of the company himself.

I had no alternative but to leave Cananea and look for work in the U.S. I still had my house and my family, so I really didn't want to leave, but there wasn't anything else I could do. It felt very bad. We fought so hard. I went a year without being able to find work. The whole economy was depressed because so many people lost their jobs.

My friends finally asked me to come with them to the United States and said they'd support me. I don't have any papers, I really have nothing. But there's a group of us here from Cananea, friends, and we help each other. We all went to school together and then came here together. We've organized this little business supplying catering trucks. I'd like to go back, but there's nothing there for me right now. The only thing I can do right now is work here in the U.S.

My children and my wife are still in Cananea. We talk on the phone a lot. It's been a very drastic change for us. I go back and forth, but it's always a big risk that they'll take away my passport or that something will happen on the road. I'd like to get legal status here. If there were an amnesty, it would help me a lot.

My wife still has her job at Telefonos de Mexico in Cananea. I don't know if we can survive here, or if it would be worth it for them to come. I'm hoping next year I'll be able to bring them. I don't think I'd go back to the mine, even if I heard they were hiring again. That part of my life is over.

JAVIER CAÑIZARES
A CANANEA STRIKER
San Francisco, California, April 2000

Javier Cañizares, a blacklisted striker, explains how economic reforms and privatization led to a massive elimination of jobs in the Cananea mine, to the strike that sought to stop that process, and to the resulting exodus of unemployed miners to the United States.

The Cananea mine, an old one, was nationalized from the 1970s to the 1990s and then sold to private owners. When the government begins to talk about the privatization of a business, it talks in terms of higher salaries and better benefits that will be possible under the new owners. But in Cananea our experience was just the opposite. After the mine was privatized we

Javier Cañizares

The workers in Cananea went on strike because of the violations of the contract, the closure of departments, and massive layoffs. When the strike started, the secretary of labor and the national leadership of our union said that we would have to accept the elimination of jobs. We refused to accept this proposal and began to organize large demonstrations throughout the state and eventually the whole country. We appealed for solidarity from many other organizations. That's how we were able to sustain our movement over the course of three months. Some of the strikers went all across the United States looking for support, and we got a lot of it.

On the ninth of February [1998], in the absence of our union representatives, the governor of Sonora and the ministers of labor and the interior reached an agreement. They said that it was necessary to close four departments and lay off a thousand workers. Eliminating a thousand jobs in a town like Cananea means turning it into a ghost town, given that the only source of jobs for the town's thirty-five thousand residents is the mine. The authorities said there was nothing we could do about it, so the workers decided to end the strike and go back to work.

The surprise for us was that after the workers decided to go back to work, the company posted lists of people who would be going back. The lists didn't include people who were very active in the strike, in addition to people from the closed departments. So we had a big meeting to discuss what had happened and decided to go in and occupy the mine. Each person was supposed to go back and occupy their job in their department.

The day after we'd gone into the mine, there was a big mobilization of the army and all the police forces in the state of Sonora. The mayor of Cananea, accompanied by the general secretary of the union, went into the mine and asked the workers to leave. They said that they were running the risk of repression.

To this day people who were active in one way or another haven't been permitted to go back. They're still out of work. These are 120 workers who were working in departments that weren't closed. The company got scared because they weren't fighting for their own jobs but for the jobs of others. The leaders of our local union went to the company and said that there shouldn't have been any problem with these people, since their depart-

began losing our benefits bit by bit. The company didn't respect our union contract or even our human rights as workers.

When they privatized the mine, there were about 3,500 workers. Today there are 2,070. The company brought in people from Veracruz, Guerrero, and Michoacan to take jobs as they became vacant. But they gave those workers lower salaries and benefits and said they weren't covered by the union contract. They were brought in as temporary workers, on twenty-eight-day contracts. So the work itself didn't disappear, but the people who did the jobs changed and weren't under the contract.

Under Mexican law, workers don't acquire seniority and become permanent and eligible for benefits under a union contract until they've worked thirty days. So with twenty-eight-day contracts these workers were never permanent. Grupo Mexico, which owns the mine, has an affiliated company called Constructora Mexico. This company was in charge of bringing in these workers.

ments hadn't been shut down. The company responded that they didn't want people who weren't in agreement with the changes. They only wanted people who would go along with their decisions.

The workers who've lost their jobs have had to leave Cananea, and even Mexico itself, to find a way to make a living. It's not possible to live in Cananea without a job. That's why I say that it's in danger of becoming a ghost town. There's no other kind of economic development there. There's just a small amount of retail business and no other large source of work. There were a couple of maquiladoras in Cananea, but they closed because of the problems with the mine.

At the end of the strike, the government said that the water system, which had been operated by the company, would now have to be operated by the town. But the town has no infrastructure or money for operating it. This is an action against the whole community. They cut off water to the whole town, and finally the women in the town occupied the water pumps and distribution plant and turned it back on.

Cananea is considered the birthplace of the Mexican Revolution. It's been a bastion of Mexican trade unionism. With the defeat of the union in Cananea, it's a bad sign for the future of unionism in Mexico generally.

Gabriel Parra

GABRIEL PARRA CORTEZ
A MINERS' UNION LEADER
Cananea, Sonora, December 2001

Gabriel Parra Cortez, an activist in the Cananea miners' union, was able to survive the strike. He describes the way the mine's privatization and the push for increased productivity led to drastic cuts in the workforce.

In the early 1990s there was a campaign against the workers of Cananea. They said that we were lazy and crybabies. The Mexican government itself campaigned against us. The Sunday supplement to the *Imparcial* released photographs that supposedly showed that we lived in wealthy homes, earned a lot of money, and didn't do anything at work. They said that we caused the company to go bankrupt with work stoppages.

It was a justification for privatizing the mine. Industrial Minera de Mexico finally bought it—part of the economic reforms. Right away there were problems because the union contract was modified to eliminate what the company said were barriers to productivity.

They started cutting back the number of mine workers. There was a cut of 100 or 110 people who were paid off and left. Then in 1998 the company said they no longer wanted to operate the dam and city waterworks, which require around sixty or eighty workers. Some thought we should organize a general work stoppage, the way we did in 1989. Others argued that those sixty or eighty workers should stop work, and that the rest of us, over two thousand of us at the time, would help maintain them for awhile. If we couldn't, just sixty workers would be lost. But there were approximately eight hundred miners left without a job in 1998.

But the workers were very brave, so we voted for the general stoppage on November 19, 1998. But it was a failure. Up until then, every time we had a stoppage the company would ask us to go back to work and talk. This time it was backwards. We wanted to go to work and talk to them, and the company administration said no. They said that we had already stopped and that there were some things we had to talk about. Once all of the issues were resolved we could return to work.

The company started by asking for a cut of sixty workers, but once this stoppage started, it demanded more massive cuts. They said they were going to close the smelter. Close to four hundred workers worked there, but they said they had to close it due to pollution problems.

Because the mine was owned by private capital, the power of the union's national president, Napoleon Gomez Sada, diminished. He wasn't able to do anything to change the minds of the private owners. We had to return with the shame of losing eight hundred jobs and not being able to solve any of the other problems that had caused the stoppage, not even lost wages for the time we were out of work or anything. It was very painful.

We were able to salvage the contract. There were occasions when the workers no longer wanted to continue the stoppage, but no one had the courage to say that stopping it was necessary. I was the one who made that proposal. That same day, I was scared that I might get beaten at the union for saying that it was necessary to go back to work. I stepped up to tell them that they had to submit the agreement to a vote. The chair of the meeting asked the people if we should lift the strike, and to everyone's surprise, it was agreed. All of us went back to work, minus the eight hundred that didn't.

My uncle, Manuel Parra, worked in the San Manuel mine in Arizona, and my cousins did, too. Many people from Cananea have migrated, especially to Tucson—at least those who were able to get their citizenship and work over there. There they pay them like they should be paid. Sometimes we talk among ourselves and say that so-and-so works in such-and-such

mine and earns so many dollars an hour. We open our eyes really wide. [*He laughs.*]

JERRY ACOSTA
BRINGING FOOD ACROSS THE BORDER TO HELP THE STRIKERS
Las Vegas, Nevada, December 2001

When the strike started in the Cananea copper mine, the U.S. union leader Jerry Acosta discovered that many families in Arizona, like his own, were connected to the strikers. He organized caravans of food to help them and got unions involved in defending people crossing the border after the strike was lost.

Both of my parents are from Cananea, and all of their families are still there. When I was a child we used to go back there, and I grew up with this knowledge of Cananea and the mine and the prosperity it brought. When I heard there was a strike there, I knew how the whole economy goes to pieces immediately when anything goes wrong with the mine. Even as a kid, I understood the mine's magnitude and its relationship to the people. The mine is everything for everybody in that town.

My grandmother Shalela Martinez used to do what they call the *fayuquera*. She'd take orders from people, cross the border to purchase American goods, come back, and deliver them. As a child I remember going from house to house and having my first experience of Mexican coffee. Everywhere you go they sit you down and you have café, no matter how young you are. I was only nine or ten. People in Cananea had money because even if you didn't work for the mine you did something connected to the people who worked there. People had money because the mine was prosperous. They had medical benefits and good jobs—it was a prosperous town.

When the strike started in the Cananea mine, I discovered some unions in Arizona were already connected to unions there, like CWA Local 7928. They are telephone workers and have come across the border to each other's meetings, had dinners together, and exchanged ideas about the impact of deregulation in Mexico. A lot of people have come across the border over the years, raised children, and kept their connection with Cananea. There is almost a blood connection between people in Tucson and people there, even Anglos.

As the Arizona state director for the AFL-CIO, I thought, How can we help the miners on strike? It was easy to generate interest in food collection and get the locals behind this issue. We got donations of food and clothes, raised money—close to twenty thousand dollars—and organized four trips with truckloads of help. After our first visit, three strikers came to Arizona to help us organize more.

I'll never forget taking food to Cananea. When we came into the city, I saw hundreds and hundreds of people waiting for us. And I thought, Oh, my God, we don't have enough food! I was overwhelmed. My cousin, Fausto, pulled up next to my van in his truck, and I hadn't seen him since I got married. We went into the school with our load of food, and the street was just full of hundreds and hundreds of people. And one of the first people waiting for me was my mom, with my uncle Genaro. It was one of the most momentous things that ever happened in my life. Right after that, we started organizing. Miners' unions in the U.S. were involved in raising the money and food, but it cut across that. There were machinists with family connections in Cananea, and Teamsters and other kinds of workers, too. I think Cananea is something special to Tucson in general. I didn't understand that until the strike. Lots of people have cousins who were born in Cananea but now live in Tucson. Everybody has family there or some connection or some history that involves the migration of people from Cananea to Tucson.

The miners in southern Arizona have a big connection. People that worked in the mines in Mexico have came across and worked in mines in southern Arizona. Miners in Arizona and Sonora have a rich culture and

history. Miners on this side of the border have a close-knit community, and the association with Cananea is part of that vital connection. There are families who work in mines on both sides of the border. Unfortunately, that's declining now. Mining in the U.S. is a pretty depressed industry. But in the family of miners, a strike is a strike and people think, "We gotta hang together." There's a special kind of solidarity between miners across the border. All along this border there are really strong connections—family, cultural, and historical.

I contacted the AFL-CIO Solidarity Center in Mexico City, and our representative, Tim Beaty, talked with the national leaders of the miners' union there. I think he found the exchange murky at best. There was something that wasn't right. Those leaders didn't want to make the strike an international battle. There wasn't cooperation from the national union, for obvious reasons, since we know what happened subsequently. In the end, they helped break the strike.

And they stopped us, too. We felt they could win the strike if they were able to last one day longer than the company, and a little more food could help them do that. But after a certain point the Mexican border police wouldn't let our trucks pass. I don't know the specifics, but the national union came in and took over, and then the relationship kind of dried up. The three workers who were coming across the border and helping us raise money and food lost their jobs in the end.

But the strike also started a relationship between labor and the community in Tucson, and I became involved in the movement to stop the deaths among workers coming across the border. People were dying every day, and that became a huge issue. Fired strikers themselves were coming north. The relationship between the AFL-CIO and people in Tucson became very close. I really don't see any difference between immigrant rights organizations like Derechos Humanos and the labor movement. And as a result of the strike we began working to get unions in the building trades to look at Latino workers as potential members. In Arizona 60 percent of the workers in commercial construction are Mexican, mostly undocumented.

Genaro Sanchez and his wife, in their kitchen in Cananea

marily to Arizona, where they were able to get a lot of help. Many organizations came and brought support to Cananea.

On the day of the caravan, we were all there at the union waiting for them to arrive. Lots of people were waiting for them, happy because of what they were bringing. Sometimes the strikers would only eat once a day, and sometimes they wouldn't even eat at all. They needed that help a lot.

There were a thousand people there when the caravan arrived, and everyone applauded. Then we went into the union hall and people spoke. The Americans could even speak Spanish. Among them was Gerardo Acosta, my nephew. He came back to his own country. His mother was there at the union, too. She'd come from the other side to welcome her son here, too, and she was very happy.

The whole world was happy that day.

GENARO SANCHEZ CAMACHO
I WAS THERE WHEN THE CARAVAN ARRIVED
Cananea, Sonora, December 2001

Genaro Sanchez Camacho describes how happy everyone felt when a food caravan arrived during the Cananea strike.

I was there in 1998 when the caravan came from the other side during the strike. The miners were seeking help during the strike because they didn't have the money to support their movement. They had put aside what they could in case of a strike, but when there's a movement like that the money doesn't last long. It runs out. So they went to the United States, pri-

MOISES ESPINOZA VALENZUELA
MINING FAMILIES WORKED ON BOTH SIDES OF THE BORDER
Cananea, Sonora, December 2001

Moises Espinoza Valenzuela grew up with Maclovio Barrajas, who became a leader of the U.S. Mine, Mill and Smelter Workers. Miners working on both sides of the border tried to help each other with problems from labor disputes to silicosis. But Espinoza did everything he could to keep his children from becoming miners, too.

During the years when the mine in Cananea was first operating, miners had to work very hard for very low pay. After the union formed, the mine was managed much more fairly. During those early years there were workers in the mine from the United States. A Mexican miner couldn't become a manager or a supervisor. In 1938 the miners began asking that the union contract

Moises Espinoza

include those jobs, so that Mexicans would have them. But it wasn't until 1950 when they were allowed to become managers and supervisors.

I went into the mine on April 22, 1937, and Maclovio Barrajas, who later became a famous leader, came to live with us. When his father died, his mother married my father, who raised him. We lived together for many years. Maclovio went to school in the U.S., but when the war came in 1942 he came here to Cananea and worked here for a long time. Later he enlisted in the U.S. Army and went to Korea.

He became a leader in the union movement in the U.S. copper mines, and in 1961 he returned to Cananea during a strike to see what we needed. He tried to bring us supplies and food, but they wouldn't let it through. The government said helping us like that was communist. It really wasn't, but that's the reason they gave for not letting the help for us get through. After this there was a miners' strike in the United States, and the miners from Cananea tried to help the strikers there.

Maclovio was as much a union man as I was. I got involved in unions, too. Every time he came we'd talk for hours. We considered him part of our family. He wanted to take Espinoza as his last name, but my father wouldn't let him. His father and my father were very good friends, and my dad said they'd killed him in the Superior mine.

I never considered working on the other side, but the company here did send me to a special course in mining over there. I could see they use the same systems on both sides of the border. The subterranean operations were identical. The workers I saw in the mines in San Juan and Bisbee [Arizona] were Mexicans, who worked first here in Mexico and used their experience to get jobs over there. A few Americans came over here to work in Cananea, but they never seemed very satisfied. That was the difference.

The mines in the U.S. were no less dangerous than the ones in Mexico, with the same rules and practices to minimize accidents. There were fewer accidents there, but this was a time of machismo, and that caused a lot of deaths here. Mexican workers would take unnecessary risks, perhaps because they needed to earn more money. You had to hold them back. When they had to put gunpowder inside a hole to blast, they'd overload it, even though we could all be buried. One had to stay close to them to keep them from doing that.

There were some things they should have fought in the U.S. as well, like silicosis. They didn't believe in it there for a long time. We knew it was an occupational disease, but it wasn't treated as one there for a long time. When I was in Denver I asked the engineers at the mine schools why. They said they were sure silicosis was an occupational disease, but that business was very powerful in the Senate and Congress, and they weren't going to allow consideration of it. Later, revolutionary people came into the U.S. Congress and were able to accomplish that. After a while, they were more interested in silicosis than we were here.

To some degree Mexican miners had an influence on miners in the U.S. They were paying attention to what we were finding out.

Bosses in the United States always liked to hire Mexicans, because we were more willing to take risks. But we paid for that. My brother-in-law died in Superior from heart problems caused by silicosis. He worked for many years in the mines. My father died in Tucson from silicosis, too, but they wouldn't recognize it as an occupational illness. We were all workers in the end, but the laws were different.

Despite the border, we've always had a lot of exchange of people between the mines on each side. When I was in Bisbee I met some young men who'd worked with me here in Cananea. It was like a celebration to get to know them and work with them again. Now the difference in wages between Mexico and the United States is much bigger, but it always was big.

All my family were miners—my father and his father, too. But I used to scare my sons about the mine so they would be afraid to work there. Now one is an attorney and the other is a chemist, so I guess I fixed it. My daughter studied accounting and lives in the United States. All of their children are professionals. I didn't want something dangerous for them. If they'd sent you to Vietnam, would you have wanted your children to go, too?

But I didn't want them to forget they're Mexican. When my granddaughter was little, she wanted to know about Mexico, from the beginning. I started to write her letters, telling her things in sequence. It was mostly to help her learn about where everything came from, and how I started. I write in Spanish and she answers in Spanish as well. In school over there they speak English, but at home Spanish. They feel Mexican and they're happy about it. I don't want them to forget the language or become assimilated.

JESUS MORALES TAPIA
A MOUNTAIN OF TAILINGS
Cananea, Sonora, December 2001

Retired miners' union leader Jesus Morales Tapia remembers the history of relations between mining communities in the United States and Mex-

ico. They're the same people, he believes, which is the reason they've been able to appeal to each other for help during strikes and conflicts.

When I was young, the most moneymaking jobs were the mines. There were other jobs, but they were badly paid for that period. All of us tried to work for the company. It didn't matter what department. The department that was most attractive was the mine, but it was also the most dangerous. There were many accidents, frequently fatal ones. But that was the area where you could earn the most money. At that time, it was shaft mining—subterranean work. All of us who were not scared went there.

All of the jobs depended on how fast we worked—on production. The jobs were paid by piece rate, no matter how small the jobs were, so that the extraction of metal would go as fast as possible. The work was dangerous because they hadn't made the advances that exist today. The machinery today is different. In any case, subterranean mines are dangerous, regardless of the machinery.

I worked two years in the shafts. Later they stopped using them, and the operation became open pit, or *cielo abierto*. I was given the opportunity to go to the concentrator, and one day I was offered a job called public service, measuring water and electricity. At that time, the company distributed drinking water and electricity to the city of Cananea. Then I became a train dispatcher and finally a confidential employee.

On my days off I worked in the smelter, because I had to support so many kids who were going to school. I worked anywhere, even on Sundays or holidays. In 1988 I retired because I could no longer work. My legs gave out.

After they started the open pit the work wasn't as dangerous. We were out in the open, with a greater chance to run somewhere in case of an emergency. In the shafts the mountain is on top of your head, always. The falls, the holes—all of it is more dangerous. People got hurt from electric shocks, metal falling, bodies falling, suffocating—there were many kinds of fatal accidents.

Today, the same companies own many of the mines on both sides of the border. It's a worldwide consortium. But the system of capital, which is in charge on both sides of the border, makes it difficult for workers to get together. The bosses are too tough. They don't give the worker anything. They're very cheap, very difficult to get money from. They all want to become millionaires very quickly. It doesn't matter what race they are—Jewish, gringos, Mexicans—it doesn't matter.

That's why workers unite. That's why unions exist in Mexico. Unfortunately, over the years they have become puppets of the government. The direction they took, and the ideas they had for workers, went bad, and the leaders no longer supported the workers. They're not like they were ten or twenty years ago, much less fifty years ago.

There was a strike here in 1961 in which miners received support from the other side, in particular from a leader of the U.S. union, Maclovio Barrajas. He had married a woman from Cananea, and that gave him ties to us. The family of his wife were miners as well. They say that he was also born here in Cananea. I'm not sure, but I do know that we were his people.

After we'd been on strike for a month or two, we sent out commissions to seek help. He arrived with half a dozen miners from the U.S. to give us moral support and later also economic support. There were people of Mexican descent with him, but also Americans. It was welcome help, if only for the fact that once the national leadership of our union knew that the miners in the United States were supporting us, there was more pressure on them to help, too. Those miners were the ones who created the space for us. Our movement was successful, in part because of the help the U.S. miners gave us. We were very grateful afterwards. A year later there was a strike among the miners in the United States, which lasted a year. With the little that we were earning in that time, we were able to come up with a good amount of dollars to send in help to the United States.

Miners on both sides of the border supported each other during that time because it's logical. In the first place, we're both communities of miners. Plus, there are family relationships among people on both sides. Family affection and fraternal feelings come into play in a strike. But the main reason we support each other is that we all work in the mine. It's the same kind of work, regardless of which side of the border you're on. When we have problems, there are no borders. We all have to work to survive. Over there they earn dollars, and over here pesos, but the basic problem is the same—work.

The system of work is the same on both sides. The companies have huge pieces of equipment for which they need the best operators, and there are lots of workers here in Cananea who know those jobs well. They can work on the other side, and the company knows they'll take good care of the equipment. Someone who's had experience on a job in a mine here can do that job in the U.S., too. The big difference is that miners over there earn twenty times more than we do.

Occasionally there have been people from Cananea who have worked in mines on the U.S. side. It's not a rare thing. Sometimes people have worked over there as long as ten or fifteen years, often without papers. During the twenties and thirties it wasn't too hard to work in the United States. It's only in recent years that crossing the border has become much more difficult.

Historically, there's been a strong connection between the Mexican workers in the mines in Arizona and those who work in this country, especially in Cananea. They were more or less the same people, driven by the same need at the same time. Miners in Mexico didn't envy others working over there, because you didn't make good money working in the mines in the United States until more recently, when the open pit started. Then people went over there because they began paying better in the U.S.

During normal times, however, there's not much relationship between miners on the two sides. Our situations are different. The relationship comes about during strikes, when the needs of Mexican miners are much greater because of the economic difference. During normal times, miners on the other side don't need our help, and the barrier of language separates us as well. The leaders of our unions change frequently, and there are a lot of political problems here in Mexico that get in the way of a stronger relationship.

I was elected recording secretary in 1970. I had the best intentions and looked for ways to better the union. But there were many difficulties caused by the national leaders who controlled the union then, and continue to control it today. They had become owners of businesses that contracted to the company, so the workers were manipulated to defend various interests.

It's difficult to have good relationships even between unions here in Mexico. When I was the leader of the union, we never had relationships even with other unions in our own mining system. We would look to each other for help only when there were problems. People have too many problems of their own to look out for somebody else's.

That's why we didn't get much help from other communities. Some supported us for political reasons—teachers, oil workers, and so on. But it was usually more moral support than economic. Actually, the students from the universities supported us more and gave more direct help to workers. The other unions were usually compromised by their relationship with the government and didn't want to jeopardize it.

During those years the mine was nationalized, and we had to fight against a government that was completely clueless about mines. Then an American company bought the mine. Working with the Americans was actually more peaceful than working for the Mexicans, even though I earned more when the Mexican government ran the mine.

When they changed to open pit production, they began covering all the land around the mine, however. Now you can see large mountains of tailings. It's necessary to strip the mountains to take out the metal. The richest ore was already extracted by the shaft mining. The open pit produces with very poor minerals, so they have to extract large amounts to produce the same amount of metal.

They've contaminated all of the rural regions of Cananea. When it rains, the water that flows through the soil gets polluted. Sooner or later, the subterranean waters are going to be contaminated. I don't believe the government is doing anything to prohibit it. In the United States the government makes the companies cover piles of tailings with fertile soil. Not here. Our government doesn't care if they pollute the land. So far in Cananea there have been no changes.

3

The indigenous Mayo and Yaqui communities of southern Sonora are the places of origin for many families who have migrated to the northern part of the state over the last two centuries and who have become miners on the border. Joaquin Murrieta, born in the village of Alamo, was himself probably a Mayo.

In Rancho Camargo, Nachuquis, and other tiny towns at the mouth of the Mayo River, indigenous people today struggle for economic and cultural survival. They feel the effects of globalization and NAFTA's neoliberal reforms as much as the miners of Cananea.

From the 1940s to the 1990s, Mayo farmers lived on *ejidos*, the collective rural landholdings created under the land reforms initiated by General Lazaro Cardenas. For decades, the system provided stability, resources, and some measure of social justice. That ejido system was virtually disbanded in the early 1990s, however, when President Carlos Salinas de Gortari rewrote Article 27 of the constitution, reinstating private large-scale land ownership. This change had a devastating impact on Mayos, many of whom lost their land and became impoverished farm workers laboring for low wages. As their income declined, so did their ability to mount fiestas and maintain their traditions.

Some contemporary cultural leaders, such as Marina Moroyoqui and Clemente Lopez Valenzuela, feel the economic pressure sharply. Ismael Cupicio Cota is also sensitive to discrimination against indigenous people, but as a labor contractor he has more faith in eventual economic progress.

Today a large percentage of Sonoran schoolteachers come from Mayo communities, not least because the teacher-training schools are located in their part of the state. Hector Moroyoqui describes his history growing up in a tiny Mayo town, the poverty of his own family and those around him, and the political struggles of the 1980s as they were played out among students.

Not everyone wants to go to the United States. Few Mayos cross the border; most of them prefer to work as migrant laborers in northern Mexico, staying within a distance that makes participation in community and cultural life possible. Pamfilo Lopez, one of the most talented of a new generation of deer dancers, is a farm worker in the Mayo heartland around Navojoa. He explains the mystical way he learned his art and how he yearns for the day he can just dance for a living instead of laboring in the fields.

Hector and Margarita Moroyoqui

HECTOR MOROYOQUI JUZCAMEYA
A MAYO HIGH SCHOOL TEACHER
Rancho Camargo, Sonora, March 2002

Hector Moroyoqui Juzcameya is one of the many Mayo indigenous people who make up most of the schoolteachers in Sonora. Mayo communities are becoming increasingly poor, yet the desire to remain close to the centers of Mayo culture keeps most from migrating across the border as other indigenous groups have done.

When I was a child I was bedridden and in excruciating pain. I couldn't stand or keep my balance, or hold anything in my hands. My grandparents recommended that we visit a curandera, and my parents saw it as their final option. They brought me to Señora Angela. She told us that we should not return to where we were living because envious people there would never permit us to be healthy. So we went to live in the community of Punta de la Laguna. I got well right away.

My parents are Mayo. My father's parents are from an indigenous town, Jiton Queca, and my mother's from a town that no longer exists, Jitombrumo. My grandparents always spoke the Mayo dialect. Unfortunately, I'm not fluent in it, but I do understand it almost perfectly. As children we were given the choice of which language to speak, and I grew up speaking Spanish. Now I regret not learning Mayo, because it would help sustain my roots.

I lived in Navolato, a Mayo town. It was peaceful but depressed because we always lacked money. Sometimes we would eat beans only twice a day, and sometimes we didn't even have beans. We would trade beans for roasted tomatoes, and that was the main course. We would savor it because the hunger was intense.

As children we would go with our parents to the fields so that we could all bring back more sacred food. We didn't have electricity or running water. That childhood was very difficult, but it gave me tools to climb the big pyramids of life.

Every time my father took us to the fields to work he would say, "If you don't want to be like me, you need to study. If you don't want to dress like me, you need to study. If you don't want to be tired all of the time like me, you need to study." I always hated working in the fields, so that inspired me.

When I went to high school, our classes were from 7 a.m. to 2:30 p.m. Monday to Saturday. I would get up at four in the morning and catch the school bus at five. The bus charged fifty cents. Then it went up to a peso, and then one fifty. I had just enough for the transportation from my house to school but no money to eat lunch, much less to pay for another bus ride home. Since we didn't have electric light, we would put gasoline in little coffee bottles and through the lid a piece of a blanket as a wick. That was what gave us light at night to study.

I was young and restless. I never thought that I would become a teacher. But when I was fifteen they gave exams to get into the Escuela Normal del Quinto [Sonora's main teacher-training school]. My friends thought the test was easy, and I thought it was really hard. But none of us got in except me. I cried, I was so happy.

My economic situation motivated me to have revolutionary thoughts. I became the treasurer of the student association, and then president. When we arrived, we had to sleep on the floor, on cardboard with a blanket. There were no dressers—we had to have our clothes in a bag. We had to organize ourselves if anything was going to change.

We told the state government that we needed windows, beds, mattresses, dressers, and services such as bathrooms, laundromats, and barbershops, and better food. Students would ask how it was possible that they fed the army's horses better than us, who were going to mold the consciousness of young people and combat all ignorance. Once they even fed us rotten beans. So we sat in the cafeteria, and hundreds of us started throwing our plates in the air. They got mad at us, but at the same time they understood, and in fact the food did improve. They gave us windows and mattresses, as well.

Professor Alberto Dueñas, of the Secretariat of Education and Culture, came to warn us about what we were doing. He said that if we wanted money or positions, they were there. But if we didn't stop our movement, we were going to disappear. We said no. Thank God, we are still alive and talking. I could have become a political prisoner or just another disappeared victim. Those were the years of Mexico's dirty war, and the government was afraid that that once students graduated from school, they would continue fighting and questioning the official parties and the military.

Knowing that I came from a very humble class and was the only hope for my family, I had to calm down. But it was an important period in my life, and despite the conditions, El Quinto did give us a very good academic education.

I graduated in 1994, and it took two months to get work. Finally, they told us that there was an opportunity to teach *telesecondaria*. I just wanted to work and was ready to take anything, even though I had no idea what telesecondaria was. They gave us positions in the most remote parts of the state, which they called positions of punishment. One of my friends was sent high up in the mountains. Another was sent to a mulatto community on the border between Sonora and Chihuahua. I was sent to the desert here in Trincheras.

Telesecondarias are high schools in rural areas where there are few students. They feature television programs shown on channel 111, a special education satellite in Mexico. I didn't understand the study plans at first, but now I can see that they are excellent. The programs in mathematics, Spanish, history, geography, civics, physical education, and art are magnificent. They are very complete and complement what we teachers give to our students.

After Article 27 of the constitution was changed, the collectivity of the ejidos where our people live has been lost. For my family, the ejido system functioned very well. They produced good crops, and everyone was together doing collective work. The ejido was divided into areas for different crops, and people got paid good money for them, so the system functioned.

Now it has all disappeared. When they changed Article 27 and gave *ejidatarios* [members of the ejido] the ability to rent or sell their properties, the collectivity was lost. The people who benefited were the large landholders. Small farmers can't pay for plowing, water, seeds, or fertilizer, so they must rent. We now call the ejidatarios the *quejidos* [complainers], because all of them complain, at least here in the Mayo region. There was also a large amount of corruption.

When incomes declined, it became more difficult for the Mayos to participate in their indigenous culture, especially the men and the youth. Take a *fariseo* [a traditional dancer in Mayo rituals]. For forty days he's supposed to be on a campaign and leave his family, while not receiving any salary. But no one can afford now to be gone for forty days. So he'll participate for a week, if at all. He can't abandon his wife and children for too long, so it makes it difficult to preserve the culture. The fiestas lose their spark, and the people don't want to come. So we're losing our traditions.

The money gathered from the community sustains the fiestas and other cultural practices, but because the economic level of the community is decreasing, there's less and less money to support them. If we have a poor community, then we're going to have poor events. If we have a stable community, then we're going to have stable events. That's logical.

When the cultural links between people in the community are strong, they don't feel the same pressure to migrate to look for work. But if the standard of living is low, many community members are forced to look for work elsewhere. And the ones that leave are the young. Looking for that illusion or that fantasy, they migrate to the cities up north. They have the idea that over there they'll find more wealth or a more dignified life than what we have here. They start working in the border cities like Nogales and Tijuana. But they still return for the fiestas, to celebrate events. The need for a job makes them migrate, but they try not to lose their traditions or customs.

Few Mayos leave the country entirely. The Mayo has a character that tries to get along. Many feel what they earn in Nogales is sufficient. If in a Mayo town I earn fifty pesos per day and in Nogales I'm earning eighty, then Nogales is better. Why go to the other side if I can make it with this? But in terms of education, we are not at all passive. We are very ambitious, and we will fight until we make our objectives a reality. Half of all the teachers in Sonora are Mayos, or Mayo/Yaqui.

People tell me that on the other side it is very good. I never wanted to go. I don't even have a passport. I'd rather go to exotic places in Durango or Michoacan, or Acapulco. I never thought that the other side was the best thing for me. I love my race and my country.

MARINA MOROYOQUI RAMIREZ
THE DELEGATE OF A MAYO COMMUNITY
Los Nachuquis, Sonora, March 2002

Marina Moroyoqui describes the poverty of Mayo communities and her fear that cultural traditions will be lost because of it.

I am the delegate, or president, of our community, Nachuquis, near Navojoa, Sonora. We had a meeting, and the indigenous people appointed me. It was a surprise. I look very indigenous to them, and I always helped them. I bring food, assist children getting a scholarship, help them with their school supplies, or get them roofing materials. We also look after the very poor people, the elders, people who are disabled, and our children.

There were no delegates in communities like Nachuquis until recently—not for the indigenous people. We would make a request to the municipal president in Navojoa, and he'd pass it on to the governor of Sonora. They treat me pretty well. Sometimes it takes a long time to get what we need, but we are getting some things, like roofs for homes or scholarships for children that have no means to go to school. Our most serious needs are for footwear, clothing, and especially food.

This is due to people's low income. Sometimes there's work, and sometimes there isn't. There are twelve hundred people in Nachuquis, but most of them are day laborers and don't have land. Only ten are ejidatarios. They receive money for renting their land, but they spend it and then it's gone.

Marina Moroyoqui Ramirez cooks a special meat stew for Easter in Rancho Camargo.

a doctor or receive medication. I would like to see them build more schools in Nachuquis, especially high schools. Then our students could graduate with better professions, and that would increase our incomes.

I help people put on the fiestas, since I am a Mayo, too. They are an important part of our traditions. But we always ask, like beggars, for donations to get the food, the *pascolas* [fiesta dancers], and the other things we need. It's hard—sometimes we get enough and sometimes we don't. I worry that in time our dialect will be lost, little by little. We need people who can teach it, so we can continue our traditions. We've asked the government to do this so our customs will continue, and now there is an indigenous school that teaches the Mayo language here.

CLEMENTE LOPEZ VALENZUELA
THE PRESIDENT OF THE FIESTAS
Rancho Camargo, Sonora, March 2002

Clemente Lopez Valenzuela describes the crisis for people trying to stay on the land in Mexico and the way it affects the ability to put on traditional Mayo fiestas.

The ejidatarios have no credit for buying what they need for farming, which is why they have to rent. Rich people rent the land from them, but they pay very little. But most still are not selling their land. They feel once it's sold and they spend their money, they won't have any more income.

The main reason income is so low is that day labor wages are low. They get paid forty or forty-five pesos daily, but that's not enough to buy food and clothing. People ask me to help when their kids get sick and need to see a doctor. They want me to negotiate with the hospital, to see if they can just pay half their bill or provide free medicine.

Day laborers don't qualify for Seguro Social [Mexico's free public health system]. You have to be employed permanently to receive those benefits, and most day laborers only get a day or two of work at a time. Their families go to the community clinic and pay something like twenty pesos to see

I am president of this church, here in Rancho Camargo. We need more money for our celebrations. It cost us eight hundred pesos for this Easter's fiesta, to pay for the musicians and everything else. You can see there is a window in the church with no glass, and we need to fix everything. That's what the president is supposed to do, but we don't have the money.

I ask neighbors to donate, and some gave a hundred pesos, but the rest can only give twenty or thirty, and some only five. Together, I still believe, our community can do it. The church does not belong to me but to them. We still try to organize traditional fiestas every year, on Easter, Saint John's

Clemente Lopez Valenzuela in the tiny church of Rancho Camargo

other daughters work here in Navojoa, one in a tire center and the other two in a factory.

My father was also an ejidatario, in San Ignacio, near here. He was born before the ejido of San Ignacio was even established, around eighty years ago, and passed away when he was ninety-two years old. My father worked hard at manual labor, not like now when we have bulldozers and Caterpillars. He grew wheat to support the family but also had to work as a day laborer. Things got better when they built the Mocuzares Dam in 1958 and created channels for irrigation. But that was the only time things got better. Since then, no one's seen any improvement.

I've had to work as an irrigation worker, tractor driver, and machinist, and I've farmed crops such as wheat, grain, and alfalfa. I have a few cows to help me out. In this region everybody has to work hard to survive. When there is no money and someone is sick, and you have gas and water bills to pay, and you know that you will run out of gas for your car, that's when you get upset.

Life is hard in Mexico.

Day, and Sacred Cross Day. We are going to have the next one on May 4, though I don't know how we are going to do it. We have no money. As the president, I struggle so we won't lose the tradition. I've been president since April, not very long. The person before me resigned. It was too difficult to organize the fiestas, so they appointed me. I'm determined they will continue every year.

I am an ejidatario, but that doesn't mean anything. My wife rents the ejido land out to a farmer. The rent is low. She gets a thousand pesos for each hectare. We have six hectares, so it is only six thousand pesos a year. There are no crops, nothing growing here. So I work as a laborer in construction to support my family. I work everywhere, wherever they ask me to go. Fortunately, my kids are all grown. My daughter Gloria lives in Tijuana. Abel and Adolfo also live in Tijuana, where Adolfo works in a tire center. They left to see what they could find, and stayed. They live better there. My

ISMAEL CUPICIO COTA
MEXICO IS NOT POOR
Navojoa, Sonora, March 2002

Despite the difficulties of making a living in rural Sonora, Ismael Cupicio Cota decided not to work in the United States but to operate a labor contracting business in Mexico instead. He believes that Mexico is capable of supporting indigenous cultures like that of the Mayos.

I live in the land of the Mayos, in Curirinpo. This town is very old. The land title dates back to 1570. My ancestors lived here: my parents and

Ismael Cupicio leans against a wall, as members of the indigenous Mayo community of Rancho Camargo listen to a police officer make excuses for arresting a man for gathering branches to build a traditional Easter altar in his home.

grandparents. I am Mayo and very proud to be indigenous. Our culture is very rich. Our dances are performed even across the border. The dance of the deer is internationally known. It was created in the wild areas surrounding the farms and then taken to another level with songs and dance.

As an ejidatario my father was able to support the family when I was young. Today the ejidatarios don't have the support they need. The interest was low back then, and you were able to pay back your loans. We all cooperated and helped on the farm. Now it is very difficult due to high interest and the devaluation of the currency.

This morning a man was beaten up for collecting branches for an altar for Easter in his house. This was very important to us, because it was an abuse. As an indigenous person, it makes me very upset. This young man

keeps the culture and tradition. He was cutting a tree, an *alamo* [aspen], for a ritual that we Mayos do. It is like the Jewish tradition where they cut leaves to cover the altar. This beating was designed to prevent indigenous people from continuing their traditions. It is important to recognize indigenous rights. Indigenous people have been mistreated, and this could happen to anyone, including myself.

We are always fighting discrimination. The problem is that the indigenous people are the ones who do all the agricultural jobs, because they don't have the education to get other jobs. But instead of people being grateful, this is what happens.

I worked in the U.S. in 1988. I was treated OK, though we had to live in the mission. In the evening we had to clean the place up—I guess that is how we paid for our food and lodging. The money might be better over there, but you need to be able to educate your children, too. We need to take care of the family. Otherwise we will be acting very selfishly.

There are organizations in the U.S. for indigenous people like myself. In Guadalupe there's one for the Yaqui, and the Yaqui and the Mayo are very similar. They asked us to go perform in their festivities in Guadalupe, which we did. We respect the authorities and don't overstay the visa so they'll invite us again. We usually do the pascola, as it is very rhythmic. When we go there the Yaquis and the Mayos are able to communicate, since our culture is very similar.

I don't think our culture is in danger. People are not going to stop their traditions just because they are afraid of being beaten up. It gives more power to the people when they have to defend it. The new generation is more interested in promoting it. Since 1990 there have been more books published in different dialects like Yaqui or Mayo, as well as books for the curanderos. There are many different projects for indigenous communities—agricultural, transport, sewing—so the job is to register in groups and request financial support.

Still, we have not had enough support or promotion of our culture. We want to encourage our people to continue the tradition. We want to advertise what we are doing here and let the government know that we are fighting for our rights.

I drive a truck and take people to work. At the big farms, I go to the person in charge and tell him I have a truck and people willing to work. If he needs farm workers, I supply the personnel, and that's how I make my money. By doing that I am supporting my people and showing that indigenous people want to get ahead. We want to succeed, we want to work, we want to preserve our culture, and we want to live in Mexico.

People say Mexico is poor, but Mexico is not poor. It is rich if we want to work together. You ask me if I want to go to work in the U.S.? There is work here, too.

PAMFILO LOPEZ OZUNA
THE DEER DANCER
Rancho Camargo, Sonora, April 2002

Pamfilo Lopez Ozuna is one of the best-known deer dancers in the Mayo communities clustered around the mouth of the Mayo River in Sonora. He says he learned the deer dance in a dream, and he tries to combine new elements from those handed down through the generations. But dancing is also a way to earn a living, like working in the fields—which is how he supports his family between fiestas.

Pamfilo Lopez Ozuna dances on the *bule*, or gourd maraca, without breaking it, during his twenty-four-hour performance at Easter.

I'm a deer dancer. When I'm dancing I think about everything. I imagine things. I think about the saint I'm dancing to, whether it's Christ, San Juan, Santa Maria, or San Jose. When the fiesta starts, I give thanks for being able to learn, for knowing what I know. I don't want to worry about what people expect. You never make people happy, but the saint you're dancing to will be happy. I focus on him, and pray nothing bad will happen to me.

We are the new people, the people of my generation. We are trying to learn what our ancestors gave us, trying to follow the culture left by the an-

cient ones. They did lovely things. The culture is beautiful, and we don't want it to end.

I've been dancing for almost seven years, since I was fifteen, at the fiestas our communities celebrate at different times of the year. My father was a deer dancer for twenty-seven years.

When I started I didn't know how to dance. I'd never been to a fiesta to see it. But without knowing why or how, wanting to dance was born inside me. My dad said, "Well, get the *sonajas* [bracelets or anklets made of nuts, which rattle when a dancer performs]. Put the deer on your head and start dancing, so I can see how you do it." But I told him, "I'm not going to dance for you. If you want to send me to perform, then send me. If you don't, I'll never dance."

Finally, he said, "Fine, I'll send you to dance at Santa Maria Baraje." And he did, so on December 12, 1995, I began. Nobody told me anything beforehand, and afterwards nobody said I did this or that wrong. My father didn't go with me either. He sent a friend to let me know what I had to do, but it turned out I didn't need him. I did everything that I was supposed to.

I never saw my father dress in his deer clothes. But before I started dancing, I saw in my dreams a large field in my hometown and a fawn jumping there. Then a large snake attacked me. At first the little animal was in shock, and then with his head he told me to follow him to his parents—a female and a male deer. I kept dreaming this, and the deer called out to me again and again. When I got to that place in my dream, I would touch all the animals. My father says that's how I picked everything up without him telling me. Then I started to dream about the fiesta and what it would be like. That's how I learned to dress myself.

He's old, and I'm new and young. I have been able to learn what he couldn't, and now we feel comfortable sharing what we know. When I started to dance, my father stopped dancing so that he could accompany me. He helps me with the *anhueja* [a drum made from a gourd that sits in a tub of water while played] and the musicians. At the same time he watches me. Before I went to the fiestas, I didn't know about the jealously among dancers and musicians. But you have to know how to take care of yourself. We take care of each other. I keep people from harming him, and if someone's harming me, he helps me.

After I began to dance, I started to see different things. At first, you don't know the different elements. But then the dance becomes like a habit. Now I see many different possibilities, and at the same time I have fun. When I dance, I sometimes get lost. I don't even know what I'm doing. Other people tell me, "You know you did this or that." But at the time I'm lost. When I dance, I dance.

A lot of other dancers don't get a crowd, but I fill the place. Many people tell me I do the dances differently. They ask me who taught me, and I tell them I taught myself. I learn by imitating the things I see in the world. You have to look for ways to distinguish yourself from other dancers. They can be new things or things from the ancestors that people are now learning again. I look forward and backwards.

Logically, to look for stuff in the past, you have to ask older people like my father or others who know how they did things before. They used to just dance to the drums, play the harp, and the anhueja. Now I get on top of the *bule* [a big maraca, or rattle] or on top of the anhueja. This is something that was done by my ancestors, but then people stopped for a long time until I began again. It's not easy, and I'm still the only one doing it. It's not only that you have to balance, but also it's very easy to break the gourd.

Then there are new things—ones I don't look for. While I was dancing in one fiesta, a man put a bottle out there where I was dancing, a beer bottle. For two hours I didn't know what to do with it. My head was spinning until I had it. I said to myself, "I'm going to open it with my mouth." I focused and I opened it. It felt good to accomplish something that others have never been able to do.

I finished high school, but I didn't go to college or SEBETIS [one of the three teaching colleges in Navojoa, which maintain indigenous Mayo student dance troupes]. I did well on the exams, but my father had no money to give me. I'd already started working before I started high school. People in my family got sick, and my parents went to help them and left me by myself. In high school I polished shoes to pay for my uniform, books, notebooks, and pens. After high school I couldn't find any good jobs, so I started working in the fields. Then I started to dance. One week I'd work in the fields. Then the next week there'd be no work, so I'd dance.

I never really liked working in the fields. But I got married, and now we have a seven-month-old baby. We didn't get married in the church. We say we got married by the Law of the Mountain, when one steals a girl and marries her without her family's permission. I had a civil marriage later, when the baby was going to be born.

With dancing there's no Seguro Social as there is with other kinds of work. Teachers have social security and can go and get treated if they're sick. With dancing, if you get sick, you learn to treat yourself. If you want to heal, then you will heal.

We don't put a price on the dance we do at the fiesta. An offering is not something that you charge for. You dance for the saints, not the people. If the people want to give something, they do it out of good will. Usually it's between two hundred and a thousand pesos, but when we dance we never know how much we're going to earn.

When I'm not dancing, I have to work in the fields. We weed and harvest zucchini, chilies, and tomatoes. The people we work for are Arabs, who give me permission to go dancing. They treat us well, and we work all year around. But a week's work doesn't even add up to two fiestas. In one fiesta, a simple one, we earn what we would in three days of work in the fields. In the fields it's only sixty pesos per day. In three days you don't earn two hundred pesos. You can earn 200 pesos in just one fiesta. We dance day and night, but I'm young and my body's used to it. I've danced for eight days straight at different places.

That's how I support my family and buy the groceries. Between the fiestas and the fields, we have enough to eat and I can clothe everyone. Thank God it's possible.

Now sometimes my wife takes my son to the fiestas when I'm dancing. When he hears the sound, he looks alert and starts moving and dances. But who knows if he'll like it in the future? Only he can decide what he wants to do.

At the fiesta today there's another young boy dancing the deer, around six or seven years old. He dances very well. He has the desire to learn. But I don't know if he will spend his time dancing or studying in school. He could do both, but no one can tell him, "You have to dance" or "You have to study." Only he can judge how far he's going to take either one.

When I dance I thank God I'm here today. I hope He will help me do a good job and that I can travel far and see other places. For my own future, I pray to God that work never ends, so that I'll be able to support my wife and my child. I ask God for work and fiestas. People come to my house and ask me to teach their son or nephew how to dance so that later someone can take my place when I no longer dance. That idea—teaching someone to do what I do, and more than I can—makes me happy.

PART FOUR

BRACEROS AND GUEST WORKERS

A HARD PAST, A HARDER FUTURE

This camp in Blythe, California, was used for braceros in the 1940s and 1950s. It housed migrant farm workers until the 1980s.

Farm workers took showers here in this former labor camp for braceros in Blythe, California.

In the 1990s migrant workers still lived in this labor camp in the San Joaquin Delta, California.

Migrant workers had no privacy in the bathroom of this labor camp.

A canal brings water from the Colorado River for irrigation in the Palo Verde Valley.

The path through the desert from Altar, Sonora, to the United States border starts north of Route 2, which crosses the Sonoran Desert just south of the line.

A worker looks over the fence between Mexico and the United States near Tijuana, trying to find a moment when the Border Patrol may not be looking so that he can go through the hole under it and cross. A Nahual legend says that when people go to the underworld, they are guided by a dog.

A memorial at the border fence near Tijuana commemorates those who have died trying to cross.

The parish of the Guadalupe Church in Altar set up a dining room for undocumented workers heading north, and outside it erected crosses as a memorial to those who have died trying to get across the border. "More than 1500 migrant brothers dead," it says on the dining room wall.

Victor Aleman, from Queretaro, says the promise of work brought him to Altar, where he hopes to cross the border a few miles north. "In Mexico, you have to work like a dog just to maintain yourself. On the other side, there are much better jobs. That's what we're all going for—looking for a life on the other side," he says.

Under the watchful eyes of a border patrol agent, undocumented workers are deported back into Mexico through the gate at the border crossing in El Hoyo in Mexicali.

This old man, who worked as a bracero in the United States during the 1950s, returned to Oaxaca permanently after deciding he didn't want to live in the north.

Edilberto Morales's father sorts through drying coffee beans in La Democracia, Guatemala. The price is so low that selling this crop will not bring the family enough money to eat.

Silvano Villatoro is the contractor who brought Edilberto Morales and fourteen other guest workers to the United States, where all except Edilberto died when the van carrying them went off the road. Since becoming a guest-worker contractor, Villatoro, who was a member of the pro-government civil guard during Guatemala's civil war, has been able to buy land planted in coffee and is now the owner of a large ranch in La Democracia.

The main highway in front of the Association of Small Coffee Farmers in La Democracia, Guatemala. Since the drastic fall in coffee prices, many residents here have started going to the United States every year as guest workers, or modern-day braceros.

1

For thousands of families in the United States and Mexico, the bracero experience was either the way they first established themselves north of the border or an experience so bitter they returned to Mexico, determined to find a way to survive that didn't depend on migration. The braceros were contract workers, recruited during World War II to work on farms and railroads in the United States at a time when the war created a shortage of manual labor. Railroad work lasted only two years, but growers liked the program so much they convinced Congress to keep it alive until 1964.

For twenty-two years the United States and Mexican governments recruited temporary laborers in Mexico and parceled them out to U.S. farmers on three-month contracts. The men who came north (the program excluded women) had the same dream—to make money and then return home to build a better life. Celestino and Amelia Garcia, Eusebio Melero, Rigoberto Garcia, and the parents of Agustin Ramirez all describe the dream in the same way.

Few, however, planned the return as elaborately as the Ramirez family. Agustin Ramirez's father worked as a bracero, brought his family north to help in the fields, and then, when the children were old enough, began to send them back to Mexico, one by one, to reestablish the family's base in Michoacan. In the late 1960s they also wanted to protect the boys from being drafted into an unjust war in Vietnam, which they opposed. Agustin, the eldest son, describes his remarkable youth as a returned student in Mexico. Just as he was ready to become a respected professional, however, Mexico's first big currency devaluation robbed him of his job and future and sent him back north to work beside his father as a farm worker in the grape vines.

Agustin Ramirez and his family were supporters of the United Farm Workers. This union of immigrants inspired the rest of the U.S. labor movement to once again begin organizing workers, a mission largely abandoned during the conservative cold war years. The UFW also trained dozens of creative organizers whose talents later helped revitalize other unions. Ramirez was one of this group. It is no exaggeration to say that the modern labor movement, regardless of its many problems, owes its survival to them.

Celestino and Amelia Garcia and Eusebio Melero describe their experience during the bracero years. Celestino and Eusebio eventually became warehouse workers and members of the International Longshore and Warehouse Union. They retired in San Leandro, California, and live across the street from each other.

Rigoberto Garcia, whose memories of his bracero experience are still fresh, lives with his wife, also named Amelia, in a small trailer in the Palo Verde Valley, one of the lush agricultural basins carved out of the remorseless desert by the great water projects flowing from the Colorado River. Although he was sixty-eight years old when he recounted his history, he continued to work picking lemons and grapefruit. A few of the bracero camps he remembered still stood on the outskirts of Blythe, although no one had lived in them for years.

Today, California growers no longer want to house the migrant workers who pick their crops. During the harvest, it's common to see cars parked on the outskirts of small farm-worker towns with whole families sleeping inside. The braceros at least had beds.

During the 1950s growers brought in these contract workers when their existing workforce struck, or threatened to do so. The threat of replacement thus allowed ranchers to undermine the ability of resident farm workers to demand higher wages. In the late 1950s and early 1960s, Alfredo Figueroa saw that impact during strikes in the fields of Blythe and the Imperial Valley.

Cesar Chavez, then an organizer for the Community Service Organization in Oxnard, California, mounted farm-worker protests over the program. Ernesto Galarza organized a national campaign to convince Congress to end it. Chavez later said that organizing the United Farm Workers was impossible until the bracero program was halted in 1964. The great grape strike in which the union was born began the following year.

But braceros did not always willingly acquiesce. California's legendary immigrant rights campaigner, Bert Corona, recalls in his autobiography not only that braceros sometimes went on strike but that local Chicano communities would bring them food and try to prevent their deportation. Rigoberto Garcia remembers those strikes. His brother organized walkouts among braceros and later used that experience to help start the first strikes by the United Farm Workers. Nevertheless, while some braceros fought to change conditions, and small rebellions may have raised wages temporarily, the threat of deportation was enough to stop any larger strike and union effort until 1965.

According to a 2002 study by the Pew Hispanic Center, 47 percent of all farm workers today lack immigration papers—about 1.25 million people. Counting their families, that number is even higher. The same study says there are about 7.8 million undocumented immigrants in the country as a whole, making up almost 4 percent of the entire U.S. workforce. A 2005 Pew Study puts the number of undocumented workers as high as 12 million.

Today's farm-worker unions therefore want a new amnesty, which would eliminate the fear of deportation when those workers try to organize. Growers, however, want guest workers, the modern equivalent of the old braceros. So far, the union has been willing to accept this, provided that the current undocumented workforce gains the right to legal status. It's a hard compromise to make.

In the days of the braceros, a few growers were able to recognize the humanity of their workers across the deep divides of economic status and nationality. Rigoberto Garcia finally got his own immigration papers with the help of a Japanese grower who saw the barbed wire surrounding the bracero camps and recognized it from his own internment during World War II.

For Garcia and many others, the bracero program was the route to a life in the United States, but it was a hard one. He's glad his children won't face it.

AGUSTIN RAMIREZ
A UNION ORGANIZER
Fairfield, California, November 2001

Agustin Ramirez, the son of a bracero, was sent back to Mexico by his parents to avoid the Vietnam War. He earned a degree in agronomy, but he wound up in the fields of California as a farm worker, when the Mexican economic collapse put an end to his family's dream of building a life in Mexico. He found his future in building unions in the United States, helping workers like his parents win security and justice.

I was born in Atacheo, a village of about eight thousand people about sixteen kilometers from Zamora, Michoacan. I was the oldest in my family. My dad began coming to the U.S. as a bracero before I was born. He came to Modesto every year until 1959. Every time he returned to Atacheo he would bring us walnuts and almonds. It was a big treat, but now I realize that's what they grow in Modesto.

We all used to wait for him. When he came, these little toys popped out of his suitcases. You put batteries in them, and they were awesome. At that time, not many kids had fathers here, so nobody else had these mechanical toys. Once he brought us a little mechanical horse. We'd take it to the town plaza, and all the other little kids would gather around. They had little wooden trucks made by people in the village. When the horse started jumping, it was the thing to see.

My father would buy clothes here and give them to his relatives. If you were a peasant in the countryside, your pants would be made of some very inexpensive material. He'd bring us checkered shirts. When we would wear them to school, even the teacher would say, "Your dad is here! He came home!"

In Atacheo most farmers were part of the ejido. The purpose of the ejido was not to make a lot of profit but to give people something to live on. The slogan of Zapata was "the land belongs to those who work it." It was that

Elvia and Agustin Ramirez

kind of idea. If you had four kids, you would apply for the extension of the ejido, so the young male adults would have a place to build their houses and future.

My father came to the U.S. as a bracero because he had no land. My parents said their goal was to stay for a few years and then go back to Mexico and start a business. Today, that's still their dream. It's just that their business is in the U.S. now.

I came to the U.S. in 1963, when I was seven. We lived in a camp near Livingston next to fields of figs and peaches. My dad bought a car, which we called El Perico [The Parrot] because it was green. We'd go out at night to chase jackrabbits. That was our thrill. We made our playground from the boxes used for picking peaches. All the families did that.

We were always with our parents. Our camp consisted of individual little houses, each with one bedroom, surrounded by the fields. We loved being

with our father, because before he was always away from home. In 1963 my parents bought a house in Merced. It was very difficult. I didn't know English, and one day in class I wanted to go to the bathroom. I asked another kid how to say that. To this day I don't know what he told me, but I raised my hand and repeated what he said. They took me to the office and whacked me with a big piece of board. In the late seventies when Cambodian people began arriving, you'd hear stories that they were mistreated in school the same way. I understand that, because that's how it was for us. People thought we shouldn't be here.

Every year we followed the seasons. First we'd pick cherries in the San Joaquin Valley. My parents and I would live in the car. We'd stay for three days, come back, and then go for another three. We'd end the season in Lakeport, and the whole family came. Even after I was married, my wife came with us a couple of times.

In 1969, when I was thirteen, I went back to Mexico. My parents were afraid that if I stayed here I would have to go to Vietnam. They said the war was not right. Every day in the news you'd see that Hispanics and blacks were the ones killed. They asked me if I wanted to go back to Mexico. At the beginning I said no, but one year after picking pears I told them I would try it for a year.

My mother drove me back to Zamora, and the first year I stayed with her friend in Zamora. Later I lived in boarding houses by myself. Now that I'm married and have kids of my own, I can see how hard it was for them. Their goal was to go back to Mexico themselves, as it still is today. But their goal was fresher then, when they hadn't been here so long.

Sending me was a first step. They told us that in Mexico, if you have an education, you could live well. A Latino working in the fields here had no future. My father would often say, "I don't want you to work here like me." By 1971, after I'd been there a few years, my sister came back. Then my other brother came. At one point there were three of us in Mexico, while my parents and four other kids were in California. The family was divided.

My parents put me in a Catholic school, the most expensive school in Zamora. It was funny. In the U.S. we were at the bottom because we were farm workers, yet in Mexico I could go to the most expensive school in town. A lot of kids loved me because I did their homework in their worst subject—English. They made fun of me because of my broken Spanish, but I was welcomed with open arms.

Later I moved to the government school, where I met my wife, Elvia, and from there to the University of Guadalajara. During those years I'd come to the U.S. in December, when I'd help my father prune apricots, peaches, and grapes, and in the summer, when we'd pick apricots and pears. My parents built a house in Zamora because that, too, was part of their dream. They planned to send one of the children each year until eventually they'd have to come too, because all of us would be in Mexico.

Soon they realized that although they loved Mexico, they couldn't make a living there. Every year they'd say, "Next year we'll come." They'd save up a few thousand dollars, but that money didn't go very far. They began to realize that to support us there, they had to work here. The idea of going back became a myth after a while.

I studied agronomy, to become an engineer. At that time, if you had a job with the government, you had it made. My dream was to get a government job, to farm, and then to open a store selling insecticides, pesticides, and fertilizers. My uncle was a deputy in the state legislature and worked in the Secretariat of Agriculture and Animal Husbandry. He told me that he could easily get me a position. In the early eighties it didn't depend on what you knew but who you knew. I wasn't a brilliant guy, but I knew the right people, so I got a promise.

When I came out of school with my agronomy degree, I was in line for a job. But the big economic crisis hit in 1981. The value of the peso went from twelve to the dollar to 560 to the dollar in six months. The government not only froze jobs but started laying people off. My promised job went down the drain. My parents didn't have any nest egg to help me start my own business. If I had to choose between being poor in Mexico and poor in the U.S., it was obvious where I should go.

That was the hardest part of my life. My parents had put me through school in Mexico for twelve years, paying for everything I needed. I lived a privileged life—I was blessed. All because my father didn't want me to do the same thing he was doing here. When I told them I was coming back, they were devastated. Everything they'd worked for seemed to be going down the drain.

I got married that year, in 1981, and my wife was with me. I needed to do something, so I ended up picking grapes in the Napa Valley. The following year my father came to work there too. There we were, working in the same field, picking grapes, side by side—the very thing he always fought to keep from happening.

I started pruning at Christian Brothers. It wasn't hard work, but I didn't know how to do it, and it was embarrassing. People would ask me, and I'd tell them I was an engineer of agronomy. But in Michoacan we studied how to grow grain, and I never saw a vine. So the workers would say, "Here's an engineer, and he doesn't know how to prune a damn vine." The first day of work I saw a lot of people I knew from Atacheo. When I'd seen them before, during the Christmas season, they'd greet me very respectfully, saying "How are you doing, *ingeniero*? You're going to make your parents proud." When I went to work side by side with the same people, they'd just look at me. They didn't say anything—they didn't know what to say. I didn't either.

In Napa we were making almost twice the minimum wage, because the United Farm Workers had been very successful there. Even in the first years when my family came to Merced and Livingston, we'd been involved with the union. My dad was a striker at Gallo in 1966. He used to walk the picket line, and sometimes we'd go with him with our little flags. Even during times when I'd come back from Mexico on vacation, we'd go to marches. My uncles were part of the union negotiating committee, and one went to work with Cesar Chavez.

I kept on working until 1983, when the workers elected me president of the ranch committee. At the ranches the union found militant people, people eager to get their rights. People who worked in the fields never had any rights. When they suddenly had power, they took it as far as they could. They were just eager to find justice.

Most of those who had land in Mexico and came to the U.S. went back after they'd been here a few years and made some money. The ones who stayed are the ones who didn't have anything to go back to. When I came, hundreds of thousands of professionals did also. Doctors with whom I'd gone to school were here, and dentists and engineers too. You'd find them working on assembly lines or in the fields—wherever they could get work. They had degrees, but because they spoke Spanish they had to take whatever they could find.

For many years my Elvia and I also dreamed we'd work in the U.S., make some money, and go back. The first year we worked here, we saved and bought some land for a house. The next year, we told ourselves we'd need a business. We decided on pigs and built sheds for raising them. The third year, we went back and bought a mill for grinding feed and a pump for a well. Then my son Edgar was born the next year, and we couldn't go. The year after that we couldn't go either. Finally we realized that we weren't going back. All our family was here. That dream of going back was just that. We made our decision in 1981, and we have to build on it.

During that time I started to work for the union. I never had a chance to repay everything my parents did for me, so maybe I just needed to give something to someone. I thought work with the UFW was a way. People just wanted to get a little piece of security, of the so-called American dream, by having a union contract. Now those who won those contracts in the 1980s have their own homes. The contracts are gone now, but people were able to achieve something. Cesar and the movement he organized did that.

My wife and I arrived with only two suitcases and landed in a room at my mother's house. Now we have a house, a car, and our kids in school. We have jobs. I think we're happy. And the best part of it is that I love what I do. I still work for unions, although not the UFW anymore. You see someone who didn't realize they had the spark in them get up and say, "This is wrong. I won't stand for it." That's an organizer's job. If you can get one person out of a hundred you touch to do that, you can say you did something good.

Our society is lopsided, and immigrants are seen as a threat. Look at me—dark skin. I'm really afraid we're going to face a backlash against all of us. Filipinos in the airports are being laid off because they're not citizens. Is that fair, to say they have no allegiance to this country because they weren't born here? I think that's wrong. Look at Timothy McVeigh. He was a hard-core American.

Society has to look at immigration as a necessity instead of putting up so many walls. This country needs immigrants to keep the wheels turning. It's filled with immigrants. But people have to be given rights.

Even though we don't have those really tight ties with Atacheo anymore, we tell our children that's where we came from. We want them to know the roots of the family are there. But we don't ever expect them to move back. None of my sisters or brothers would ever think of moving there. This is our land. This is where we're going to die and be buried. Our roots are in Mexico and Atacheo, but the way I see it, it's like in agronomy. When you transplant a plant and you treat it right, it's going to grow roots. That's what happened to us. We were transplanted. Our roots are over there, but the tree that grew up is over here. And my kids' roots are here now. This is where they're going to grow, where they're going to flourish.

Our family is very close. That's what counts, what helps us get through things. That's why we're all here and why nobody's going back.

RIGOBERTO GARCIA PEREZ

A BRACERO

Blythe, California, December 2001

What was it like to work as a bracero? Rigoberto Garcia was one of many thousands of men who came every year, and his memories document brutal exploitation and callous treatment. But other memories puncture stereotypes. Some braceros went on strike and suffered deportation as a result. Their experiences laid the groundwork for later strikes by the UFW after the bracero program was abolished. And Garcia remembers a Japanese grower, interned during World War II, who finally helped him win his legal status.

Amelia and Rigoberto Garcia, with the contracts Rigoberto signed as a bracero on the table in front of them

My father owned some land in my hometown, Lalgodona, Michoacan, but he had to keep selling it off. In the end, he sold almost all of it, and he became a bracero when the war started with Germany in 1941. They always made good money, the braceros. He rebuilt his house and tried to recover his land, but he couldn't. But he was a fighter, so he started a small store and went into business. And he never went to the U.S. again.

When I began to think about crossing the wire, my father was against it. It was as if I had told my parents I was going to work down in the mine. His idea was that when you work for someone else, you never get free of it. For him, when we worked on the land we were working for ourselves, not someone else. When you work for someone else, the profit from your work stays with them. That was his advice, and it was true. Because here you work just to survive, and you don't own anything. You just survive and survive, but someone else owns your labor.

I was an *alambrista* [undocumented immigrant] the first time I went to the U.S. We got to Mexicali and got on a train. There were two trains that went from San Diego to Phoenix and traveled quite a ways on the Mexican side. At the border you'd have to get off because immigration was there. So you'd get off outside town and cross the border on foot. It wasn't a big

problem like it is today where they're keeping such a watch. The border was almost free then.

I worked in Stockton, in the cherries, where the migra caught me twice. After that I didn't want to go back. I decided to work in Calipatria, where if they caught me, I was closer to the border and it wasn't as hard to get back. Because we were so near Mexicali, when we'd hear on the radio that some famous artist would perform there, we'd all go. We didn't need papers. We'd go to Mexicali and have a good time. And that night, we'd cross back over. It was easy. Now it costs a lot of money for everyone to cross. Poor people suffer a lot.

I went back home and got married, and I stayed home a year. Then I decided to cross again, but as a bracero. Instead of hopping freights and all that, we could go a different way. I went to the contracting station in Sonora, in Empalme. It was very easy to get work. There were people there who would sign you up, for three hundred dollars a month at that time. They'd get a thousand or two thousand people a day.

I went as a bracero four times, but I didn't like it. We got on the train in Empalme and went all the way to Mexicali, where we got on busses to the border. From there they took us to El Centro. Thousands of men came every day. Once we got there, they'd send us in groups of two hundred, as naked as we came into the world, into a big room, about sixty feet square. Then men would come in masks, with tanks on their backs, and they'd fumigate us from top to bottom. Supposedly we were flea-ridden, germ-ridden. No matter, they just did it.

Then quickly, they took a pint of blood from every man. Anyone who was sick wouldn't pass. Then they'd send us into a huge bunkhouse, where the contractors would come from the growers associations in San Joaquin County, Yolo, Sacramento, Fresno, and so on. The heads of the associations would line us up. When they saw someone they didn't like, they'd say, "You, no." Others, they'd say, "You, stay." Usually, they didn't want people who were old—just young people. Strong ones, right? And I was young, so I never had problems getting chosen. We were hired in El Centro and given our contracts, usually for forty-five days.

It was an agreement from one government to the other. The contract had to have the signature of the mayor of your town, guaranteeing your reputation. You also had to have experience picking in Mexico. It was a kind of blackmail. My wife's father had to work in the Yaqui River Valley to complete his period of time before he could go to Empalme and sign up. When your contract was over, they'd put you on a bus back to El Centro. And there they'd give you the passage back to Empalme.

One year I went to Santa Maria, where we picked strawberries. From there they renewed our contracts and sent us to Suisun, and we picked pears there. When we were through the rancher said, "Now we're going to Davis." And from there they sent us back to Mexico.

I think at that time our wage was eighty cents an hour. In the tomatoes it was piecework—twenty cents a box. That was pretty good if you could pick a hundred boxes. But the work was a killer, really hard. They'd give you two rows, which could give you fifty boxes, and you could do that in half a day.

In Tracy I was with a crew from Juajuapa de Leon, in Oaxaca, and one of those boys died. Something he ate at dinner in the camp wasn't any good. The kid got food poisoning, but what could we do? We were all worried because he'd died. What happened to him could happen to any of us. They said they'd left soap on the plates, or something had happened with the dinner, because lots of others got diarrhea. I got diarrhea, too. But this boy died.

We slept in big bunkhouses. It was like being in the army. Each person had his own bed, one on top of the other, with a mattress, blanket, and so on. They'd tell us to keep the place clean, to make our beds when we got up. We woke up when they sounded a horn or turned on the lights. We'd make our beds and go to the bathroom, eat breakfast, and they'd give us our lunch—some tacos or a couple of sandwiches, an apple, and a soda.

When we got back to camp, we'd wash up before we went to eat. In the tomatoes, you really get dirty, like a dog, so you'd want to go in there clean, with your clothes changed.

We could leave the camp if we wanted to go into town. In Stockton there was a Spaniard who had a drugstore and a radio station. He would send busses out to the camps to give people a ride. He was making a business out of selling us shirts, clothes, and medicine.

The foremen really abused people. A lot was always expected of you, and they always demanded even more. We were obligated to really move it. There were places where braceros went out on strike or stopped work. One of my brothers went on strike in Phoenix because they were picking cotton and the crop was bad. They always said you could never make money doing it. A lot of work for nothing. They threatened to send them back to Mexico. They put them on a bus to El Centro, and from there they sent them to Fullerton, to work in the oranges.

My brother was one of the leaders. He got it into his blood and later worked with Cesar Chavez for many years. There was always exploitation then. They would say that a bucket would be paid at such and such a price, and you'd fill it up, and then they'd pay less. When the farm workers' movement came along, we already knew about organizing and strikes from people who'd participated in those movements. My father had been on strike in Mexico too. He'd tell me that when the boss doesn't understand, you have to hit him where it hurt, in his pocketbook. If you don't, he won't see you. I think it's that way everywhere in the world.

Those who can exploit, do it. That's what Cesar said when he died in San Luis. "Hay que educar a que pisa, y hay que educar a les deje pisar. Hay que educar a los dos." You have to educate both—the exploiter and the exploited. If you don't educate both sides, you can't have a future.

I was a bracero from '56 to '59. I was in Watsonville six months before I got married. That was when my wife and I were just lovers. We'd write each other, and I'd ask her to wait for me until I returned. So we got married. She didn't like my leaving, but she stuck with me. I told her, "I'll just go this once, and I'll be back in time to do the planting." I went off to work, but always with the idea I'd come back and we'd use the money to do more on our farm. We had four hectares of onions, but the price fell and the crop just stayed in the ground. So I said, "Well, I better go to the United States."

The next year, when I came back, we had a good crop of camote—sweet potatoes. We put our backs into it and irrigated, and we had no competition. We were the lords of the market. But afterwards I thought again, "Well, I better go to the United States." A human being is never satisfied. We all have one thing and want another.

The last time I came as a bracero, I was in San Diego. There I worked for a Japanese grower named Suzuki, a good man. During the war they had put him into one of the camps. He talked a lot about it. He told us, "I know what your life is like, because we lived that way too, in concentration camps. They watched over us with rifles." So he got papers for all of us. He fixed us up and told us to come work with him. That was the last contract I worked.

When I fixed my immigration status, I decided I wouldn't go back, because my father had died, and I decided to bring my wife here instead. I was tired of being alone. That was the hardest thing—the loneliness. You have

the security of three meals, a place to stay, your job. But you get depressed anyway. I missed my land and my wife. And since I met her, I can't go with another woman. My parents and grandparents gave me that tradition. One wife for one strong family.

But it was important to send my kids to school. That's what I was trying to do as a bracero. I wanted a real future, and we knew that we were just casual workers—I would never be able to stay. I had to look for another future.

It was the beginning of the life I'm leading now. Thanks to those experiences, we survived, and here I am. I have two countries—just me, one person. I can cross the border and live in my own land, and I can live happily in this country too. I came first as an alambrista and then as a bracero. Eventually I got my papers and lived like any other person. But I always remembered how I got here. Illegal, a bracero.

I still have a house on the land my father gave me. And I haven't let it go, because that's where all my children were born. Anytime we want to go to Mexico, we have a place there. I tell my son, your grandfather was a visionary. Don't sell the place, he said, because we don't know what will happen. Maybe one day we'll go back.

CELESTINO AND AMELIA GARCIA
A BRACERO AND HIS WIFE
San Leandro, California, November 2001

Celestino Garcia was a bracero who lived apart from his wife and family for fourteen years. Then they got visas, came to live in the United States, and became citizens.

CELESTINO: I went to the U.S. for the first time in the mid-1940s. Lots of people from my hometown in Durango, Sandias, were going to the U.S. then. They would recruit people and fix our papers so that we could come.

Amelia and Celestino Garcia, at the home they share with their children in San Leandro, California

in Woodland. It was better working here than in Mexico. We would earn more money and we could save.

AMELIA: But it was only seasonal. They would only give you a few months, not the whole year. And then you'd have to go back to Sandias.

CELESTINO: We'd stay in the U.S. about six months, and then they'd send us back. But if someone didn't want to go back, sometimes they'd leave him here. It was hard work. In Santa Paula we picked lemons and oranges for four months. We lived in a camp, but not a very big one. Other workers there were also from Sandias. Sometimes it was good, and other times it was bad. We would send the little we earned to Mexico for the family. We just spent a little money here going around.

AMELIA: With the money from the first three trips he made to the U.S., we built a house. We got married after his first trip. Eventually we got documented and came up together. Thank God, we are citizens now. [*They both laugh.*]

CELESTINO: We got fixed. Because I came and worked, they said that we could get our papers fixed.

AMELIA: It took a long time, though. By the time we got our papers our youngest son was fourteen. For many years he worked here while I still lived in Sandias. He would send money for me to live on. It was difficult. They paid them very little, but he would send what he could. And that's how we survived. We suffered in Mexico, and he suffered here.

CELESTINO: The longest we stayed away was a year. In one way, it was good because we could work and immigration would not bother us. When we didn't have a passport, sometimes we would only work for a week or two, and we'd get deported. But sometimes I'd work four or five months, and if they didn't catch me, I'd voluntarily go home. If they caught me while I was leaving, I'd tell them I would go voluntarily. Sometimes they'd say, "Okay. Go ahead." Other times they'd put me in jail for one or two days. But they didn't do anything more than just send me back.

AMELIA: After I came here, at first we'd return often, because we had a daughter who was mentally ill. Now we go back every year or two. The whole family is here. Sometimes we go back to check the house. We still

AMELIA: In 1941 we got married. [*She laughs.*] That's why he came here—we got married. But he had come before. I still stayed in Mexico during that time. The contractor, the owner of the work here, was from our town, Leonardo Galindo.

CELESTINO: Yes, but he never came with us. He was there waiting for us. He was a boss. They would put us in trains in Mexico, and once we got here he would take us off at the places where we were needed. Leonardo worked have a nephew and a brother there, but now we feel we are from this country. We are still Mexicans because we were born there and we love our country. But we are U.S. citizens, and this is where we made a living. We consider ourselves both Mexicans and North Americans. Otherwise, think of how much worse off we'd be. We have six children. Five daughters and a son, right? I better not get confused. [*She laughs.*] We have around eleven to fourteen grandchildren, and great-grandchildren too. [*They laugh.*] We're getting old. They live here, and most likely they'll stay here.

CELESTINO: It's better here because there's no work there. There's nothing to do.

AMELIA: There are no jobs in Sandias. When it doesn't rain, there is no corn. There's nothing. Most of the people come here to work.

CELESTINO: But it's good to have memories.

EUSEBIO MELERO
FROM BRACERO TO UNDOCUMENTED
San Leandro, California, November 2001

Eusebio Melero explains why many braceros preferred to leave their contracts once they arrived in the United States and work without papers until they were deported.

My family were farmers in Sandias, Durango. We had all kinds of animals and our own land. My father left to go to the mines because he needed work, and he died in Tonopah, Nevada, in 1936. He died because of the dust. I was twelve years old, so my grandfather took care of me. He watched over all five of us until we started working. I was close to my grandfather.

There wasn't a high school in Sandias, so when I was fifteen I quit school. I thought I had to live life. In Sandias there was only work for short periods of time. My grandfather passed away, and my mother was left with five children. Since I was the oldest, I left for the U.S. to look for money, for life, to help my family. This was in 1943, and I was nineteen.

I felt good because I was going with people from the same town, ten of us traveling together. I guess there weren't enough people during that time in the fields in the U.S. to pick the oranges and the rest of the crops. So they brought braceros from Mexico to work on contract for three or six months. We signed the contract in Mexico City. People would gather to get a contract and then thousands of us would leave from there.

The contractors recruiting people scheduled a time and place to enlist us. We had to come with our birth certificates. Then they'd examine us to see if we were good for work. If not they would tell us to go home.

From Mexico they brought us to Pasadena in a train. There were hardly any buses then. Once we got off, the ranchers were waiting for us and took those they needed. From Pasadena I was taken to Salinas, where they had a camp ready with lots of beds. We started working there. Each rancher had a specific number of men they wanted, and they would take us to the place every morning where we worked. Every day they'd give us our lunches there, and we'd come back at the end of the day.

The foreman, Luis, was short and dark skinned. He lived in Los Angeles and spoke English. He was a good man, and so was the farmer. They treated us very well.

We lived in a workers' camp, like a military camp, in a big barracks with many rooms. Around a hundred men lived there. All of us were Mexican. Every morning, Luis would take us to the farm to pick oranges. The work was heavy because the trees were too tall. The ladders were twenty-four-feet long and unsteady. Sometimes the ladders would fall. We would use scissors, not our hands, to pick the oranges. The bags were long, and when they were full we could hardly get down.

They'd pay us by the box. The food at the camp was cheap, but it wasn't very good. Still, they didn't charge us to live there. They paid every week and took money out of our checks, which we were supposed to receive when we returned to Mexico. We never did, though.

On Sundays we'd go downtown, buy a shirt or a pair of pants or whatever we needed. Sometimes girls would come to the camp looking for men.

I picked oranges for a short time and then left to work with a friend in Los Angeles, where they ran the streetcars. We picked up along the tracks and fixed the rails. It was good work, but different from the farms. They gave us only the job, and we had to feed ourselves. I lived with an uncle who'd been living many years in Los Angeles with his family. Back then there were many jobs because of the war—the city was full of work. We left our contracts because we thought we could make more money working without papers. It was something a lot of people did. Most people would work as a bracero for a month or two and then work somewhere else until they were deported. We worked on the streetcars for about a month, when immigration deported us, too. They didn't do anything to us because we didn't do anything bad. We were just looking for a better life.

When you're young you can work hard. I didn't go out a whole lot. During that time Los Angeles had a lot of *pachucos*—people in gangs who wore long hair and long chains. They never did anything to me. We didn't live there long enough to get involved. We didn't speak English then, and I still don't.

The next time I came as a bracero, I went to Canby, California, near Klamath Falls, Oregon. There were people there from my hometown, but we didn't live all together. We'd see each other every month and all worked on the same railroad line, not as farm workers. I worked there for a year on a bracero contract. There were houses on different track sections where we could cook and do everything for ourselves. It wasn't like in the camps, where the food was cooked for you. The boss lived in the same area we did, but in a different house.

I was working for Southern Pacific. We lifted up the tracks, removed old ties and replaced them with new ones. Our first contract was for six months, but they gave us permission to do another. If they liked the way you worked, they'd renew your contract, and if they didn't, they'd tell you that you needed to go. But at the end of our second contract there was no

more work, and we returned to Mexico. When I left, the war had already ended.

I came here many times without any papers. Sometimes I'd get deported, and other times I wouldn't. But I liked life here because it's easier. In Mexico, it hardly ever rained, and water was limited. When the water was gone, we'd have to move. When I would get deported, I would go back to my hometown, but I'd return that same year.

Here there was more work, but it was still work done with your hands and your lungs. I don't know how to explain it to you. I lived life as a worker, and life here was good. I liked it here. At the beginning I always wanted to better myself and return to Mexico. But then I started liking living here too much to go back.

2

The bracero experience is part of U.S. and Mexican social history and the personal history of thousands of families. Today, however, it has acquired a broader meaning. Not only do similar programs still exist but new proposals seek to reestablish a contract labor system very similar to it.

Instead of recognizing the existence of transnational communities like those of the Mixtecs and Qanjobales and changing the laws that deny them equality and legal status, Congress and large corporate interests are bent on channeling migration into new temporary worker programs. After the bracero program ended in 1964, other schemes for importing temporary contract labor took its place. One of them is the current H2-B visa program, under which tens of thousands of workers come to the United States yearly, mostly to work in the pine forests of the east and south.

Many of the workers recruited into this program are the same indigenous people from the Guatemalan highlands whose relatives and neighbors are consolidating transnational communities and fighting for labor rights in the meatpacking plants in Nebraska. U.S. immigration policy is at a crossroads. It can either support those transnational communities or become a vehicle for supplying single men on temporary visas to large employers.

The experience of the H2-B workers from the tiny highland towns ironically named La Democracia and La Libertad [Democracy and Liberty] suggests that these migrants will become trapped in a cycle of debt and obligation. This debt will harm their families in Guatemala and act as a whip forcing the workers to take risks and exhaust themselves during their stay in the United States.

In September 2001 a group of migrant temporary workers from Guatemala and Honduras were traveling in a van through the forests of northern Maine. As it crossed a bridge, the van veered off the roadway and into a river. Of the fifteen men inside, all drowned except for Edilberto Morales. His description of what happened that day makes plain the terrible human cost of this labor system. He describes not just the accident but also the enormous debt he accumulated in order to get to the United States. As a result he was in no position to object to having to travel two and a half hours at high speed on dirt roads through the Maine forests to get to work. In fact, he and his companions sought to eke out as many hours of labor as they could in order to pay off their loans, keep their homes, and have a little money left for the welfare of their families. Florinda Sanchez and Natividad Maldonado, widows of men who died that day, describe how difficult it is to be the ones left behind.

Esteban, an older man who worked in a similar program, explains how he was cheated and could not protest effectively. Yet he still thinks about going back to the United States, even though he knows that nothing has changed.

Critics of U.S. immigration policy have said for decades that its purpose is not really "welcoming your tired, huddled masses, yearning to breathe free," but providing an ample labor supply. "It's all become an issue of the price of labor—how it will be regulated and how much it will cost employers," says Lourdes Gouveia, who heads the Center for Latino and Latin American Studies at the University of Nebraska in Omaha. U.S. immigration policy doesn't affect the number of people coming across the border as much as their status once they're here.

While the conditions faced by Morales, Esteban, and the dead husbands of the two widows are not exactly the same as those remembered by the braceros, the purpose of the contract labor programs is identical—supplying temporary workers to employers.

The chains binding these workers are much the same as those of the braceros. They and their families accumulate enormous debts in order to come. Their recruiters exercise great power over them, not least because they control whether workers can return year after year (some recruiters maintain a legal blacklist of troublemakers). Once workers are in the United States, protesting unfair conditions or organizing to change them is dangerous. They are far from cities and most sources of legal and organizational help. And their employers can deport them if they strike or refuse to work.

In 1986 Jamaican contract sugarcane workers in Florida stopped work to try to raise the piece rate. Growers called in the sheriffs, who sicced dogs on the strikers. The dispute became known as the Dog Wars. The workers were loaded onto planes back home. More recently, in 2000, in Leamington, Ontario, a group of Mexicans brought in under the Canadian guest-worker program stopped work, protesting abuse by a foreman on a local farm. Sixteen workers were deported as a result.

"Growers justify a new guest-worker law by saying there is not enough labor available," says Lucas Benitez of the Coalition of Immokalee Workers, a community-based project organizing farm workers in south Florida. "But it's a lie. Every day in the papers you read about the high numbers of unemployed workers. The problem is that most workers do not want to do the work we do for the wages we're paid. We average $7,500 a year, and the conditions of exploitation are such that any reasonable person would prefer receiving unemployment benefits. Instead of new braceros, we need to raise wages and improve working conditions."

EDILBERTO MORALES

A SURVIVOR OF A TERRIBLE ACCIDENT

La Democracia, Guatemala, January 2003

Edilberto Morales came to the United States on a special H2-B visa as a contract temporary worker. Because of the large debts incurred to finance their trips, he and his coworkers were under intense pressure to get as many hours of work as possible. Morales describes how the speeding van in which they were traveling fell into a river, and fourteen men drowned.

Edilberto Morales and his wife in front of the drying coffee beans from their harvest in La Democracia, Guatemala

My parents were farmers who grew corn and coffee. I completed three years of schooling and began working with them. When the price of coffee was high, we could make a living, but when the price dropped we had to do something. I heard from my friends that in the United States you earn more money. They would come back, build houses, and buy land. I wanted to do the same. Here I could earn only twenty quetzales [$2.50] per day, or 120 a week.

I started talking with my wife to see if she was open to the idea. She supported my decision because she is my wife, but she was worried because she would have to stay here by herself with the children. My children go to school in Villa Gloria, and they charge forty quetzales each per year at the beginning, and later they usually ask for more.

At first I tried to go to the U.S. illegally. I reached San Cristobal [Chiapas, Mexico] twice, but I was caught and sent back to Guatemala. As a result, I was in debt about ten thousand quetzales. I asked Mr. Villatoro if he would take me to the United States. He said he would, and in December he told me my visa had been approved.

My debt of ten thousand quetzales had, through interest, increased by about seven thousand. Then I had to borrow another ten thousand. In total I owed almost thirty thousand quetzales and had to sign over the deeds to my house and land.

We left from Guatemala with twenty-four people on the plane. When we got to the U.S., I was sent to Louisiana, where I started planting pine trees.

We carried a bag and a small hoe to make holes for the small trees. We could carry a thousand of these small pines on our backs, and we planted about fifteen hundred per day. It was hard, and the bag was very heavy. The first two weeks my body was very sore, but I didn't have any other option than to keep working. When we were finished planting, we fertilized the pines, carrying a tank on our back. We had no masks, only gloves, and were breathing in the liquid we sprayed. The first days I felt very faint, but I soon became accustomed to it.

We were paid twenty-five dollars for planting a thousand trees, but with all the deductions it worked out to nineteen dollars. For the most part our check would come to three or four hundred dollars every two weeks. When we worked in Mississippi we were paid more, about six hundred dollars every two weeks. There we were paid in cash. There were a lot of inspectors.

If they didn't like our work they would send us back and have us do it again. They would not pay us for that time, because they said that we did it wrong in the first place and it was our fault that we had to return.

After working in the U.S. for a while, Mr. Villatoro said that the company had approved an additional five months on our visas if we were willing to travel to Maine. Since I needed the money I decided to go. In Maine we cut pines with a chain saw, every fourth tree. Five of us worked together, four from my hometown who died and myself. I knew them all—they were my neighbors, and one was my nephew, Juan Sellez.

They paid us between forty-eight and ninety-five dollars per acre, depending on the thickness and number of the trees. Our biweekly checks were between five and seven hundred dollars. We liked working there because we were paid a lot better.

The accident occurred on a Thursday. Our supervisor called us at three o'clock in the morning. He told us we had to leave early because we had not worked the day before, due to rain. We made our lunch and left at 5:30, stopping at the gas station to buy snacks. We all fell asleep during the ride, but at 7:55 I woke up. We were traveling down a dirt road, and I thought we were going too fast, so I told Juan to slow down. The others teased me, asking if I was scared. They all wanted to get in a lot of hours and didn't mind going fast.

I fell asleep again and woke up when I heard our back tire pop. I saw we were on an old bridge with no side railings. We were almost to the other side when I felt us go off the bridge and fall into the river below. When I came to, the van had come to rest at the bottom of the river with the tires upward. The front windshield was shattered and water was rushing in, but we had no way to get out, because the side and back windows were still intact. I started pounding and broke a window. I felt someone tugging at my pants, but I couldn't do anything for them because I couldn't breathe.

I finally came up to the surface. After taking a breath, I went back down and touched the hand of a coworker, but they were dead. I went up again and swam to shore. I had lost my pants and shoes. I looked toward the river and saw blood and gas come up to the top. I began to cry and scream. The water was so cold, and I was so scared and I didn't know what to do. Twenty minutes later I saw a truck approaching. I stopped them and told them what had happened. The forest rangers put me in the cab and turned on the heater. And later they took me home and fed and clothed me. They told me to call my family and tell them what happened.

Later they took me back to the accident site, and I saw them pull the van and the bodies out of the water. The next day they took me to identify them. I told the authorities the names of the men and where they were from. I went to our apartment and separated all their belongings to send to their families.

It's been four months since the accident. I think about it when I'm going to sleep. I remember what happened and think about why I was the only one who survived. Maybe we all should have died.

I live in my parents' house now. I paid my loan, but I did not have as much money as I thought I would when I returned to Guatemala. If I go again, I will have to take out another loan. I don't think I will, though, because I still don't feel well. Mr. Villatoro recently took another group to the U.S. He already has a list of seventy other people who are signed up to go on the next trip. He is doing all of us a favor.

FLORINDA SANCHEZ PEREZ AND NATIVIDAD MALDONADO DOMINGO
TWO WOMEN WIDOWED BY AN ACCIDENT
La Democracia, Guatemala, January 2003

Both Florinda Sanchez Perez and Natividad Maldonado Domingo lost their husbands in the terrible accident in Maine when the van carrying them plunged into a river. Both families had incurred large debts to finance the trip the men made as contract guest workers and would have lost their homes and land had they not paid them off just before they died.

enough money for our second plot, we worked our own land and sold the harvest. Back then the price of coffee was a thousand or eight hundred quetzales, but in the last three years it fell a lot. It's just not worth much anymore. Many people just don't harvest coffee at all because the price is so low. We all suffered, since the price of other products rose at the same time, and we couldn't buy much.

My husband then decided to go to the U.S. We knew it was very dangerous, but he left anyway. That is why many people decide to go, and the reason my husband left.

He tried going to Tapachula and Comalapa in Mexico, which was a lot closer, and even to Guatemala City. But he knew he would earn more money in the U.S., and then we'd be able to build our children the house they wanted. I didn't want him to leave, but he insisted. My husband borrowed about twenty thousand quetzales. Ten thousand were for Mr. Villatoro and another ten thousand for expenses on the way. The man who lent my husband the money knew he had always paid him back. He charged 15 percent interest. Juan borrowed the money in November and left on New Year's Day.

Many people go and return, so I didn't think anything was going to happen to him. We talked on the telephone. Edilberto Morales had a cellular phone, so when he called his wife, he would let my husband use the phone and I would talk to him.

He was supposed to return October 15, but the accident was September 12, and he never came back. Mr. Villatoro has taken people before and says this had never happened. It was my husband's first trip.

Before Juan died, he had already paid off the debt. We had initially put down the deed to our house in case we couldn't pay it. My sons and husband were very adamant about paying the money back as soon as possible so that we wouldn't have our house taken away.

I don't feel well because my son also passed away two years ago. He was riding his bike and was hit by a drunk driver. He was helping me financially before that happened. Now both my son and husband have died in accidents. My other sons tell me not to cry. They tell me we all have to die sometime and that the body dies but the soul doesn't. When I leave the

Natividad Maldonado Domingo and Florinda Sanchez Perez at the parish hall in La Democracia

FLORINDA SANCHEZ PEREZ: I was sixteen years old when I left my parents' home with Juan Mendez. We later married in the church. He grew beans and coffee and liked to farm. He spoke Mam and Spanish and was very playful. When we married we rented land together. When we had our two children I told him that we couldn't continue renting, that we should try to buy a few acres. We worked to buy a little piece and then bought another.

Until then Juan worked for very large coffee growers. When we gathered house I am okay, but when I return and see their pictures I start to cry. Sometimes I just want to go far away.

My son Ismar wants to go to the U.S. now. He wants to see where his father died. I told him he isn't going, because I am scared. I visited Mr. Villatoro because Ismar wanted to go with him, and he told me Ismar couldn't go because he is too young. Ismar was mad, and he says he wants to go next year.

I lived with my husband for twenty-seven years. I was not mad that he went to the United States. He was a good man, and I didn't think anything was going to happen to him. That was God's plan, and that was his destiny. When he left, he said that if it was God's will he would return and if not, that everyone had to die at some time. He said that if he died working he would be happy, and that is how it happened. He was on his way to work.

NATIVIDAD MALDONADO DOMINGO: I grew up here in Democracia. At fifteen I got married and went to live with my husband, Cecilio Morales Domingo. Cecilio grew beans and corn. We had land but not enough to sustain us.

My husband went to the U.S. to work. We didn't think he would die in an accident. It was the first time he had gone. Everybody knew that Mr. Villatoro took people to the United States. He came to the house because he knew my husband wanted to go. It cost ten thousand quetzales, and Cecilio borrowed the money, hugged our children, and left.

We gave the deeds to our two pieces of land to the moneylender, and he let us borrow the land back. He charged 12 percent interest.

After Cecilio left, I was here with no money. Because we are so poor, my son, who is twelve, and I went to cut coffee. My husband felt very bad, and he told me to be patient. Fortunately, he was able to pay off the loan when he was in the United States.

Our home is not the same. It is very sad not to have him around.

ESTEBAN
A MODERN-DAY BRACERO
Huehuetenango, Guatemala, January 2003

Esteban asked that his real name not be used, since he was thinking of returning to the United States. He thought he might have trouble getting a contractor to hire him if he became known for speaking publicly about the conditions under which he worked.

I got the job through a company looking for people to transplant pines. I applied and went over there. The person in charge of hiring only took people recommended by another worker who had gone the year before. Every year he forms a group to take to the U.S.

We were sixteen people the year I went. We paid eight thousand quetzales and the fees for the passport and the visa, and the tickets to get to the capital and catch the plane. Most of the people had to get a loan to go. After I arrived in the U.S. I never saw the contractor again. Since we were all scattered in different places, we didn't see many of the people in the group.

I worked in Georgia and Mississippi. The name on our paycheck was Ellers. Our job was to plant pines. They gave us a tool they called a "talache" [mattock] and a bag made of sailcloth to carry the trees. With one hand you open a hole in the soil, and with the other you'd throw in the tree. Then you'd cover the hole with soil with the tool and press it down with a kick of the heel. Sometimes, if the soil was soft, I could plant 3,800 pines in a day. I'd start working at 6:30 or 7 a.m. and would continue until 5 or 6 p.m.

When the tree is small you can fit six hundred pines in the bag, which weighs about seventy pounds. As you carry the bag the weight starts diminishing. You plant a tree and take two steps forward to plant the next. It was fast; otherwise you don't plant enough trees.

Esteban holds the notebook in which he recorded, every day, the number of pine trees he planted, and knew, therefore, how much he was cheated by the contractor.

They told us they'd pay $27.50 per thousand trees. In the end we'd receive a check for one hundred dollars a week because they'd deducted money they said we owed them for the equipment we were using. They weren't deducting money to give us at the end of our job—they were taking that money away from us. We never received a sheet listing the deductions; otherwise we'd have known how much money they were taking from our paycheck. After I was planting for two months, they still told me that I owed them an installment.

We kept track of how much we were earning, calculating an average 2,500 pines daily. To our surprise the checks would only amount to a hundred dollars! There was not one week that we received more than that.

We bought food with that hundred dollars and paid for lodging. They charged forty dollars a week per person for the hotel, and five of us had to share the room. We were eating, but we couldn't send any money to the family in Guatemala. We were left with almost nothing.

We didn't protest because we couldn't. We were far away from the company office, and maybe the next year they wouldn't give us the chance to go to the U.S. again. A lot people left the company and worked elsewhere. Some came back when it was time to return to Guatemala, and others would just stay. My idea was to come back to Guatemala and go back the next year to do the same. I thought I should escape from the job right away. Otherwise, I wouldn't make any money. But I couldn't go the following year, so I'm still here.